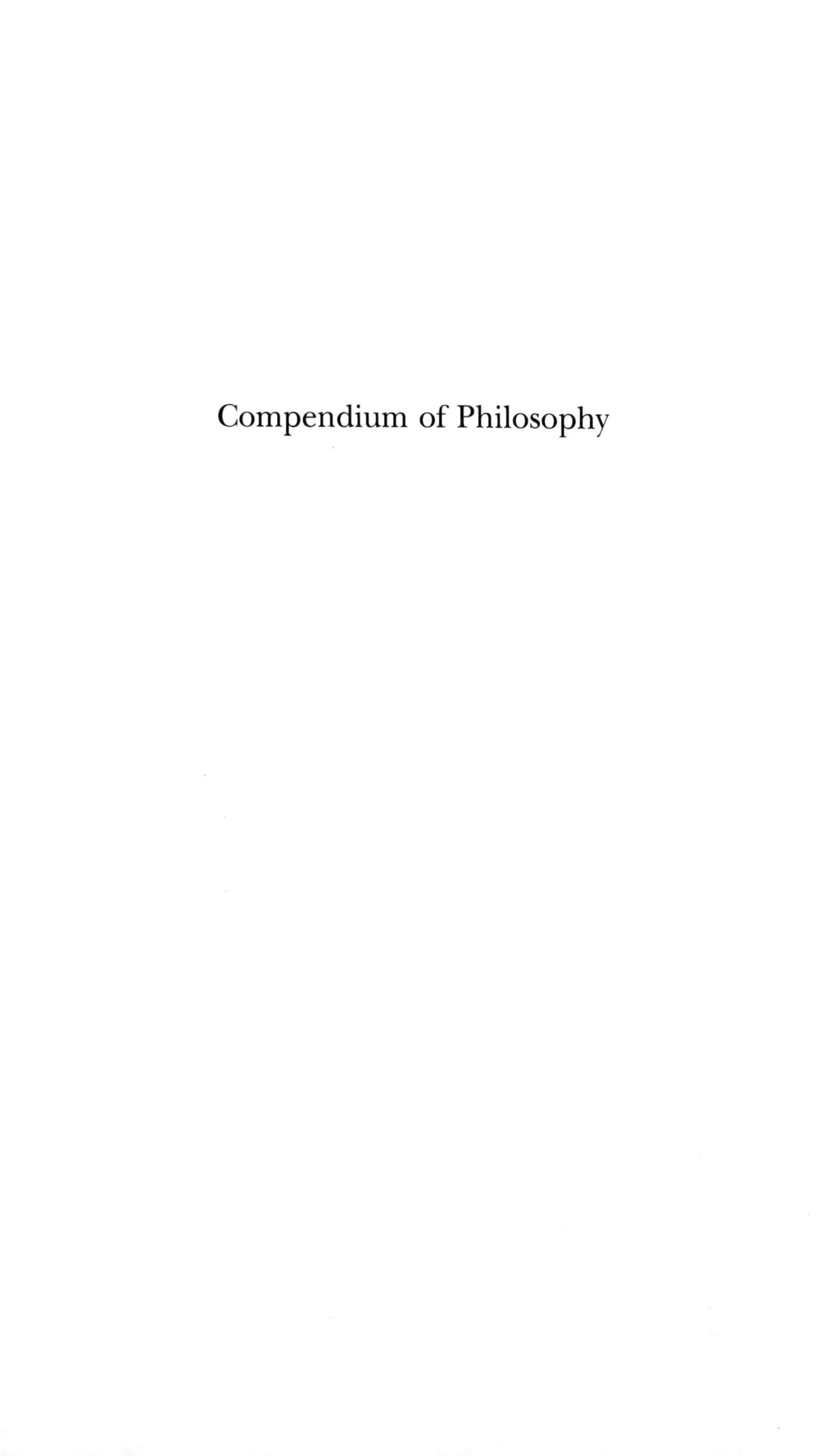

Compendium of Philosophy

MLBD

SACRED BOOKS OF THE BUDDHISTS SERIES

Reprinted Under License from **Pali Text Society**

- **A Buddhist Manual of Psychological Ethics** : Translation of the First Book in Abhidhamma Piṭaka entitled Dhammasaṅgaṇī—With Introductory Essay and Notes by *C.A.F. Rhys Davids.*o
- **The Book of the Gradual Sayings** : Translation of Anguttara Nikāya, the Fourth Collection of Sutta Piṭaka **(5 Vols.)**—Tr. by *F.L. Woodward* and *E.M. Hare.*
- **The Book of the Kindred Sayings** : Translation of Saṁyutta-Nikāya **(5 Vols.)**—Tr. ,Ed. & Introduction by *C.A.F. Rhys Davids,* Tr. by *F.L. Woodward.*
- **The Collection of the Middle Length Sayings** : Translation of Majjhima Nikāya, the Second Collection of the Sutta Piṭaka containing 152 suttas. **(3 Vols.)**—Tr. from the Pali by *I.B. Horner.*
- **Compendium of Philosophy** : Translation of Abhidhammattha-Saṅgaha)—With Tr., Introductory Essay and Notes by *Shwe Zan-Aung,* Rev. & Ed. by *C.A.F. Rhys Davids.*
- **Culavaṁśa** : Translation from German Translation by Wilhelm Geiger. A Continuation of *Great Chronicle of Ceylon* (Mahāvaṃśa) : **(2 Pts. in One)**—by *C. Mabel Rickmers.*
- **Dialogues of the Buddha** : Dīgha Nikāya, the First Collection of Sutta Piṭaka **(3 Vols.)**—Translation from the Pali by *T.W. Rhys Davids* and *C.A.F. Rhys Davids.*
- **Dictionary of Pali Proper Names (2 Vols.)**—*G.P. Malalasekera.*
- **English-Pali Dictionary** —*Venerable A.P. Buddhadata.*
- **The Expositor** : Translation of Atthaśālinī, Buddhaghoṣa's Commentary on Dhammasaṅgaṇī, the First Book of Abhidhamma Piṭaka—Tr. by *Pe Maung Tin,* Rev. & Ed. by *C.A.F. Rhys Davids.*
- **Conditional Relations [Paṭṭhāna] (2 Pts.)** Part I : Guide, Part II : Translation of Caṭṭasaṅgāyana Text of the Seventh Book of Abhidhamma Piṭaka—Tr. by *U. Narada Mula Patt Thana Sayadow,* Assisted by *U. Thein Nyun.*
- **The Jātaka or Stories of the Buddha's Former Births (6 Vols. in 3 Pts.)**: Translation from the Tenth Book of Khuddaka Nikāya of Sutta Piṭaka—Ed. by *E.B. Cowell,* Tr. by *Robert Chalmers, W.H.D. Rouse, H.T. Francis* and *R.A. Neil.*
- **Pali-English Dictionary**—*T.W. Rhys Davids* and *William Stede.*
- **Pali Metre** : A Contribution to the History of Indian Literature—*A.K. Warder.*
- **Points of Controversy** (Subjects of Discourse) : A Translation of the Kathāvathu from the Fifth Book of Abhidhamma Piṭaka—Tr. by *S.Z. Aung* and *C.A.F. Rhys Davids.*
- **The Sutra of Golden Light** : Translation of Suvarnabhasottamasūtra—*R.E. Emmerick.*

Pali Text Society
Translation Series No. 2

COMPENDIUM OF PHILOSOPHY

Translation from the Original Pali of the
Abhidhammattha-Saṅgaha

with Introductory Essay and Notes by
SHWE ZAN AUNG

Revised and Edited by
MRS. RHYS DAVIDS
Special Lecturer in Philosophy at Manchester University

MOTILAL BANARSIDASS PUBLISHERS
PRIVATE LIMITED • DELHI

First Indian Edition: Delhi, ***2016***
7th Reprint, Wiltshire, (UK), 1995
First Published: Wiltshire, (UK), 1910

ISBN: 978-81-208-4035-5

Also available at
MOTILAL BANARSIDASS
41 U.A. Bungalow Road, Jawahar Nagar, Delhi 110 007
8 Mahalaxmi Chamber, 22 Bhulabhai Desai Road, Mumbai 400 026
203 Royapettah High Road, Mylapore, Chennai 600 004
236, 9th Main III Block, Jayanagar, Bengaluru 560 011
8 Camac Street, Kolkata 700 017
Ashok Rajpath, Patna 800 004
Chowk, Varanasi 221 001

MLBD Cataloging-in-Publication Data
Compendium of Philosophy
Translatd by Shwe zan Aung
Revised and Edited by Mrs. Rhys Davids
in *MLBD Sacred Books of the Buddhists Series*
ISBN : 978-81-208-4035-5
Includes introductory essay, notes, translation from Pali of the *Abhidhammatha Saṅgaha*
I. Buddhism II. Abhidhammattha-Saṅgaha
III. Translation from Pali IV. Aung, Shwe zan
V. Mrs. Davids, Rhys

Published by
Motilal Banarsidass Publishers Private Limited
www.mlbd.com • mlbd@mlbd.com
Printed by Replika Press Pvt. Ltd.

TO

THAT SMALL BUT DEVOTED BAND OF SCHOLARS,

LIVING AND DEAD,

WHOSE SELF-SACRIFICING LABOURS HAVE PAVED THE WAY

FOR THE

APPRECIATION BY WESTERN ARYANS

OF THE TEACHING

OF THE

GREATEST OF THE ARIYAS,

THIS WORK IS GRATEFULLY

DEDICATED BY

S. Z. A.

EDITOR'S PREFACE

In so far as a book may be pronounced useful which has ministered to a continual demand, the utility of the *Abhidhammattha-sangaha* ranks very high among the world's historical documents. For probably eight centuries it has served as a primer of psychology and philosophy in Ceylon and Burma, and a whole literature of exegesis has grown up around it, the latest additions to which are but of yesterday. In at least three Pali books of history and bibliography, of uncertain, if not very early date, but based on older works now lost,[1] the manual is ascribed to a teacher named Anuruddha. Of him nothing further is recorded, save that he was the author of at least two other works on philosophy, the former[2] of which (and possibly the other two also) was compiled at Kāñcipura, or Conjevaram, on the Madras coast, a seat of learning associated at an earlier date with the name of Dhammapāla Ācariya, the Commentator. According to the Burmese tradition, Anuruddha was a Thera (elder) of Ceylon, and wrote the Compendium at the Sinhalese Vihāra, founded by Somādevī, Queen of King Vaṭṭagāmanī (88-76 B.C.), and the Minister Mūla, at Polonaruwa. When Anuruddha lived is not recorded, but it is believed to have been earlier than the twelfth, and later than the eighth, century A.D. In the chronological list of saintly and learned men (rahans) of Southern India, given in the Talaing records,[3] his name

[1] *Sāsanavaŋsa*, ed. Mrs. Bode, P.T.S., 1897, p. 34; *Gandhavaŋsa*, ed. Minayeff, J.P.T.S., 1886, p. 61; *Saddhamma-Sangaha*, ed. Saddhānanda, J.P.T.S., 1890, p. 62; *Buddhaghosuppatti*, ed. J. Gray, p. 26.

[2] *Paramattha-vinicchaya*. See next page.

[3] J. Gray, *op. cit.*

and works are given not only after those of Kaccāyana, who is believed to have flourished in the seventh century, but also aftor those of two intervening worthies. And it was in the twelfth century that the Compendium is said to have superseded, as a textbook, Dhammapāla's *Sacca-sankhepa* ('Outlines of Truth').[1]

Wherever or whenever written, the Compendium is, in Burmese bibliography, classed under a group of classical summaries, or compendia, entitled Let-than, or Little-finger Manuals, nine in number, and having, most of them, an exegetical literature belonging to each work. The other eight are the following, belonging, all of them, to a time contemporary with our so-called 'Dark Ages' of culture, or to the epoch immediately succeeding them:

1. *Paramattha-vinicchaya*,[2] by Anuruddha (our author).
2. *Nāmarūpa-pariccheda*,[3] by the same.
3. *Abhidhammāvatāra*,[4] by Buddhadatta,[5] of India, contemporary of Buddhaghosa.
4. *Rūpārūpa-vibhāga*, by Buddhadatta.
5. *Sacca-sankhepa*,[6] by Dhammapāla, of India, author of the *Visuddhi-magga Ṭīkā*.
6. *Mohavicchedanī*, by Kassapa, of Ceylon.

[1] This from the translator, to whom I am indebted for all the following bibliographical materials, but who gives no documentary authority. This work is ascribed to Dhammapāla (not the Commentator who is called ā c a r i y a) in *Sās. Dīpa*, ver. 1,220. The *Saddhamma-sangaha* ascribes a work called *Saccasankhepa* to one Ānanda Thera, cataloguing it *next after Abhidhammattha-sangaha* (p. 62), and not ascribing any such work to Dhammapāla. This list, however, is in other respects shown to be unreliable.

[2] Having an original Ṭ ī k ā, by Mahābodhi of Ceylon, and a sub-Ṭ ī k ā by an anonymous writer of Ceylon (*Sās. Vaṃ. Dīpa*, 1226).

[3] Having an original and sub-Ṭ ī k ā, both by Vācissara-mahāsāmi, of Ceylon (*fl.* A.D. 1250). *Gan. v.*, J.P.T.S., 1886, 62; Geiger, *Dīp. Mah.*, 94.

[4] Having an original Ṭ ī k ā by Vācissara-mahāsāmi and a sub-Ṭ ī k ā by Sumangala, of Ceylon, author of the *Ṭīkā-gyaw* (see below).

[5] On his literary relation to Buddhaghosa, see Gray's *Buddhaghoshuppatti*, pp. 4, 49 *ff*.

[6] Having an original Ṭ ī k ā by Vācissara-mahāsāmi, and a sub-Ṭ ī k ā by Mahābodhi, of Ceylon.

7. *Khema-pakaraṇa*,[1] by Khema.

8. *Nāmacāra-dīpaka*, by Saddhamma Jotipāla, the only author of note from Burma, who ranked as Commentator (atthakathācariya).

The *Abhidhammattha-saṅgaha*, whether on account of its completer survey of what is known as Abhidhamma, or because of its excessively condensed treatment, or because of its excellence as a handbook, stimulated a larger growth of ancillary works than any of the foregoing. The translator has supplied me with the following list:

A. Four Ṭīkā's (sub-commentaries):

1. *Porāṇa-Ṭīkā* (old commentary, considered quite superannuated), by Nava-Vimalabuddhi, of Ceylon.

2. *Abhidhammattha-Vibhāvanī*, by Sumangala, of Ceylon, a late medieval work. This is the most popular and most authoritative, and is known in Burma as the famous Ṭīkā, or *Ṭīkā-gyaw*. It has been freely quoted in our footnotes and Appendix as the 'Ceylon Commentary,' or C.C.

3. *Sankhepa-Vaṇṇanā*, by Saddhamma Jotipāla, author of the *Visuddhi-magga-Gandhi*, a commentary on that monumental work. He was a native of Pagan, of the Bassein district in Burma, and pupil of the Burmese teacher, Vajira Uttama, and visited Ceylon for purposes of study.

4. *Paramattha-dīpanī Ṭīkā*, by Ledi Sadaw (teacher) of Monywa, Upper Burma, who is a writer of the present day. The long list of his works, grammatical, ethical, religious, and philosophical, may be read in Mrs. Bode's *Pali Literature of Burma*, London, 1909, p. 97. This Ṭīkā has recently created some sensation in the philosophical circles of Burma, from the dissent expressed in it from most of the commonly accepted opinions of the *Ṭīka-gyaw*. The innovations put forward in it have not yet met with any general acceptance among readers trained in the established commentarial traditions; nevertheless, it also is frequently quoted in the present volume.

[1] Having a Ṭīkā by Vācissara-mahāsāmi.

B. A 'key' to the *Ṭīkā-gyaw*, entitled *Maṇisāramañju*, by Ariyavaṃsa, of Sagaing, Upper Burma.[1] The author also wrote a key to the *Atthasālinī*, Buddhaghosa's Commentary on the *Dhammasaṅgaṇi*.

C. A Commentary entitled *Madhu-sārattha-dīpanī*, by Mahānanda, of Hanthawaddy, Burma. The *Piṭakatthamain*, a Burmese bibliography (1906), places this work in the sixteenth century, during the reign of Bayin Naung, who united Burma and Pegu in one kingdom.[2]

D. Lastly, a number of works not in Pali, but in Burmese:

Abhidhammattha-saṅgaha-madhu, a modern work by Mogaung Sadaw.

Abhidhammattha-saṅgaha-gandhi, a modern work by Payagyi Sadaw.

A number of analytical works entitled *Akauk*, all more or less modern, and too numerous to find place here.

Paramattha-sarūpa-bhedanī, by Visuddhārāma (or Ingan) Sadaw, a commentary with a practical object.

Abhidhammattha-sarūpa-dīpaka, by the late Myobyingyi, of more theoretical import.

As compared with the older and more famous classic, Buddhaghosa's *Visuddhi-magga*, the present Compendium covers very largely the same range of subject-matter as that work, though without the same amplitude of treatment. But the object of each work, and hence, to some extent, the order and emphasis of treatment in each, is different. The Compendium is a concise statement of a view of things, with purely theoretical analysis. The 'Way of Purity' is ethical in its end, and is psychological only in order the better to teach ethics, and the way to saintship. The two works are thus to some extent mutually complementary, and as such still hold the field as modern textbooks for students of Buddhism in Buddhist countries.

As such they should have been made accessible to

[1] On this fine-souled writer of the fifteenth century, see the pleasant biography in Mrs. Bode's, *op. cit.* (from *Sāsanavaṃsa*, pp. 95 *ff.*), p. 41 *f.*

[2] Mrs. Bode, *op. cit.*, p. 47.

cultured readers in European tongues before now. The Pali Text Society, at its very birth, was admonished to be forward with editing the original of the Compendium, as the best introduction to the study of the *Abhidhamma.* One of the four distinguished Theras of Ceylon, who sent a written benediction to the first journal of the infant society (1882)—Srī Saddhānanda Thera—wrote in Pali to this effect: 'Compressing the whole subject-matter of the *Abhidhamma* contained in these seven books, the great Thera of old, Anuruddha, made the very brief Compendium of the *Abhidhammattha.* Whoever shall learn this Compendium by heart from his teacher's lips is already skilled in the seven books, with ease and certainty. . . . I believe that the most proper way, in the study of *Abhidhamma,* is to learn its method in the Compendium with its two Ṭīkā's, as well as in the *Sucittālankāra* and the *Abhidhammāvatāra,* and then only to take up the seven books.'

The Pali Text Society was so far mindful of this injunction that, when it had barely completed its third year, its founder published in the Journal,[1] 1884, the text of the *Abhidhammattha-Sangaha.* At the same time he also met and incited the late Henry Warren to devote his crippled but indomitable energies to the study of Pali. That was over a quarter of a century ago. Ten years passed away. Warren was spending his ebbing strength on the text of the *Visuddhi-magga,* and translating passages for his *Buddhism in Translations.*[2] And his excellent summary of its contents was in our hands.[3] I had prepared a similar analysis of the Compendium, but, not aware of the Ceylon Thera's advice, judged it better to get on with the *Abhidhamma* sources themselves. Another ten years passed. Warren had passed away, leaving a mass of material in type or manuscript, and a successor competent and willing, but laden with work having earlier claims upon his leisure.[4] But the Buddhist Society of the Buddhasāsana Samāgama

[1] J.P.T.S., 1884.
[2] Harvard Oriental Series, 1896.
[3] J.P.T.S., 1893.
[4] I refer, of course, to Professor Charles R. Lanman.

had been formed at Rangoon, and its Director, Bhikkhu Ānanda Metteyya, placed me, as one wishing to translate the Compendium, into communication with one who had not only written a manuscript translation, but was also acquainted with the best commentarial explanations of the text, without which its intensely concise sentences are extremely hard to understand. I welcomed the idea of a collaborated translation, but had myself to plead for delay on account of other work. With the utmost courtesy and patience Mr. S. Z. Aung placed his manuscript in my hands, offered most generously to defray the expenses of printing, and waited for three years—till the autumn of 1908. I thereupon wrote my own translation, and in three months' time sent him both manuscripts, leaving him to collate the two and decide as to choice of renderings. I also invited him, as one well trained in Buddhist philosophy, to contribute an expository essay, on the lines of his all too brief article in *Buddhism*, the organ of the Samāgama, entitled 'The Processes of Thought.' In the autumn of 1909 I received from him not only a third translation—the outcome of our respective previous attempts—together with the essay, but nearly three hundred folio pages of comment and criticism, written in brief intervals of leisure with a flying pen, but showing mastery both of subject and of idiomatic English. It were ill-judged to overload a translation with footnotes. We have kept these within narrow limits. But I am persuaded that the comments and criticisms so generously poured out concerning my own efforts at translation, printed or in manuscript, cannot but prove a valuable contribution to Western inquiry in Buddhist philosophy, in elucidating some of the terms and concepts that most puzzle inquirers. I wish to lay on others some of my own considerable debt to the translator. I have therefore transcribed a selection from these notes and included them in an Appendix.

To the best of my belief, this volume, the antecedents and the making of which have been herewith written down, is the first attempt to treat of Buddhist philosophy by East and West working hand in hand, and I trust it may prove the forerunner of many another similar collaboration. Even in the present little work, a very cursory perusal will reveal it as fairly bristling with points needing more adequate investigation, but which, in the compass of a 'Compendium,' it was not possible to thresh out more fully.[1] We can only claim to have made one step forward out of what appeared—to myself, at least, after some ten years of inquiry—as almost a deadlock in this field of research. We have set down the *living tradition* of many philosophical concepts, as handed on in the most eminent school of Buddhist philosophy.

For the last fifteen years my colleague has been, as a student,[2] in close touch with several very learned monks, including the distinguished Doctor, Ledi Sadaw, in a country where the study of Abhidhamma, or philosophy, is cultivated more than elsewhere. Bhikkhus from Ceylon come now, as in days of old, to study philosophy under the Theras of Burma, so renowned are the latter for proficiency in this subject. Mr. Aung has also, through a course of study necessarily limited, and not yet including our latest departures in thought, assimilated a notable purview of our own philosophic tradition. He is thus

[1] *E.g.*, notably the hypotheses, *to us* so obscurely expressed, of consciousness in the sequence of death and rebirth.

[2] Shwe Zan Aung was born in 1871 in Akyab, Burma, the second son of U. Shwe Tha, A.T.M., K.S.M. Officiating District Superintendent of Police. From his tenth year he was educated at the High School, Akyab. He entered the Rangoon College in 1887, and graduated B.A. in 1892. It was there that, for the first time, Pali was learnt under Dr. Forchammer, and subsequently under Mr. Gray, Pali lecturer. He joined the Government service in 1892, and has been this summer appointed Treasury Officer and Headquarter's Magistrate at Henzada. In 1895 he began the study of Buddhist philosophy (as well as of Western philosophy), his teacher being one U. Gandhamā. A few years ago the idea of translating the Compendium into English, as a basis for all future efforts in the same field of research, was suggested to him by a fellow-countryman renouncing his original intention of doing so. He then wrote a draft translation himself, which eventually was entrusted to my revision.

better fitted than most Oriental students to translate into our vehicles of expression the living meaning, as distinguished from the *etymological* connotation, of Buddhist philosophical terms. Western philology, as far more advanced, can accomplish the latter task well enough, and better than the East. But it is a well-known fact that in England, *pace* other nations, words may be used in a sense which has very little direct relation to the etymological sense—for instance, the word 'sense' itself, or 'interest,' or 'condition,' or 'emotion,' and so forth. And it is a funny hash an Oriental translator would make among these, if he had to depend for accurate renderings, and with a varying context, solely on philological competence. There is this further pitfall for the unaided Western, that commentaries often give two kinds of explanation: one etymological, the other exegetical. In the latter, a term is defined in its relation to a special point of discourse, edifying or otherwise—like Armado's 'Love is a familiar; love is a devil; there is no evil angel but love.' In getting at a meaning, we need to keep the two methods apart, and aim beyond them, at the 'place' in the speaker's or writer's mind occupied by a meaning when he expressed it by a given term. Here I suggest that we need the living tradition to help us; and this, in the following pages, we have tried to set down.

It will be objected that, at the best, we have but recorded the modern usage in Burmese colleges, built on a medieval tradition which has very possibly diverged from such interpretations as the compilers of the Pali Canon would have made. This is possibly quite true. But it does not improve the case for our unaided etymological inferences as to original meanings. We should not commend the judgment of a Burman, who sought to get at the meanings of early Greek philosophers in the original, without reference to the mass of European comment thereon, grown up out of medieval learning.

But if we of Central and Western Europe can feel justified in claiming, for our interpretations of early Greek philosophy, that we can adequately reproduce the ideas, and correctly render the language, of those thinkers, the Burmese have at the very least as strong a claim to a corresponding adequacy and accuracy. For us, the thoughts of Plato, Aristotle and their forerunners, are, as we have them in our tongues, somewhat of a grafted hybrid. But for Buddhists, the doctrine called Abhidhamma has sprung from the very tree itself of the Dhamma. It is, for them, of no pagan stock, pruned and trained by doctors of the Church in assimilating the philosophic culture of Hellas to the tenets of a faith come otherwhence to birth and power. To realize the unity in the Theravādin tradition, we must imagine the first few centuries A.D. put at the back of the age of Sokrates and the Pre-sokratics! Make Christians of those Greek thinkers, and picture how venerable a structure we should see in Christian philosophy, genuinely so-called. Then turn and contemplate an Indian vista like this of Buddhism!

India has not yet taken back the faith of her Emperor Asoka. Burma and Ceylon and Siam are the spiritual children of her wonderful missionary enterprise set on foot by him in obedience to the Founder's injunctions, and the Order's loyal and devoted career of service and self-sacrifice. They are not the daughters—*orasā jātā*, mouth-born, of the Exalted One's own ministry. Yet I am persuaded that we shall not understand Buddhist philosophy as it appears to a Buddhist, till we have learnt to see life and mind as these see them who have been nourished on its age-long, yet living and growing tradition of culture.

If, indeed, we shall even then understand! We approach the subject wearing the spectacles of our own Greek tradition. Our perspective is based on space rather than on time; on substance statically filling space, rather than on movements and moments; on permanence and identity, rather than on change and transmitted force. Here is no contrast drawn between European and Indian thought. Herakleitus was the 'Dark One,'[1] to the tendencies of

[1] Ὁ σκοτεινός, ὁ αἰνικτής.

contemporary thought. And these tendencies prevailed and were wrought up into the philosophies of those magnificent reactionaries,[1] Plato and Aristotle, so that the works of Herakleitus were allowed to perish, even as the works of Leukippus and Demokritus were 'willingly let die.' But so, too, has Indian Parmenideanism, using spatial and static concepts in its turn, ever said of Buddhism: How can you build upon nothing? How can 'that which is' proceed, become, from 'that which is not'? Thus did 'Ptolemaic' philosophy grow out of the myth of world-on-elephant-on-tortoise, and laid the foundations of its soul no less solidly.

So India turned a deaf ear at length to her Protestants, and only the scenes of her past missionary labours carried on their message. Meanwhile, the ever-changing baseless earth flew on her way round Helios, who also flew on his own wider way. And one day Copernicus arose and saw. Since then our concepts of the visible universe have changed. And our concepts of things invisible, of life and mind, of birth and dissolution, of subject and object, will change, are changing, in their turn. For these concepts are derivatives from those. Now, it is my conviction that if the way in which the tradition of the Theravādins—it is often called Southern Buddhism—has philosophized, and still philosophizes, on these fundamental questions, could be adequately expounded so as to be intelligible to Western philosophy, tendencies in the former might become apparent which are not a little sympathetic with much in certain notable departures now showing themselves in France, America, and England.

Here and now more definite comparisons were out of

[1] Most Europeans will dissent from this term. And it is no doubt true that for Plato the problem of knowledge was precisely how to transcend the antithesis between the views of Herakleitus and Parmenides (G. C. Robertson, *Elements of Philosophy*, p. 31), and that Aristotle sublimated the concept of soul from materialistic animism (*ibid.*, 218 *f.*). Nevertheless, they both philosophized on an animistic basis; they both started out with a 'substance' called psyche, and in this essential feature they are, for a Buddhist, and for some of us, reactionaries.

place and over-previous. The present little volume is but a forerunner of better work by those who will profit by our halting efforts. It is but as some essay by a Peripatetic of old, long known and taught, but only in Byzantium, borne thence to Italy in the robe of a Christian bhikkhu fleeing from decadence or Turk, and fain to let it meet the eye of some sympathetic De' Niccoli or Pico della Mirandola.

We must have materials. And in this Compendium we see a famous and venerable digest of that more abstract, analytical, advanced teaching which the Buddhists called Abhidhamma, or 'ultra-doctrine,' wherein the narrative and the homily of the Suttanta discourses found no place. The title of the work, literally translated, means 'Compendium of the subject-matter of Abhidhamma.' But this rendering is not only cumbrous; it does not give us that which the title conveys to a Buddhist of Burma or Ceylon. To him Abhidhamma is not very far from being synonymous with metaphysic, to what extent 'meta' means *after* or *beyond* ('abhi') 'physica.' But 'metaphysic' has got itself largely tied up with theories of noümena and the Absolute. I have read a book where this pre-emption of the term was carried so far that the rejection by Buddhism of the *ātman*, or noümenal ego, and of an Absolute in general, was called 'the sore spot in its metaphysicless view the world.'[1]

If this be the tether of the term, let Buddhists cheerfully make a present of it to Absolutists, and fall back on the word 'philosophy' as, on the whole, the best equivalent for Abhidhamma. They will hereby be no farther from the truth. The culture that is distinctively Buddhist of the Theravādin sort is mainly comprised under the twin branches, philosophy of mind (psychology and logic) and philosophy of conduct or ethics.[2] We have no word coincident with Dhamma, let alone Abhidhamma.

[1] Dr. G. Walleser, in his spirited and pioneer sketch, *Die philosophische Grundlage des älteren Buddhismus*, Heidelberg, 1904.

[2] It is only in Mahāyānist Buddhism that Buddhology attains to the eminence of a third branch.

Nevertheless, to teach the one or the other amounted to imparting, with this or that emphasis, the philosophic attitude over against the mystery and the menace of life. There is in Buddhist culture not only that absence of specialization, which is characteristic generally of ancient learning; there is also a oneness of interest, cult, and ideal that is unique. Its schools had no Faculty of Theology. Its teachers of philosophy were not expected to consider divinity and religion *tabu*. It saw no conflict between science and religion.

Hence the translator has wisely decided to give to the term *Abhidhammattha-sangaha* the comprehensive rendering of Compendium of Philosophy. The manual gives us no systematic digest of the seven books comprising the *Abhidhamma-Piṭaka*, and only alludes to one of them by name.[1] But it gives us in outline the form which the teaching of the Dhamma took, when for Buddhists it became Abhi-dhamma. In its dry, terse categories, condensed still further into mnemonic summaries,[2] we discern a psychological and an ethical philosophy in outline. We see a philosophy which *starts* with an analysis of (1) what we find (*a*) within us, (*b*) around us, and of (2) what we aspire to find. (1) Mind is analyzed and catalogued. The visible world, and that which we associate therewith, is similarly treated. This includes things invisible, but conceived as analogously existing: worlds beyond our ken, beings infra-human, superhuman. Scientific thought knows of no beginning nor ending. For Buddhist thought the universe has never been homocentric. It has never held that, to say: a watch, if picked up, implied the existence and work of a watchmaker, constituted a sound analogy as to anything *beyond*

[1] The *Paṭṭhāna*, called elsewhere the 'Great Book.'

[2] It is scarcely necessary to remark that the doggerel rhymes correspond to blank verse in the original. We thought that rhyme was more characteristic of English mnemonics. These 'mnemonics' are so very elliptical that I have expanded them considerably, in translating, in the interests of meaning and metre and rhyme.

such temporary rearrangements of things as it termed unreal.[1]

The curt, dry method of the Compendium and the unfamiliar perspective are not calculated to attract. For that matter I anticipate that the cursory reader, even if not unversed in our own psychological method, will not get past a feeling of repulsion and impatience. The little work will reward only those who can patiently soak the mind in the peculiar method of treatment. The numerical character of the psychological analysis will seem to us somewhat crude and bizarre; nor shall we, at this time of day, find much appreciation for a classification of consciousness, wherein ethical and philosophical concepts seem to encroach on the field of psychological analysis, as much as, and more than, they did in the mental classification of Sir William Hamilton and other bygone teachers among ourselves.

On the other hand, we cannot but be struck (*a*) by the marked distinction drawn between the flux of individual organic life including subconscious mind, subjectively viewed as *bhavanga*, and the emergence of sequences of moments of conscious mind called *citta's*;[2] (*b*) by the relatively strong microscopic power of the introspection employed, and by the results it is made to yield. I refer to the theory of *cetasika's*,[3] or factors in any *citta*, that is. in any distinguishable unit in the continuance of consciousness, and also to the duration-theory of *citta's*.

(2) Then, the Ideal, and there-under chiefly the way thereto; for under this head the subject is no more things as they are, but work that has to be done, travail of thought and will to lift the whole being to a higher plane of existence, if so be it lie in him to experience moments of ecstasy which may transform and purify all his earthly vision. Herein Buddhism approximates to the mysticism of other religious philosophies, both of East and West.

[1] See Appendix: A t t h a.

[2] Pronounce chittas.

[3] Pronounce chaytas'ĭkas.

And hence another definition of mysticism is called for than that which sees in mysticism a craving for union of the human and the divine.[1] The Buddhist sought in his discipline to attain, not union with a deity, but super-normal vision and power in himself. Whether man, and woman, originally made gods in their own image or not, the Buddhist—the Indian generally—held the human mind and will to be potentially god-like. Given the right antecedents and the right training, to man belonged the powers that had been projected into deities. Thus do we see, in the complex ideal of Arahantship, or Nibbana-under-present-conditions, a super-normal evolution of faculties combined with, not to say resulting from, ethical purity.

One is tempted to speculate whether we might not have thought, or even wrought, along this line in the West but for two hindrances: our divorce of intellect and 'heart,' and our cramped conception of life. We have never allied genius and morals. We incline, on the contrary, to associate transcendent powers of creative and interpretative imagination with that unstable mental equilibrium which essentially implies 'incomplete moral sanity.'[2] In the East, though men of high gifts (Devadatta, *e.g.*) might be immoral, he who is pure and holy is, *as such*, the 'canning' man (to use Carlyle's word). In the more child-like creeds he could wither with a curse. In the more virile philosophies his intellect and will were supernormal. He had sloughed off infirmities of heart and character *in process and by dint of* making unfaltering efforts 'to see things, by perfect reason, as in themselves they really are.'[3]

[1] *Cf.* Dr. Lehmann's *Mysticism*, London, 1910, p. 7: 'The oneness of the human soul with the Divine is the conceit (*Wahn*) of mysticism; it is this that makes mystical things into mysticism.' Under 'Indian Mysticism' no consideration is given to Buddhism. So also in Royce, *The World and Reality*, vol. i.

[2] Maudsley, *Body and Will*, p. 284.

[3] A phrase repeated throughout the Pali Nikāyas. One of our own poets has expressed a sense of what such insight would involve. I refer to Tennyson's 'Flower in the Crannied Wall':

Godlike insight, for the Indian, and bestowing godlike powers.

Then, as to the two different perspectives of life: As Mr. Aung shows, the Buddhist conception of personal identity is in accordance both with what we infer to have been the Herakleitean standpoint, symbolized by the flowing river—the same, yet never the same—and with our own conception of all great physical forces—heat, electricity, and so forth—in which identities are series of *informed* or *charged sequels*.[1] Thus, 'my life as endless' did not mean, for Buddhists, a transmigrating essence, adopting one fleeting vesture after another.[2] Yet it could still be spoken of as my life, not yours. And in maintaining the right (in virtue of a re-constructed principle of identity) to speak of 'my life' as infinite, the possibilities of development in it are immeasurably greater than they can be by a theory which conceives 'my life' to have begun a few years ago, whatever inherited powers we may concede for it. The expansion of memory down the long past, the supernormal range of vision and hearing, telepathic, or rather telenoetic power, the mastery of will over the body, and beyond that:—all this abnormal faculty to which Buddhist tradition has ever testified, is, at least as theory, only so many logical corollaries of its view of life. Any life is infinite as to its past. Therefore it has had infinite possibilities, each death and re-birth constituting, in Leibnitzian phrase, mere 'envelopments and diminutions.'[3] And if development of thought and character has not been invariably frittered away again, one

---

'If I could understand
What you are, root and all, and all in all,
I should know what God, and man is.'

And if we *know* as much as that, what could we not *do!*

[1] Introd. Essay, pp. 11, 42.

[2] 'He that has no clear idea of death and rebirth . . . comes to conclusions such as: "A living entity dies and transmigrates to another body."'—Buddhaghosa, *Visuddhi Magga*, ch. xvii.

[3] *La Monadologie*, § 73.

may eventually, even as man, attain to some such efficiency of faculties as is, in other creeds, vaguely believed to be restricted to life in its otherness *hereafter*.

But these be themes too far-reaching to be fitly dealt with in introductory remarks. Moreover, the sceptical and scientific reader—one of whom is better worth holding than a hundred over-credulous temperaments—will not stay content at hearing attestations brought into consistency with the logic of a theory. He will ask for verification, nor be satisfied with the testimony of long bygone instances in ancient documents. He will demur that some of the commentarial assertions are obviously only the work of imagination playing around a theory, since they are not only unverified, but unverifiable. The Buddhist may reply that had the sceptical attitude never been expunged by the discipline entitled Purity of transcending doubt,[1] there had been no attainment of supernormal cognition by any one of his teachers. It was precisely in the flashes of intuition won in Abhiññā that unverifiable observation and experience had been won.

Then will his Western fellow-man round on him and say: 'Ah! but we too once stood where now, as to such matters, you still stand. Your faith in the validity of these fetches of insight in your most saintly teachers, your faith in the omniscience of your greatest teacher, has kept you down to this day in durance of intellect to your traditions. The fact that you have so long retained this hoary little Manual as the nucleus of your philosophizing speaks for itself. The most curious mixture of subtlest psychological analysis and crudest mythological cobweb-spinning, it has been suffered by you in its entirety for centuries as the educator of your youth. You have evolved from it no textbook pruned, by a more adult criticism, of dogmas respecting demonic destinies and the long careers of Cloud-cuckoo-town devas. In the science of the analysis and criticism of historical evidence, you have remained as a child. Over-late to commit your oral literature to the registra-

[1] Kankhā-vitaraṇa-visuddhi. See p. 65.

tion of ink and stylus, you have transmitted your childlike trust in the truth of your seers' words to the validity of the written letter—a trust apparently as implicit as that of a British Protestant of untrained intellect in the Jacobean Bible as the register of a verbally inspired revelation.'

For the moment let us leave the last word to the critic. Our task is not to debate after this sort, but to investigate and make known a great, and by us hitherto neglected, field in the growths of human ideas. Both we and the direct inheritors of this field have yet too much to learn of each other's evolution of thought before we are competent to criticize. Buddhists of different countries are fast learning something of ours. We shall watch with ever-growing interest whether, if they penetrate beyond the curious blend of scepticism and dogmatism, which so greatly mars the scientific position among ourselves, they will assimilate such good fruit of historical criticism as we have to offer, and in applying it to their own thought, retain their own wonderful perspective of the possibilities of life and being. And for ourselves, we have yet to see how far, apart from isolated cases of thorough-going conversion here and there, we are capable, as lovers of philosophy, of acquiring sympathetic but critical knowledge of their standpoints.

I believe that Buddhists are not likely to shrink from honest inquiry, as if the secrets of their wisdom rested on some 'great medicine' or priest-driven oracle of primitive culture. The broadly scientific bases of their philosophy, and its freedom from ecclesiastical sanctions, dispose them to meet questioning from the West halfway,'[1] if only the questioners meet them in the attitude required by the Buddha himself: Ye keci sikkhâkāmā, 'Whosoever of them are desirous to learn!' Once let this disposition replace patronage, cynicism, and self-complacency, and who can foretell what good things for philosophy may not result in the future when they, whose tradition heard but

[1] *Cf.* the translator's own attitude, p. 284.

lost the only scientifically based philosophy of Hellas, meet and commune with them, whose tradition both heard the sister utterance of Northern India,[1] and has upheld it through the ages to the present day!

C. A. F. RHYS DAVIDS.

ASHTON-ON-MERSEY,
July, 1910.

---

[1] It is probable that Herakleitus and Gotama Buddha were nearly contemporary, the former perhaps younger by a generation or so. Leukippus and Demokritus flourished nearly a century later than the Buddha.

The Buddhist standpoints unconsciously approached by Lotze in some of his critical discussions, notably, *e.g.*, those on 'Becoming and Change' (*Metaphysic*, I. ch. iv.), etc.—*consciously* influenced by Herakleitus alone among the ancients—suggest that the intercourse desiderated above might bring about interesting developments in Lotzes' successors.

SOME CORRIGENDA

Page ix (*line* 24).—*Read* Uttarājīva *for* Vajira Uttama.

Page x (*line* 1).—Read *Maṇisāramañjūsā*.

Page xix (*line* 26).—*Read* contunua.

Page xxiv (*note*).—*Read* Lotze's.

Page 6 (*last paragraph*).—*Read* Anatta *for* Annatta.

Page 8 (*line* 4).—*After* state *add* or rather condition.

Page 9 (*note* 3).—*After* street *add* track,

Page 11 (*line* 2).—*After* identity *add* continuity for succession.

(*line* 2).—*Read* all *for* al.

Page 18 (*line* 6).—*After* is *add* not.

Page 24 (*note*).—*Read* tortured petas *for* absurd objects *and delete* but not a Peta.

Page 64 (*line* 25).—Read Aruppa *for* Aruppa.

Page 101 (*line* 12).—*After* kinds *add* namely twelve.

(*line* 13).—*Omit* in the.

(*line* 14).—*Omit* in the.

Page 138 (*lines* 12, 13).—*Read* Brahmā.

Page 144 (*line* 6).—*For* function *read* order of precedence or effect.

Page 152 (*line* 6).—*After* rebirth *add* , in Rūpaloka.

Page 154 (*note* 2).—After *Bud. Psy.* add *Eth.*

Page 178 (*line* 13).—*Read* the life we know *for* life we know.

Page 179 (note 3).—*Read* six nīvaraṇa's *for* six Nibbana's.

Page 182 (*note* 2).—*After* is made, *supply* ':—

Page 196.—*Here the footnotes are wrongly numbered; 2 and 3 belong together; n. 4 refers to* § 6, '*grasped at*'; *n.* 5 *to the passage marked* 4; *n.* 6 *to that marked* 5.

Page 203 (*line* 22).—*Read* cracked *for* crackled.

Page 212 (*line* 14) to page 213 (*line* 1).—*Read* [respective] characteristics,[6] functions or properties.

Page 212 (*note* 6).—*Read* the nature or essence of a thing *for* the ordinary feature of *each* thing.

Page 218 (*note* 2).—*Read* confined to the world of men (manussaloka), the fifth class of Sakadāgāmin's being intended here *for* applicable to . . . Kāmaloka.

Page 219 (*line* 19).—*After* entitled *add* The Chapter on.

Page 228 (*line* 15).—*Read* eight *for* eighteen.

Page 276 (*line* 9).—*Read* -samudayena; (*note* 1) *read* -samudayo.

A few other misprints in accents, commas, etc., the reader will himself correct. I desire he should also bear in mind that the translator has read none of the proofs except those of his Introductory Essay. Hence he must not be held solely responsible for everything contained in the Appendix, or in the footnotes, not signed Ed., although I have tried to present his MS. as faithfully as possible.—Ed.

Some additions to the original 'Some Corrigenda' have been incorporated above; they have been taken from a copy of the *Compendium* corrected by S. Z. Aung.—I. B. H.

AN INTRODUCTORY ESSAY TO THE COMPENDIUM OF BUDDHIST PHILOSOPHY

THE Abhidhammattha-Sangaha, the Compendium of Buddhist Philosophy, has now been translated. This important work is so highly condensed that it consists, for the most part, of terse, jejune sentences, which may not be easily intelligible to lay readers; and a reprint of my article, entitled 'The Processes of Thought,' which appeared in *Buddhism*, vol. i., No. 2, has been suggested by my respected and valued colleague as an introduction to this manual. I have therefore taken this opportunity of revising and expanding that article in order to make it, more or less, a complete résumé of the present work. At the same time, I must myself condense and be brief, so that this succinct exposition of Buddhist philosophy, from the psychological standpoint, may be kept well within the limits of an introductory essay.

Definition of Mind.

'By the mind of a man, we understand,' said Reid, '*that* in him which thinks, remembers, reasons, wills.' Bain considered this definition as at once defective and redundant.[1] Hamilton wrote: 'What we mean by mind is simply *that* which perceives, thinks, feels, wills, and desires.' This definition is also redundant. And if Buddhists were to frame their definition by the fifty-two mental attributes or properties enumerated in Part II. of the Manual, it would be similarly unsatisfactory. Nothing would satisfy Bain unless the definition of mind were also a division of mind.

[1] *Mental Science*, p. 3. *Italics are mine.*

The vedanā-ñāṇa-sankhāra-bheda[1] of our author, however, corresponds to Bain's division of the mind into Feeling (vedanā), Will, or Volition (sankhāra or cetanā), and Thought or Intellect (ñāṇa).

But the grammarian's definition of the term citta (mind) is ārammaṇaŋ cintetīti cittaŋ (thought = thinking of an object). Here the word cinteti (to think) is used in its most comprehensive sense of vijānāti (to know). Mind is, then, ordinarily defined as *that* which is conscious of an object. This is called the kattu-sādhana definition, or definition by which an agency[2] is attributed to the thing denoted by the term. It is no doubt the most convenient mode of defining terms.

Consciousness defined. From this definition we get our definition of viññāṇa (consciousness). Consciousness may therefore be tentatively defined as the relation between ārammaṇika (subject) and ārammaṇa (object). This relation is spoken of in the language of the Paṭṭhāna as ārammaṇa-paccaya. 'Paṭṭhāna' is the title given to the Seventh Book of the Abhidhamma-Piṭaka, which treats of the related modes of existence. It is, therefore, essentially the Buddhist Philosophy of Relations, covering more ground than the Association Philosophy, which deals with the association of *ideas* only. 'Ārammaṇa-paccaya' means the relation of presentation. In this relation the object presented is termed paccaya (the relating thing) and the subject, paccayuppanna (the related thing).[3] Thus, these two terms are relative, one implying the other—that is to say, the subject cannot exist without the object, and *vice versâ*. It will be noticed that greater prominence is given to the object. From this fact Buddhism cannot be exclusively classed as Idealism. We might therefore begin with the consideration of the object.

1 Bheda = division.—Ed.

2 Kattu = to do or act.—Ed.

3 Paccaya is lit. paṭi = back to, and aya = going. Paccayuppanna is lit. uprisen-as-related, or -in-relation.—Ed.

The object of consciousness is either object of sense or object of thought. Object of Consciousness.

The former subdivides itself into five classes—sight, sound, smell, taste, and touch. Sight, or rather light, and sound are classed together by Buddhaghosa as asampatta-rūpa,[1] because their objective *source* does not come into physical contact with our organism. Smell and taste, on the other hand, being but modifications of touch, are classed under sampatta-rūpa. Touch consists of any or all of the Three Essentials, or Primary Qualities of body, namely—pathavī (extension), corresponding to the sense of locality; tejo (heat), corresponding to the sense of temperature; and vāyo (motion), corresponding to the sense of pressure. Extension means occupation in space. As no two atoms can occupy the same space at the same time, we associate with extension our idea of the impenetrability of matter. And this attribute, in turn, implies the Buddhist 'characteristic mark'[2] of kakkhaḷatta, or hardness. Object of Sense.

Locke gave the name of 'Ideas of Sensation' to these five classes of sensibles, which in Buddhist philosophy are collectively termed fivefold-object (pañcārammaṇa).

The object of thought also consists of five sub-classes: (1) citta (Mind); (2) cetasika (mental properties); (3) pasāda-rūpa and sŭkhŭma-rūpa (sensitive and subtle qualities of body); (4) paññatti (name, idea, notion, concept); and (5) nibbāna.[3] These are collectively termed dhammārammaṇa, a term which corresponds to Locke's 'Ideas of Reflection.'[4] Object of Thought.

The fifty-four classes of Kāma-consciousness enumerated in Part I. of the Manual, together with the fifty-two mental properties which severally enter into their composition, as well as the twenty-eight qualities of

[1] Lit., material-object which-is-not-reached.—Ed.

[2] Lakkhaṇa.

[3] Better known in its Sanskritized form as Nirvāṇa.—Ed.

[4] Dhamma here means mental-presentation, as distinct from special sense-impression.—Ed.

Body enumerated in Part VI., are collectively termed kāma-object. The twenty-seven classes of rūpa- and arūpa-consciousness, together with the thirty-five mental properties which severally enter into their composition, are collectively termed mahaggata-object.[1] The forty classes of transcendental consciousness, together with the thirty-six mental properties, which severally enter into their composition, as well as nibbāna, are collectively termed transcendental object.

Paññatti explained.

The paññatti-object is of several sub-classes, as enumerated in Part VIII. of the Manual. The subject covers a wide field, but we might discuss it here briefly. Paññatti is either (1) that which makes known (paññāpetīti); or (2) that which is made known (paññāpiyatīti). Or, as our author puts it, sadda-paññatti[2] is so called because it makes known (paññāpanato), and attha-paññatti is so called because it is made known (paññāpiyattā). From these two definitions it is clear that sadda-paññatti, which makes attha-paññatti known, and attha-paññatti, which is made known by sadda-paññatti, are relative terms.

Sadda-paññatti is a name (of a thing) which, when expressed in words, or represented by a sign, is called a 'term.' Hence it may mean a name, word, sign, or term. It is synonymous with nāma-paññatti.

Now, every term, according to our logico-grammarians, is connotative. Therefore attha here may be either dabbattha[3] (denotation) or sakattha (connotation). Hence attha-paññatti is the idea or notion of a thing denoted by, and of its attributes connoted by, a term. In other words, attha-paññatti is the idea or notion of the attributes of a thing made known, or represented by a

[1] Lit., great-gone-to, *i.e.*—become large, or developed. Hence lofty or sublime, and so rendered in the Manual.—Ed.

[2] Sadda = sound, or word; attha = sense or meaning.—Ed.

[3] Dabba-attha = meaning of a thing; saka-attha = meaning of attribute, own, intrinsic meaning.—Ed.

name (nāma-paññatti), which is expressed by a word (sadda-paññatti), or signified by a *sign*.

Concept appears to us to be the nearest English equivalent term to express this attha-paññatti. Concept is defined by Mansel as 'a collection of attributes united by a *sign*, and representing a possible object of intuition.'[1] Concept, viewed objectively, is an attribute or collection of attributes; but, viewed subjectively, is an idea or notion corresponding to that attribute or collection of attributes. In a particular conception, as distinguished from general conception, a concept may be an idea corresponding to an individual thing. Concept.

Now, let us see whether the term 'concept' is applicable to the following classes of attha-paññatti's:

1. Tajjā-paññatti[2] is the idea or notion *corresponding to* things—namely, in their ultimate sense (paramattha-dhamma's).

2. Upādā-paññatti is the *derivative* concept, being an idea or notion derived from things in their ultimate sense.

3. Samūha-paññatti is the *collective* concept, being an idea or notion corresponding to a group or collection of things or attributes.

4. Jāti-paññatti[3] is the *general* concept, being a *class-notion* corresponding to a genus of attributes possessed in common by a number of individuals.

5. Saṇṭhāna-paññatti is the *formal* concept, being an idea corresponding to the form of a thing.

6. Disā-paññatti is the *local* concept, being an idea or notion of locality.

7. Kāla-paññatti is the concept of *time*.

8. Ākāsa-paññatti is the concept of *space*.

9. Nimitta-paññatti[4] is the conceptualized after-

[1] *Prolegomena Logica* (1860), p. 66; *Metaphysics*, p. 204.

[2] Tajjā=(tat-yā, tassa bhāvo, that-ness) appropriate, suitable.

[3] Jāti=birth, lineage, family, or kind.—Ed.

[4] Nimitta=sign, or sensuous impression, or percept. Paṭibhāga =similar to. Uggăhā=taking up—viz., by the mind of the initial

image (paṭibhāga-nimitta), being an idea corresponding to the image (uggaha-nimitta), which is an exact *copy* of the original (parikamma-nimitta). The paṭibhāga-nimitta cannot itself be depicted to sense or imagination, though it forms one element of an image which is so depicted.

10. Natthi-bhāva-paññatti[1] is the concept of Nothingness.

11. Santati-paññatti is the idea of the identity of a thing on the ground of its *continuity.*

12. Sanketa-paññatti is the idea of the *conventional* sign by which a thing is generally signified.

Paññatti *versus* Paramattha.

In the paññatti, as distinguished from the paramattha,[2] if we resolve the former into two classes named above, we have nāma-paññatti (names, or the Nominal), attha-paññatti (ideas, or the Conceptual), and paramattha (things, or the Real). The two former are so closely connected together that we are reminded of Cousin's words: 'If Nominalism sets out from Conceptualism, Conceptualism should terminate in Nominalism.'

External Objects.

The object of sense is always *present*—that is to say, it is intuited as something present. Nibbāna and the paññatti-objects are kālavimutta (out of time);[3] the rest are either present, or past, or future.

A thorough analysis of the object would exhaust the entire universe. Thus the object, comprehending, as it does, the subject, is wider, more extensive than the latter. This is probably one reason why greater prominence is given to the object in the Paṭṭhāna.

Annatta doctrine.

Before speaking of the subject, a word on the Annatta-theory, which forms the central doctrine of Buddhist philosophy.

---

impression as an after-image. Parikamma, lit., preparation, is the original, initial impression. See Part IX., § 4, of the Manual.—Ed.

[1] N'atthibhāva=lit., not-is-state.—Ed.

[2] Parama=lit., highest, supreme, ultimate.—Ed.

[3] Lit., freed from time.—Ed.

English Idealism. Berkeley, the greatest idealist of the West, reduced matter to a mere group of qualities, and proved (for us Buddhists, quite convincingly) that the hypothetical substance or substratum, in which the qualities are supposed to inhere, is a metaphysical fiction. But the mind-stuff proved refractory in his logical crucible. Hume, however, was sceptical as to the existence of this very mind-substance, for, whenever he tried 'to catch himself,' he always 'tumbled on a particular perception.' But both Berkeley and Hume were forestalled, three-and-twenty centuries ago, by the Buddha, who had 'got rid of that shade of a shadow of the substance' by pushing the Berkeleyan arguments a step farther to their rigid, logical conclusions. If Hume stands refuted to this day, it is probably because Humean philosophy does not contain the elaborate 'Laws of Relation,' which the Buddha propounded and expounded in the Valley of the Ganges two centuries before Aristotle sowed the seed of the Association Philosophy. The triumphant vindication of Aristotle's claims to be regarded as the earliest expositor of the Theory of Association is therefore not justified. Had Sir William Hamilton known the existence of a body of the Laws of Relation in the Paṭṭhāna, he would surely have accorded that honour to the Buddha.

Association Philosophy. Aristotle's claims questioned.

In Buddhism there is no actor apart from action, no percipient apart from perception. In other words, there is no conscious subject behind consciousness. Indeed, the subject loses itself in the very relation of which it has been supposed, in and by our tentative definition to be a correlate. This is probably another reason why greater prominence is given to the object. Hence, the kattu-sādhana-definition of mind by Buddhist grammarians must be recast into the bhāva-sādhana-definition[1] of Buddhist philosophers—viz., 'Mind is simply the consciousness of an object.' Although it is a convenient mode of speech to adopt (or indulge in) the kattu-sādhana-form, every philosophical term defined in

[1] *I.c.*, in terms of state or being, as opposed to action.

Buddhism must be understood in the bhāva-sādhana-sense. Whenever, therefore, the term 'subject' occurs in this essay, it *must be understood* to mean, not the self-same permanent conscious subject, but merely a transitory *state* of consciousness.

Import of the term 'Subject' in Buddhism.

The object of the profound analysis known as Abhidhamma, is to show generally that such state of consciousness is no simple modification of a mind-stuff, and, above all, that there is no soul or ego which is apart from the states of consciousness; but that each seemingly simple state is in reality a highly complex compound, constantly changing and giving rise to new combinations.

Buddhist view of Life.

It is only of late years that it has come to be recognized in the West that for no two consecutive moments is the fabric of the body the same; and yet this doctrine was taught by the Buddha more than twenty-three centuries ago. 'Nadī soto viya' ('like the current of a river')[1] is the Buddhist idea of existence. And the theory of the ceaseless change or flux of things, the anicca-dhamma,[2] applied alike, in the Master's teaching, to the body (wherein it is said to occur by the continual replacement of kalāpas, or groups),[3] and to the mind. In the latter, indeed, the flux was held to be more rapid, the impermanence more marked; so that it were truer to speak of the body, which at least seems to persist for a few fleeting years, as attā (permanent soul or ego), than so to regard mind, which endures not the same for any two consecutive instants of time.[4]

Anicca-doctrine.

Life, especially the life that we term conscious existence, is indeed like the current of a river, which still maintains

[1] Judging by the contents of the Pali canon, the river-simile was not put into the mouth of the Buddha himself, but is of later date. The simile used by him to illustrate the constantly changing nature of mind or consciousness is that of the leaps of an ape from bough to bough.—Ed.

[2] Anicca=not-lasting, im-permanent.—Ed.

[3] Kalāpa, again, I have not met with, as a philosophical term, in the Pali canon.—Ed.

[4] S. ii., 94, 95.

one constant form, one seeming identity, though not a single drop remains to-day of all the volume that composed that river yesterday.[1] A person standing on the bank of such a river would, of course, think that the river is the same, though not a particle of water which he sees at any point remains where it was a moment ago. And as the beginning and the end of a river receive the special names of 'source' and 'mouth,' though they are still composed of the same material as the body of the river itself, even so the source and the mouth of this River of Life are respectively termed 'birth' and 'death,' though still composed of the same water of life.

Now, what is this 'water of life'?

When the mind is entirely vacant, as in the state of dreamless sleep, its vīthi-mutta (thoughtless, lit., thought-free) existence is termed bhavanga[2] (being). Bhavanga therefore corresponds to Leibnitz's state of obscure perception, not amounting to consciousness, in dreamless sleep. If this term be rendered by its etymological equivalent 'being,' the latter must be understood subjectively, as in the Hegelian identity of thought and being. In Buddhism, however, thought and being are not identical. Being, which is vīthi-mutta, is opposed to thought, which is vīthi-citta.[3] Though there is thus a contrariety, yet there is a similarity between the two, in that both are subjective.

Being opposed to Thought.

Bhavanguppaccheda, the *dividing line* between

[1] *Cf.* the well-known line of Herakleitus: 'You cannot step twice into the same rivers, for fresh waters are ever flowing in upon you.' —Ed.

[2] Lit., bhavassa anga, part (anga) of being, or becoming (bhava). For earlier post-Pitakan occurrence of this term, *cf.* *Nettip.*, 91; *Milinda*, 300. The bare expression occurs, indeed, in *Anguttara-Nikāya*, ii., 79, as one in a category of four anga's: rūpa, vedanā, saññā, bhava. (Catukka-Nipāta, Apaṇṇaka-Vagga, 75.) See Appendix: Bhavanga.—Ed.

[3] Vīthi=lit., a line, road, street, or course. It was not yet used philosophically in the Abhidhamma-Piṭaka, but I have found it so used in the Commentaries—*e.g.*, that on the Kathā-Vatthu. —Ed.

Threshold of Consciousness. Being and Thought, is termed mano-dvāra, the Threshold (lit., door) of Consciousness. Consciousness below this threshold may be termed, after F. W. Myers, subliminal consciousness, and that above, supraliminal.

There are nineteen classes of subliminal consciousness among the classes of 'resultant' consciousness (vipāka) described in Part I. of the Manual. Of these, only ten are said to be *potentially* possible in the kāma-loka, five in the rūpa-loka, and four in the arūpa-loka.[1] But only one or other of these is *actually* possible for each individual life, according to circumstances. These are described in Part V. of the Manual as paṭisandhi's, but will be referred to as kāma-, rūpa-, or arūpa-bhavanga's, while discussing the forms of consciousness, when the connection between bhavanga and Being will be more apparent. The investigation of these circumstances will lead to the determination of which class, or classes of subliminal consciousness can take part in the processes of thought to be described later.

A flow of the momentary states of subliminal consciousness of a particular class constitutes the bhavanga-sota, the stream of being, bounded by birth (paṭisandhi) and decease (cuti). And as decease is but a prelude to another birth, the continued flow of the stream of being from life to life, from existence to existence, constitutes saŋsāra,[2] the ocean of existence.

These momentary states of subliminal consciousness of an individual being are like one another in certain respects—to wit: plane of existence (bhūmi), kind [of consciousness] (jāti), concomitant mental properties (sampayutta-dhammā), conditions precedent (sankhārā), and object of consciousness (ārammaṇa). And because of the continuity of such similar states or temporary selves,

[1] Loka is world or sphere of existence. On the three loka's, see Manual, p. 81, *n*. 2, and below, p. 12. Paṭisandhi = lit., re-connection, is the usual term in Abhidhamma for re-birth (or re-conception). —Ed.

[2] Lit., continual going.

men, under the blinding influence of ignorance (a v i j j ā) mistake similarity for identity, and are apt to think of al this 'river of life' as one enduring, abiding soul or ego, even as they think the river of yesterday identical with that of to-day.

While the object is regarded as constantly changing, the subject is still held in the West to be an abiding, enduring entity. But in the Buddhist view, both the subject and the object are alike transitory, the relation alone between the two impermanent correlates remaining constant. This constancy of relation, which, according to our tentative definition, is consciousness itself, gives rise to the erroneous idea of Personal Identity. **Personal Identity.**

If the subject be self-same, it should always regard an admittedly changing object as different at different times; but never as the same for any two consecutive moments. But the fact that we can regard a changing object as identical at different times, even after a lapse of a long interval, shows to the Buddhists that the subject cannot possibly remain the identical self for any two consecutive moments throughout that interval.

The phenomenon of self-consciousness is not an exception. Self presented in this consciousness is, like any other object, variable, but regarded as identical. **Self-Consciousness.**

The Stream of Being, then, is an indispensable condition or factor, the *sine quâ non* of present conscious existence; it is the *raison d'être* of individual life; it is the life-continuum; it is, as it were, the background on which thought-pictures are drawn. It is comparable to the current of a river when it flows calmly on, unhindered by any obstacle, unruffled by any wind, unrippled by any wave; and neither receiving tributary waters, nor parting with its contents to the world. And when that current is opposed by any obstacle of thought from the world within, or perturbed by tributary streams of the senses from the world without, then thoughts (vīthi-citta's) arise. But it must not be supposed that the stream of being is a sub-plane from which thoughts rise to the surface. There is juxtaposition of momentary states of consciousness, subliminal and supraliminal, throughout a life-time and from existence to existence. But there is no superposition of such states.

Life, then, in the Buddhist view of things, is like an ever-changing river, having its source in birth, its goal in death, receiving from the tributary streams of sense constant accretions to its flood, and ever dispensing to the world around it the thought-stuff it has gathered by the way.

Primary classification of consciousness.

We have seen that subliminal consciousness is either **kāma**, **rūpa**, or **arūpa**. Supraliminal consciousness may be classified as normal, supernormal and transcendental. Normal consciousness is termed **kāma-citta**, because it generally pertains to the **kāma-loka**, so called because desire (**kāma**) prevails on this plane of existence. Supernormal consciousness is termed **mahaggata-citta**, because it has reached the sublime state. And it is further distinguished as **rūpa-**, or **arūpa-citta**, according as it is generally found in the **rūpa-** or **arūpa-loka**. **Rūpa-loka** is so called because the subtle residuum of matter is said, in that plane of existence, to be still met with. **Arūpa-loka** is so called because no trace of matter is held to be found in it. Transcendental consciousness is termed **lokuttara-citta**, because it is altogether out of all the three **lokas**, or worlds.[1]

Universal mental properties.

Consciousness, in this fourfold classification, is primarily composed of seven mental properties (**cetasika's**)—namely: contact (**phassa**), feeling (**vedanā**), perception (**saññā**), will or volition (**cetanā**), oneness of object (**ekaggatā**), psychic life (**jīvitindriya**), attention (**manasikāra**). These seven mental properties are termed **sabba-citta-sādhāraṇa**, or Universals,[2] because they are common to every class or state of consciousness, or every separate act of mind or thought.

[1] **Uttără**=beyond, outside of.

[2] Lit., common to all consciousness.

Each of them is therefore consciousness and *something* more. If we were to represent a state of consciousness by a sphere composed of these seven mental properties, their common consciousness would be represented by the outer shell of the sphere. And if each sphere of consciousness were composed of only these seven and no more, there would be only a single class of consciousness. But there are forty-five different properties distinguishing one class from another. And these, in varying combinations, give rise to the eighty-nine classes of consciousness enumerated in Part I. of the Manual, or, according to a broader classification, one hundred and twenty-one.

Different properties and classes of Consciousness.

A type of consciousness analyzed.

If we take as our example the first automatic (asaṅkhārika) class of thought out of the eight appetitives (lobha-mūla's), and subject it to an analysis according to the methods of Buddhist psychology described in Part II., we shall find that this class of consciousness is compounded of no less than nineteen mental properties. These māy be grouped as follows: Seven Universals, or sabba-citta-sādhāranas (already named); six Particular properties, or pakiṇṇakas, common to some only; four Bad Universals, common to all evil thoughts (sabbākusala-sādhāraṇa's); appetite or greed (lobha); and error (diṭṭhi—*i.e.*, micchā-diṭṭhi).[1]

Now, in Buddhist logic adequate analysis of any *datum* includes an examination of its—(1) characteristic mark (lakkhaṇa); (2*a*) function (kicca-rasa), (2*b*) property (sampatti-rasa), (3*a*) reappearance as phenomenon (upatthānākāra-paccupaṭṭhāna), (3*b*) reappearance as effect (phala-paccupaṭṭhāna), and (4) proximate cause (padaṭṭhāna).[2] Space, however, does not permit such a detailed inquiry into each of these nineteen mental properties, nor into those other properties given in

[1] Diṭṭhi = lit., view or views; micchā = wrong, bad.—Ed.

[2] On this logic of definition, see Manual, Part IX., § 7, 8, *n*. Reappearance (paṭi-upaṭṭhāna, hence paccupa°) is 'habitual' phenomenal appearance.—Ed.

Part II.), and I must confine myself to a brief consideration of their most salient features.

The seven universal properties. First of all, then, the subject is aware of the presence of an object. And in the case of the type of thought under discussion the object is either an agreeable sight, sound, smell, taste, touch, or concrete mental object (dhammārammaṇa)—agreeable in the sense that it

1. Phassa explained. is desired by the subject (iṭṭhārammaṇa).[1] This awareness of the objective presentation is termed contact (phassa).[2]

2. Vedanā. The subject is next aware of itself as being affected as an animated organism (nāma-rūpa, where rūpa, or matter, is conjoined with mind)—in this case pleasurably, by the agreeable contact or impact. This awareness of subjective affection in some way, either pleasantly, painfully, or indifferently, is termed 'feeling born of contact' (samphassa-jā-vedanā). The term 'vedanā' is not confined to the hedonistic aspect of sensations, but includes such emotions as joy and grief. It covers all kinds of feeling, physical and mental. Vedanā is either bodily (kāyikā), or mental (mānasikā, cetasikā). Under the aspect of feeling (anubhavana-bheda), vedanā is either pleasure (sukha), or pain (dukkha), or neither pain nor pleasure (adukkham-asukha). The last-mentioned is also known as upekkhā—*i.e.*, hedonic neutrality or indifference.[3] But this hedonic element is distinct from that equanimity or balance of mind (tatramajjhattatā),[4] which implies a complex intellectual state.

The sense of touch alone is accompanied by the positive hedonic elements of pain and pleasure; the other four senses are accompanied by hedonic indifference. This exceptional distinction is assigned to the sense of touch,

[1] Lit., wished-for object.—Ed.

[2] More, lit., still, 'tact,' the etymological equivalent of con-tact being sam-phassa.—Ed.

[3] Lit., looking-at—*i.e.*, contemplating, not pursuing.—Ed.

[4] Lit., there-middleness. *Cf.* below, p. 66.

because the impact between the sentient surface (pasāda-rūpa) and the respective objects of other senses, both sets of which are secondary qualities of body, is not strong enough to produce physical pain or pleasure. But in the case of touch there is contact with one, or other, or all the three primary qualities (locality, temperature, pressure); and this is strong enough to affect those primary qualities in the percipient's own body. Just as cotton-wool striking cotton-wool on an anvil does not affect the latter, but a hammer striking cotton-wool imparts its shock to the anvil also.[1]

If to pleasure and pain we add excitement, we get joy (somanassa) and grief (domanassa). Thus, there are five classes of vedanā considered as controlling faculties (indriya's). The excess of pleasure over pain constitutes the sentiment of happiness or bliss (sukha), and the excess of pain over pleasure, the sentiment of misery or ill (dukkha). We have digressed a little here, so as to prevent a possible confusion between the hedonic upekkhā and the intellectual upekkhā, on the one hand, and between the simple sukha and the complex sukha on the other.

3. Saññā. Next, the subject refers the sensation proper to a sense-organ—*e.g.*, the eye in the case of sight—and is aware that the vatthu, or the physical basis of this sensation, is extended so as to receive contact—*i.e.*, occupies space. This recognition of the localization of sensation proper is termed 'perception (proper) born of contact' (samphassa-jā-saññā).

But here also the term saññā should not be confined to external perception. If it is rendered by 'perception' in this Manual, the term 'perception' must be understood in the widest significance of the term, somewhat after the manner of Descartes, Malebranche, Locke, Leibnitz, and others, before its limitation by Reid. Saññā, in Buddhist psychology, means the awareness of the marks, real or

[1] A simile derived by the commentators from Buddhaghosa (*Asl.* 263; *cf.* my *Buddhist Psy.*, lvii., 127, *n.* 1).—Ed.

imaginary, by which an object either of sense or thought is, or may hereafter be, recognized.

4. Cetanā. The function of volition is twofold. In its psychological aspect it merely determines the activities of its concomitant properties, eighteen in number in the present case. In this aspect it is called co-existent volition (sahajātā-cetanā). In its ethical aspect it determines its own consequences, subject to conditions (hetu's). In the class of consciousness under consideration the exercise of volition is conditioned by the two so-called 'roots': Ignorance (moha) and Greed (lobha). Under favourable circumstances volition is transformed into action, or kamma—that is to say, the particular state of consciousness in which volition is translated into action may manifest itself as thought (mano-kamma), which in turn may lead to, and result in, speech (vacī-kamma) or deed (kāya-kamma). When it is so transmuted, entailing moral consequences, it is designated asynchronous volition (nānakkhaṇika-cetanā).[2] And the action (kamma), into which this volition is transmuted, is termed 'course of action' (kamma-patha).

5. Ekaggatā. The mental property by which the Object of consciousness is *necessarily* regarded as an individual, occupying a definite position in space, or time, or in both, is termed 'individuality of object' (ekaggatā).

Time and Space are Subjective Elements. Without entering into the celebrated examination, by Kant, of the question whether time and space have objective reality, we may say that, in Buddhism, both are regarded as subjective elements. Ākāsa (space) is a permanent *concept* (nicca-paññatti), by which the mind is enabled to distinguish objects in external perception. What space is to matter time is to mind. Time is the concept (kāla-paññatti), by which, first and foremost, mental states are distinguished in internal intuition. It is the *sine quâ non* of the succession of these mental states.

This mental property of objective delimitation, or

1 *I.e.*, volition differing in time from its consequences. *Cf.* Part VIII., § 9.

okaggatā, when cultivated and developed, is designated concentration of thought, or samādhi.

6. Manasikāra.

The selective or co-ordinating activity of attention (manasikāra) may be aroused from within or from without, and, in the present case, spontaneously (*i.e.*, without any volitional effort on one's own part or on the part of another) from without by the object itself. And it is directed to this one object. It is the *alpha* and the *omega* of an act of consciousness. This is probably the reason why it comes last in the list.[1]

7. Jīvitindriya.

We have said that will determines the activities of its concomitant properties (p. 16). But the activities of will itself and the rest of the concomitant properties are due to the psychic life (jīvitindriya), which infuses mental life into one and all, and constitutes the whole into a psychosis or psychical state.

In this way all the seven Universals should be accounted for in every class of consciousness, though they may be unequally roused into activity, according to circumstances, in different states of consciousness.

Six particular cetasikas.

Of Specific or Accidental properties, first the six particulars :

1. Vitakka. 2. Vicāra. 3. Adhimokkha.

Vitakka is the directing of concomitant properties towards the object. Vicāra is the continued exercise of the mind on that object. Adhimokkha presupposes a certain amount of hesitancy on the part of the mind whether it shall attend, or not, to a particular object out of many presented. As its name implies, it is the 'freedom' from the wavering state of the mind between two courses open to it. It is the property by which the mind *decides*, or *chooses* to attend to this, rather than that, in the field of presentation.[1] It has nothing to do with judgment, which

[1] Imam evāti sanniṭṭhānakaraṇaŋ:—'Making the conclusion: "Just this one."' The work quoted is the Thera Subhūti's Index, *Abhidhānappadīpikā-sūci* (Colombo, 1893) to his edition of *The Abidhānappadīpika* (Colombo, 1865), a Pali dictionary compiled about A.D. 1200 by Thera Moggallāna.—Ed.

is not formed till the process of thought called vinic-chăyă is reached; for it obtains also in any purely presentative process. And such a process does not admit of any comparison whatever between two concepts compared in a judgment, as, *e.g.*, when an unknown object is presented for the first time, and representative cognition is

4. Viriya. involved. The effort of conation or will is due to viriya.
5. Piti. 6. Chanda. Pīti signifies an interest *in the object;* chanda constitutes the intention with respect to act. Effort, intention, or knowledge, may predominate at the time of the commission of an act, and, when it does so, the 'predominant' factor is termed adhipăti, to which we shall revert later (p. 60).

Four universal bad cetasikas. 1. Moha. Of the four Universal Bad Properties, moha (illusion) is present as the root of every form of evil, creating confusion as to the true nature of the object, or the consequences of an act. The evolution of evil from avijjā (ignorance) is discussed under the doctrine of Paṭicca-samuppāda, in Part VIII. of the manual.

The absence of shame in the commission of an evil act
2. Ahirika. is ahirika; while the absence of fear of its consequences
3. Anottappa. Conscience. is anottappa. Their opposites correspond to conscience or the moral faculty. The distraction of the mind is
4. Uddhacca. accounted for in uddhacca, the property antithetical to attention.

Two specific cetasikas. 1. Lobha. 2. Diṭṭhi. Of the two Specific Properties, greed and error, greed covets the object and supplies a motive for the act of getting at it. In doing so it conditions its concomitant properties, principally volition (cetanā) in the production of the desired effect.

The class of consciousness under examination is termed
Sahetuka. conditional (sahetuka), because it contains a condition —*i.e.*, two *conditioning* properties and seventeen *conditioned* properties.[1] The specific characters of this class of consciousness are, that it *automatically springs into being* (on

[1] 7 Universals + 6 Particulars + 3 Bad Universals + Error.

the presentation of an agreeable sight, etc.), that it is *associated with erroneous views* (as to the consequences, etc.), and is *accompanied by joy.* From these special characteristics this class of consciousness has been styled 'consciousness accompanied by joy, connected with error, automatic.' This many-worded term is a definition rather than a mere name. And it is a definition which fulfils Bain's requirements, to which we have alluded at the beginning of this essay.

This type of thought may manifest itself in seven of the ten courses of bad action (akusala-kammapathā, sometimes called ten duccarita's), described in Part V. of the manual—*e.g.*, in theft, adultery, etc., but not in murder, harsh speech (pharusa-vācā), and hostile thought (byāpāda). Again, this class of thought generally occurs to one who is of a joyous nature by birth (somanassa-paṭisandhika), or to one who has not a deep (agambhīra), philosophic turn of mind. But when such an one holds a wrong view of the universe, or associates with another who holds such a view, and when the absence of sloth and torpor is brought about by suitable foods, etc., then this class of thought may arise in any individual, except the eight classes of the elect (ariya-puggalā), under the above circumstances, at *any* time and at *any* place.

Such is the complexity of the mechanism of a single class of consciousness. The salient features of the remaining mental properties will have to be studied under other classes of consciousness; but space does not permit me to enter into them here.

Classes of Consciousness grouped.

Of the eighty-nine classes of consciousness to be studied in this way, some are karmic (*i.e.*, function as karma, or as causes); some function as resultants (vipākā); and some are non-causal (kriyā). Or, considered from the point of view of energy, some are actual or potential, some are in course of manifestation as work, and some are static. The term 'inoperative' has been introduced into the translation as a substitute for the last (kriyā).

Unconditional (a h e t u k a) consciousness is either resultant or non-causal; while conditional consciousness (s a h e t u k a) is either causal or non-causal. Causal classes of consciousness are either good or moral (k u s a l a), or bad or immoral (a k u s a l a), and are therefore determinate; while resultant and non-causal classes are neither moral nor immoral, and are therefore neutral, unmoral, or indeterminate (a b y ā k ā t ā).

Kriyā. Non-causal or static consciousness is characteristic of the Buddha and his Arahants only. Their non-causal volition (kriyā-cetanā) does not modify the character ethically one way or another, because it is now subject to good hetu's (conditions)—namely, absence of greed (a l o b h a), absence of ill-will (a d o s a), and the absence of illusion (a m o h a), and is entirely free from the *latent* principles of evil (a n u s ă y ă ' s).

Hasituppāda. Of the non-causal classes of consciousness, the 'genesis of mirth' (h a s i t u p p ā d a, or æsthetic faculty) bears on the Philosophy of Æsthetics. Of the three branches of this Philosophy—the Beautiful, the Sublime, and the Ludicrous, which are so closely connected with one another —we propose to discuss here briefly the first and the last.

The Beautiful. The Beautiful does not appear to be defined anywhere in Buddhism. The obvious reason is that it is largely subjective. Hence to us it is not surprising that moralists in the West have now abandoned the idea of searching after the common quality or qualities of the Beautiful.

In Buddhism the term 'the beautiful' (s u b h a or s o b h a ṇ a) is opposed to evil (p ā p a). Hence 'the beautiful' is synonymous with 'the good.' And 'the good,' when applied to an object, is equivalent to the desirable (i ṭ ṭ h a). Thus the beautiful is more or less a matter of *taste*. In other words, the Philosophy of the Beautiful is identical with the Philosophy of Taste*; for what is pleasing to one may be painful to another. Notwithstanding this relativity, the Buddhists do recognize a common sense of beauty, by virtue of which *average* minds are similarly affected by the same object. In fixing the standard of objective beauty, Buddhists avoid the two extremes.

The one extreme is that cultured minds may regard even a corpse which is ugly or foul (a-subha) as useful, suitable, good, and agreeable for the purpose of his meditation. They also perceive the loathsomeness of food (āhāre-paṭikūla-saññā), which ordinary mankind are in the habit of regarding as wholesome. Hence the Buddhists consider that such a sense of beauty is too refined to be of any practical value for a common standard. The other extreme is that uncultivated minds often look upon the beautiful as ugly. Heretics, for example, were offended with the personal beauty of the Buddha, who was held by one-third of mankind as the supremely desirable object (ati-iṭṭhārammana). The lower animals also often relish most abominable foods. Their sense of beauty, therefore, cannot serve as a standard either.

Another test of beauty is, according to Buddhists, in the sense-organs. A fine spear, they say, is very pleasing to the eye, but very disagreeable when it pierces the skin. A fruit may be palatable to taste, but offensive to smell. A bitter fruit may be very pretty. In short, what is agreeable to one sense may be disagreeable to another.

Now the pleasures of the senses are regarded by mankind as desirable, but excess of pleasure is painful; for there is a limit to everything that is in this world. Light or sound, for instance, is pleasing to the eye or ear up to a certain limit, beyond which it is positively painful. This limit, of course, varies with individuals, but there is a common limit fixed by the average majority.

The third criterion by which Buddhists judge of the pleasurableness or painfulness of an object is the amount of effort required to get a desirable object, or to resist or repulse an undesirable one. The most pleasant is then in the line of least resistance. Buddhaghosa has accordingly summed up, in his Commentary on the Vibhaṅga,[1] as follows: 'The desirable and the undesirable are decided by means of (or with reference to) either the common sense of mankind, or the sense-organs, or the amount of effort required.' Of all the senses, sight and hearing are regarded as most æsthetic. Sight is compared by Buddhists to a snake which delights in a hole full of rubbish. Thus art-paintings with variegated colours are preferable to a plain drawing. The same remarks apply to hearing, which takes delight in music, but not in a monotonous noise.

The Ludicrous.

Now we shall see how the Theory of the Beautiful bears on that of the Ludicrous from the Buddhist standpoint.

Laughter is held to be but an expression of pleasurable feeling. There are six classes of laughter recognized in Buddhist works: (1) sita: a smile manifesting itself in expression and countenance; (2) hasita: a smile consisting in the slight movements of the lips just enough to reveal the tips of the teeth; (3) vihasita: laughter giving out a slight sound; (4) upahasita: laughter accompanied by the movement of the head, shoulders, and arms; (5) apahasita: laughter accompanied by the shedding of tears; and (6) atihasita: an outburst of laughter accompanied by the forward and backward movements of the entire body from head to foot. Laughter is thus a form of bodily expression (kāya-viññatti), which may or may not be accompanied by vocal expression (vacī-viññatti). Of these, the first two classes are indulged in by cultured persons, the next two by the average man, and the last two by lower classes of beings.

Laughter is caused by one or other of the thirteen classes of joyful thoughts named in Part I. of the manual—namely, by four of the 'Appetitive' (lobhamūla) class, by four of the 'Great' main classes or types of good consciousness

[1] Iṭṭhāniṭṭhāni majjhassa vasā dvāravasena vā payogassa vasenāpi nicchitānīti āgataŋ. *Sammoha-Vinodanī.* There is as yet no European edition of this work.—Ed.

(mahā-kusala),[1] by four of the great classes of inoperative consciousness (mahā-kriyā), and by the one sense of æsthetic pleasure termed 'laughter-genesis' (hasituppāda).

In the case of ordinary average persons (puthujjănă's), the first eight classes of joyful consciousness obtain. Of these eight, the two erroneous classes of appetitives do not obtain in the case of the four 'attainers of the paths' (maggaṭṭhānā) and the three lower 'enjoyers of the fruits' (phalaṭṭhānā). The last-mentioned five classes of joyful consciousness are the prerogatives of the Buddha and his Arahants. And as the Buddha is supposed to have only indulged in the sita class of laughter, the term hasituppāda must be understood to be a contraction of sitahasituppāda.

We have said elsewhere in this essay that either an agreeable object, or the inborn or innate sense of pleasure, or the want of seriousness, gives rise to joyful consciousness of the Appetitive class. But we cannot here enter into the complicated causes that bring about joyful thoughts in other classes of consciousness. Suffice it for the present to observe that laughter is not caused by joyful thought in cognition on occasion of sense (called 'five-door cognition,' pañcadvāra-vīthi). The sight of an agreeable object gives rise to a sudden accession of pleasure. Pleasure accompanied by excitement is joy, and it is this joy which is reproduced in the reproductive processes, to be described later, that excites laughter. Thus there is a certain amount of reflection, comparison, discrimination, etc., when we laugh.

It is generally said that the Buddha smiled on seeing the Subtle (anoḷārika). But Buddhadatta, the contemporary of Buddhaghosa, would substitute the Degraded[2]

Anoḷārika *versus* anuḷāra.

[1] See p. 86, *n.* 3. Twenty-four classes of kāma-consciousness are so-called because they have the most extensive field of action.

[2] Chasu anuḷāresu ārammaṇesu hasituppādānakiccă. *Abhidhammāvatāra.*

(a n u ḷ ā r a), as opposed to the Sublime (p a ṇ ī t a), for the Subtle. Herein this much-abused author seems to us to be describing more aptly Moggallāna's smile on seeing a P e t a,[1] because P e t a s are very low in the scale of beings, and all of them were more or less ugly and awkward. It has been argued against this view that Moggallāna, from his compassionate nature, could not possibly have been exulting over the misfortune of another. But this argument has been met by the answer that the thera merely rejoiced over the idea that he himself had escaped the rounds of such miserable existence.

Hobbes anticipated. In this view, then, the Buddhists forestalled Hobbes, according to whom 'laughter is a sudden glory arising from a sudden conception of some eminency in ourselves by comparison with the infirmity of others or with our own formerly.' This implies some gratification of the sentiment of power; for the pleasure, whether excited by the Beautiful, the Sublime, or the Ludicrous, is nothing but a sense of superiority over certain other things in nature. If, on the other hand, we are pleased on account of the superiority of others, our pleasure, now termed m u d i t ā, is sympathetic and appreciative. If the Ludicrous be the Degraded, the degradation is not sufficient to provoke pity or ill-will, or grief. That is to say, it is not an undesirable object in itself, but a mean between the Desirable and the Undesirable. But in the absence of the Ludicrous, as when a man is always of a smiling face, we attribute his smiling countenance to his innate sense of pleasure or naturally happy temperament.

Finally, when a child, from the wantonness of youth, bursts into laughter at the slightest cause, which is not sufficient to provoke even a smile from an adult, we say that the child's hilarity is due to a want of seriousness,

[1] A race of hungry shades or ghost-beings: one of the unhappy forms of rebirth. This episode has apparently grown out of P ā r ā - j i k a IV. (*Vin.* iii., 104 *f.*), and L a k k h a ṇ a - S a ṃ y u t t a (*S.* ii., 254 *f.*), where Moggallāna sees a variety of absurd objects and smiles, *but not a Peta.*—Ed.

which somewhat corresponds to Bain's 'Reaction from the Serious.'[1]

Now, there are two elements in every consciousness, the Constant and the Variable. V ī t h i is, figuratively speaking, the road along which the mind travels by marked, well-defined, permanent stages (ṭ h ā n a ' s). The fixity and constancy of these stages gives rise to that Order of Thought (c i t t a - n i y ā m a), which corresponds to Mansel's 'Form of Consciousness.'[2] The form of consciousness, the constant element, is opposed to the matter of consciousness which, as supplied in this or that experience, constitutes the variable element; but it must be borne in mind that, in Buddhism, both subject and object are variable at every moment. With Mansel, who holds that the subject is the constant element, there is only one form. But in Buddhism there are several forms of consciousness, each of which will be designated a 'process of thought' whenever it takes place as a fact.

Order of Consciousness (Vīthi).

The Form and Matter of Consciousness.

We have said that time is the *sine quâ non* of the succession of mental states. To every separate state of consciousness (c i t t u p p ā d a), which takes part in a process of thought as a functional state, either in the subjective form of the stream of being, which we have described as free from process (v ī t h i - m u t t a), or in the objective form of a conscious act of mind or thought, which we shall describe as process-consciousness (v ī t h i - c i t t a), there are three phases—genesis (u p p ā d a), development (ṭ h i t i), and dissolution (b h a n g a). Each of these phases occupies an infinitesimal division of time—an instant (k h a ṇ a)—so that to every separate state of consciousness there are three instants, in which successively it becomes, exists, and disappears. These three instants —nascent, static, and cessant (or arrested)—together form one mental moment (c i t t a k k h a ṇ a), the period occupied by any single state of consciousness, or any separate act

Three Phases of Thought.

A Thought-Moment of Three Instants.

[1] *Mental Science*, p. 317.
[2] *Metaphysics*, p. 58.

of mind or thought. And it pleases commentators to say that there are more than one billion of such thought-moments in the time that would be occupied by the shortest flash of lightning.

Life-term of Matter.

The life-term of the qualities of body (rūpa) has been deduced from the longest time required for complete consciousness of an object. We shall see that seventeen thought-moments are held to be requisite for a complete process of consciousness. Thus Buddhists have come to speak of matter as lasting for seventeen thought-moments. These, they say, constitute the normal duration of a material phenomenon—normal, because six out of the twenty-eight qualities of body (enumerated in Part VI. of the Manual)—viz., the two communicating qualities of body, or media of communication (viññatti-rūpa's), and the four characteristic marks of matter (lakkhaṇa-rūpa's), are of less than seventeen thought-moments' duration. These may be styled 'short-lived qualities.'

Some authorities (*e.g.*, the Mūla-Ṭīkā[1]) dispute the existence of a static phase of thought, and regard it as merely hypothetical. They hold that, in becoming, a thing simply grows and decays, with no static stage.

We have so far cleared our way for the description of different thought-forms. These will not be clearly understood unless I add some such preliminary survey of the Buddhist view of life, and of the salient character of Buddhist psychology.

Paṭisandhi-vīthi.

The term paṭisandhi (re-birth or conception) is applied to the resultant consciousness, as determined by the past efficient action (janakakamma), of that which is being conceived as an individual. From and after the moment of conception the current of being is said to be renewed in the form of a series of fifteen or sixteen subconscious moments (or bhavanga's). These have for their object either the past efficient action itself, or a symbol of that past action (kamma-nimitta), or a sign of the

[1] Sub-commentary on Buddhaghosa's Commentaries by Ānanda of Anurādhapura in Ceylon.

tendencies (g a t i - n i m i t t a) that are determined by the force of that past action. The explanation of these three technical terms is better postponed till we come to the consideration of the philosophy of death. Suffice it for the present to state the Buddhist hypothesis of decease and re-birth—namely that, whatever object was presented to the mind at the stage of apperception immediately before death in the *previous* existence, there is invariably presented, or re-presented, to the new consciousness, all the sub-conscious moments and the re-decease (c u t i) of the existence immediately following.

Bhavanga-calana. Next, the new sphere of existence, as an object, enters the field of presentation, and produces perturbation in the stream of being, causing this, as it were, to vibrate (as a lamp flickers before it goes out) for two moments. The first of these moments is termed 'vibrating' (b h a v a n g a - c a l a n a), but the second is termed 'arrest' (b h a v a n - g u p p a c c h e d a), because at the end of the latter the stream is 'cut off' by the faculty of reflection, or mind-door cognition—*i.e.*, mind proper (m a n o d v ā r ā v a j - j a n a). And this faculty is capable of reflecting on the new existence. The 'arrest' is thus, as has been already observed, the threshold of consciousness, by which thought is divided from mere being.

Bhavanguppaccheda.

Mind-door faculty.

This reflecting in turn is followed by a series of seven apperceptives, accompanied by a strong desire to live the new life (b h a v a - n i k a n t i - l o b h a - j a v a n ā n i).

Consciousness thereafter loses itself in *living* (b h a v - a n g a); sinks, as it were, into the stream of being, until its current is interrupted by some new thought-obstacle or sensation.

Intuitive Process of Sight in Presentative Consciousness. Suppose now that a visible object (r ū p ā r a m m a ṇ a) is presented.[1] It first enters the stream of being at the nascent instant of a life-moment, which is termed 'past'

[1] The European reader should remember that in the following description the *duration* of each stage is, through analysis, magnified from infinitesimal to appreciable quantities, even as happens to minute sections of material structure under the microscope.—Ed.

Atita-bhavanga. (a t ī t a - b h a v a n g a). This is so called because it completes its three phases and passes away *before* any marked perturbation is produced in the calm flow of the stream. Then the object begins to assert its influence by impeding the stream, with the result that the latter begins to vibrate, as a spinning-top when its velocity is failing. In other words, the vibration is due to the initial impact between the object and the organs of visual sentience (c a k k h u - p a s ā d̥ a - r ū p a's), the sentient surface springing into activity at the nascent instant of the moment of the object's entry into the stream.[1] This vibration lasts for two moments, as in the preceding case, after which the stream ceases to flow as such, because it is now arrested by the so-called 'Five-door-turning-towards' of cognition on occasion of sense, in which attention is more active than its concomitant mental properties. At this stage the subject merely *turns* for one thought-moment to something that arouses its attention after having produced a disturbance in the stream of being, but knows no more about it.

Pañca-dvārā-vajjana.

Cakkhu-viññāṇa. Following upon it, the specific sense of sight, or visual sensation (c a k k h u - v i ñ ñ ā ṇ a), comes into play, when the subject *sees* a certain object, as to the nature of which it does not as yet *know* anything. At this stage, then, the subject is merely aware of the fact that a certain object is seen.

Sampaṭic-chana. This sense-operation is followed by a moment of *reception* of the object so seen—*i.e.*, of the whole scene presented to the eye, when the receptive faculty passively receives, as it were, the sense-impression caused by the external stimulus. Two modes of recipient reaction are distinguished—reception of an agreeable, or of a disagreeable object.

Santīraṇa. Next comes the investigating faculty, or a momentary *examination* of the object so received. Three modes in it are distinguished, according as the object is very agreeable, moderately agreeable, or disagreeable.

After this comes that stage of representative cognition

[1] See on physical base of consciousness, p. 31.

termed 'fixing,' or, as we might say, *determining*. This is the arranging of the investigated material in such a manner as to constitute it into a definite object. This is done by differentiation and limitation, by discrimination and definition. A mango-fruit, for instance, to be discerned as such and as nothing else, must have certain definitive and constitutive features and attributes of its own. By this faculty these are separated from the surroundings for final apperception in the next stage. Up to this stage the subject is not yet intelligently aware of the nature and character of the object. Voṭṭhabbana.[1]

Now intervenes the *apperceptive* stage, or full cognition,[2] wherein the object, determined or integrated by the foregoing activity, is apperceived, or properly cognized, as, *e.g.*, in the 'first automatic type of thought' analyzed above. This is held to occupy ordinarily seven thought-moments. It is a Buddhist rule of thought that an apperception occurs for either seven moments, or none at all, except in the cases of death, stupefaction, creation of pnenomena, and other special cases, when a less number of moments than seven obtains. Javanā.

At this stage of apperception the subject interprets the sensory impression, and fully appreciates the objective significance of his experience.

After this psychologically important stage there follows a *registering*, or identifying, for two moments, of the object thus apperceived, eleven modes of the process being distinguished according to the nature of the object, etc. The Buddhist theory is that this identification operates for two moments, or not at all. Tadārammaṇa.[3]

Consciousness then loses itself once more in the stream of being; or, to adopt Western phraseology, an objective

[1] In the purer Pali of the Sinhalese term, voṭṭhappana (vi-ava-ṭhap)=thorough, settling-down; hence *establishing* or synthesis.—Ed.

[2] See Appendix: Javana. Twenty-nine modes of javana are distinguished in Kāmaloka experience.

[3] Lit., *that* object, just that same and no other.—Ed.

thought sinks below the threshold of subjective consciousness.

The Simile of the Mango-tree.

The simile of the mango-tree may here serve to illustrate the above process. A man, lost in the deepest sleep, is lying at the foot of a mango-tree with his head covered. A wind now stirs the branches, and a fruit falls beside the sleeping man. He is in consequence aroused from dreamless slumbers. He removes his head-covering in order to ascertain what has awakened him. He sees the newly fallen fruit, picks it up, and examines it. Apprehending it to be a fruit with certain constitutive attributes observed in the previous stage of investigation, he eats it, and then, replacing his head-covering, once more resigns himself to sleep.

The dreamless sleep corresponds to the unperturbed current of the stream of being (b h a v a n g a). The striking of the wind against the tree is like the 'past' life-moment, during which the object enters the stream and passes down with it, without perturbing it. The swaying of the branches in that wind represents the vibration of the stream of being. The falling of the fruit corresponds to the arrest or interruption of being, the moment at which the stream is 'cut off' by thought; the waking of the man to the awakening of attention in the act of cognition on occasion of sense; the removal of the head-covering to the sense-reaction of sight. The picking up of the fruit is comparable to the operation of receiving; inspection of it recalls the examining function. The simple apprehension of the fruit as such, with certain constitutive attributes of its own, corresponds to the discriminative or determining stage; the eating of the fruit resembles the act of apperception. Finally, the swallowing of the last morsels that are left in the mouth[1] corresponds to the operation of retention, after which the mind subsides into mere vital process, even as the man once more falls asleep.

The Tadārammanavāra process.

The above is the normal process of a very vivid (a t i m a - h a n t a) object. The object is so called because it completes

[1] The after-taste had perhaps been an apter simile.—Ed.

its normal life-term of seventeen moments, from the moment of its entry into the stream till the uninterrupted flow is resumed.

The Physical Basis of consciousness. The physical basis of the sense of sight (cakkhu-vatthu) is composed of the optic nerve-ends (cakkhu-pasāda-rūpa's), which spring into activity at the nascent instant of the moment when the object enters into the stream, and are collectively termed 'of mean,' or 'medium duration' (majjhimāyuka), because their functioning is coeval (or synchronous) with the duration of the object itself.

All other states of consciousness that take part in the process have for their physical basis the nerve-cells (hadaya-vatthu's),[1] which spring into active being at the nascent instant of the next previous thought-moment of each.

Mahantārammaṇa. In the case of an object causing only a moderately vivid impression, the vital vibration does not commence till after two, or, in the case of a still less vivid impression, three, of the so-called 'past' moments. In neither case is there retention. The object continues for one moment after apperception in the former, but ceases with the seventh moment of apperception in the latter, after completing its life-term from the moment of its entry into the stream.

Parittārammaṇa. In the case of an object causing only a slight impression, there are four so-called 'past' moments before vibration sets in, and two thought-moments of determining; but these are not followed by apperception. And in direct ratio with the slightness of the impression, the object flows with the stream for five to nine 'past' moments without perturbing it.

Atiparittārammaṇa. There are six modifications of process when the object causes hardly any impression at all. In these the arrest of the stream of being is followed immediately by its

[1] Hadaya-vatthu is, literally, heart basis, but modern Buddhist psychology has apparently clothed the newer physiology in the garment of the older concept. See Appendix: Dasaka, Hadaya.—Ed.

resumption. The object here continues in the stream for from ten to fifteen 'past' moments before vibration sets in, and it ceases to exist after the fifth, fourth, third, second, and first moments of the cognition process in the first five cases respectively, but ceases with the arrest of subconscious life itself in the last. The sense-impression in these so-called 'futile' term-processes (m o g h a - v ā r a) is so weak, that it is not even translated into sensation, but remains a simple undifferentiated irritation of the nerves.

Thus there are four principal classes of reaction to each of the External Senses.

Pañca-dvāra-vīthi, or Five-door-Cognition. This completes the description in outline of presentative consciousness in cognition on occasion of sense (p ā ñ c a - d v ā r a - v ī t h i, or 'five-door process').

External or Acquired Perception. In an actual concrete case of external perception, such as is called by Mansel Acquired Perception,[1] a process of thought never occurs singly. Each externally intuitive process of presentative consciousness is not only repeated several times, but is also followed by several sequels, termed 'consequent' (t a d - a n u v a t t a k a), or 'associated consecutive,' mind-door process (a n u b a n d h a k a - m a n o d v ā r a k a - v ī t h i).

Anubandhavāramatta. The latter group is either (*a*) simple or (*b*) complex, according as it is not, or as it is, accompanied by sign and speech. In order to enable a man to say 'I see a rose,' no less than four classes of the simple group of sequels are required, each of which may be repeated several times. He must first of all perceive a rose, presented in one or other of the forms of external intuition already described. Each process is followed, with a brief moment or two of the subconscious continuum intervening, by the process called 'grasping the past,' in which there is necessarily a depicting to the imagination of the past object which he has just perceived, the images alone of the different parts of the rose being present in mind. These two processes may alternate with each other several hundred thousand times before the synthetic process takes place. The

Atītaggahaṇa-process.

[1] *Metaphysics*, p. 116.

alternation of these two processes may be compared to that of makes and breaks in the connection of an electric dynamo.[1]

Samudāyaggahaṇa or samūhaggahaṇa.[2]

In the third process, also repeated several times, he forms the entire composite image of the rose into a *synthesis* out of the different, component parts which he has just depicted alternately.

Atthaggahaṇa.

In the next stage, called 'grasping - the - meaning,' also repeated several times, he forms an idea of the object corresponding to that image which is representative of the original.

Nāmaggahaṇa.

Lastly, in the stage called 'grasping-the-name,' he invents a name to represent that idea. But if the name happens to be already known to him, three more processes may intervene between this stage and the last.

Sanketa.

That is to say, in the process, called 'convention' (s a n k e t a), he thinks of the conventional sign by which such an idea is usually signified; in the process called 'comparison' (s a m b a n d h a), he compares the idea in question with the former ideas signified by that sign. If, in this comparison, he discriminates certain resemblances between the common attributes, he forms a judgment: 'This is a rose,' called 'the process of judgment' (v i n i c - c h a y a). And, finally, in the process of 'name-grasping,' he applies the class-name to the object. In other words, he brings the concept under a known class.

Sambandha, process of comparison.

Vinicchaya, process of judgment.

These complicated processes of imagination, reproductive and constructive, memory, conception, discrimination, judgment, classification, all follow one another so rapidly in succession that the percipient considers that he 'sees' the rose almost instantaneously. Such is the complexity of processes distinguishable in an act of external perception.

After each external perception the stream of being flows on until it is once more disturbed by a new sense-impres-

[1] Ledi Sadaw cites the ancient and well-known simile of the circle of fire caused by a moving point, to show the persistency of an image.

[2] *I.e.*, grasping of what 'rises up together,' or of a 'collective whole.'

sion, when the whole complex process is once more resumed. In waking life, of course, these complex groups of processes follow each other with hardly an intervening break of unconscious life.

To each process in these sequels to a concrete act of perception there are four classes of reaction, according as the object is very clear (a t i v i b h ū t a), clear (v i b h ū t a), not clear (a v i b h ū t a), or very far from clear (a t i - a - v i b h ū t a. The Manual recognizes only the second and third classes (Part IV., § 2), but the above classification is put forward by the Ledi School. Space, however, forbids me from trying to analyze each class in detail. Briefly indicated, the specific difference is as follows:

Ativibhūtārammaṇa. We have seen that the stream of being, after the two usual moments of vibration, which is here *at once* set up by the object's entry, is arrested by the 'adverting' of the mind door, which reflects on (lit., 'turns to') the object for a moment. Later, the activity whereby the object is apperceived is aroused for seven thought-moments; and, lastly, an act of retention or identification records it for two moments, after which the stream resumes its flow. This is the process when the object is very clear.

Vibhūtārammaṇa. When the object is moderately clear, the vibration and arrest are similar to the corresponding process described above, a hypothetical distinction being drawn with reference to prior and posterior moments of subconscious life (*cf.* pp. 27, 28).

Avibhūtārammaṇa. In the case of an indistinct, vague object, apperception is not at all aroused, and cognitive activity operates for two or three moments only. We shall refer to this class when we come to discuss 'dream-consciousness.'

Ati-avibhūtārammaṇa. Lastly, a very dim object merely sets up vibration in the stream, but with no perceptional result.

The Complex Anubandhaka. Kāyaviññatti. In the complex associated processes, as when a man communicates his wish to another by sign or gesture, two more forms—namely, 'grasping-the-sign' (v i ñ ñ a t t - i g g a h a ṇ a), and 'grasping-the-intention' (a d h i p p a y - a g g a h a n a)—obtain.

Suppose a man beckons another. The movement of the hand is first of all noticed in a visual process of perception, followed by the process of 'grasping-the-past,' in which the past movement of the hand is depicted to imagination. After the alternation of these two processes for several hundred thousand times, as the hand moves forward and backward, the past movements are now imagined as a composite whole in the process of 'grasping-the-synthesis' (s a m ū h a g g a h a ṇ a). Then an idea of the moving hand is formed in the process of 'grasping-the-meaning,' which is followed by the process of 'grasping-the-name,' in which the name 'hand' is thought of.

Viññattiggahaṇa-process.

Now, in 'grasping-the-sign,' which may be in any one of the forms under the four classes of reaction described above, a certain peculiarity in the movement is regarded as a sign. Similarly, in the process of 'grasping-the-intention,' the person's wish is understood.

Adhippāyaggahaṇa-process.

The processes termed above 'convention,' 'comparison,' and 'judgment' may intervene between the last two.

In the case of hearing, the processes of 'name-grasping' and 'meaning-grasping' are reversed. In the case of hearing a foreign language not wholly familiar, the process called 'customary-meaning,' in which the foreign word is translated into the hearer's vernacular, intervenes between the two. But this process is not possible to one who is as yet unacquainted with that foreign language; nor is the process of 'grasping-the-meaning' possible to one who has no previous knowledge that the word in question represents a particular object. When the word is a compound term, the processes are further complicated.

Vohāratthaprocess.

When a person recognizes another by the sound of him without seeing him, the 'synthetic' process is followed by the process of 'grasping-the-sound,' in which the sound ordinarily made by that person is attended to before the 'convention' and the rest of the processes take place. In the case of a speaker, he first of all conceives the idea of the object in the 'meaning-grasping' process; he next thinks of his name in the process of 'name-grasping';

Saddaggahaṇa-process.

then of the sound of that name in the process of 'sound-grasping.' This is lastly followed by the process in which the 'movement' of the vocal organ, together with its resulting sound, are attended to. The last two processes may occur millions of times in the utterance of a single long vowel. But these four processes—grasping of name, meaning, sound, and attention to movement—belong not so much to the subject of perception as to pure representative cognition, to which we shall presently come.

Copana process.

When a person forms an idea of the object from the sight of a written name, the same sequels of the sight of a written word occur as in the case of the object itself.

Vaci-viññatti.

When a man communicates his wish to another by speech, the same processes of the complex group occur as in the case of communication by sign, with this distinction, that the process of 'grasping-the-sign,' in which the peculiarity of the sound uttered is regarded as a sign of communication, is not preceded, but succeeded, by the process of 'grasping-the-name.' Further, in the case of communication by means of a foreign language, the process of 'customary meaning,' in which the foreign language is translated into the vernacular, intervenes before the process of 'grasping-the-meaning.'

The sequels to perception on occasion of smell, taste, and touch are not usually complicated by processes of communication.

Thus there are several links between cognition on occasion of sense and reflection by way of the mind-door in a chain of thought.

Suddhika-mano-dvāra-vīthi.

We have now to consider the forms of Internal Intuition and Reflection Proper (suddha-manodvāra-vīthi).[1]

The possibility of the 'internal' presentation of all the six classes of objects named at the beginning of this essay is

[1] Suddha = pure or clean; hence = bare, 'pure-and-simple,' viz., here, 'not on occasion of sense'; -ika forms the adjective of a quality, the Greek ικος.—Ed.

laid down in the P a ṭ ṭ h ā n a, and in Part III. of the Manual. In other words, the Buddhists hold, that a sensation can be experienced without the corresponding objective stimulus, *e.g.*, a flash can be seen with eyes closed and without the objective ether-waves, as when electricity is applied to the temples. **Sensation without an objective stimulus.**

The possibility of Reflection proper is attributed to the force of the relation termed 'proximate sufficient cause,'[1] by virtue of which (*a*) a sense-impression once experienced in a sense-cognition by way of the five doors, or (*b*) a previous experience of an internal intuition or cognition by way of the mind-door, or (*c*) the idea once formed in the sequels of either, can never be lost.

Any sense-impression once actually experienced in the present life is now classed among Things Seen (d i ṭ ṭ h a),[2] and the processes of reflection connected therewith are grouped under the category of Things Seen (d i ṭ ṭ h a-v ā r a). But when an object that has not been actually sensed is constructed out of, and connected with, these seen objects, it is termed 'object associated with things seen' (d i ṭ ṭ h a-s a m b a n d h a). And the processes of thought connected therewith are classed in the category of objects associated with things seen. **Diṭṭha-vāra-processes.**

The six classes of objects once reflected upon in the present life, from information gained either by hearing others or reading books, are classed as Things Heard (s u t a).[3] And the object constructed out of and connected therewith is termed 'object associated with things heard' (s u t a s a m b a n d h a). **Suta-object.**

· Any apparently *a priori* object that may enter the field of presentation from any other sources except the last two —*e.g.*, when developed by culture—is classed as Things Cogitated (v i ñ ñ ā t a). Any object constructed out of them **Viññāta-object.**

[1] A n a n t a r ū p a n i s s a y a - p a c c a y a.

[2] The sense of sight representing all sense. *Cf.* the French phrase *choses vues*, things of 'real' life.—Ed.

[3] The remarkable conservatism of India in deferring the adoption of writing in all intellectual matters is betrayed in this term.—Ed.

and connected therewith is termed 'associated with things cogitated' (v i ñ ñ ā t a-s a m b a n d h a).

An object in the category of Things Seen may be either past, present, or future. When it is present, it is intuited as a vivid reality. The forms of this internal intuition, or cognition by way of the mind-door, are the same as those described under the 'Sequels.'

The same forms hold good for all kinds of thought or reflection, and may be applied to English concepts of the same as follows:

Reproductive Imagination.

When an object belonging to Things Seen is past, or is reflected upon as past, its image is now presented. And when the presence of the image is accompanied by a belief in the possible existence of a corresponding object in an intuition, thought is an exercise of reproductive imagination. If the image reproduced be not vivid enough, imagination fades into fancy, which 'moves on a lighter wing.' But when the belief amounts to a conviction that the corresponding object had actually existed in a past intuition, reproductive imagination is changed into memory or remembrance. The conviction here is fostered by the Buddhist principle of recognition (s a ñ ñ ā). With a less vivid image, memory fades into reminiscence; and when it has to be recalled with a certain amount of effort, reminiscence becomes recollection. When the Thing-Seen is future—*i.e.*, when the presence of the image is accompanied by a belief in the possible existence of the corresponding object in an intuition not yet experienced—thought is an exercise of anticipation, and hope is weak anticipation.

Paṭisallakkhaṇavīthi.

In the processes belonging to the category of Associates-with-Things-Seen, if a new concrete image—*e.g.*, a unicorn—be constructed by a combination of the parts of several past intuitions, thought is an exercise of constructive or creative imagination. The object of this process may be any one of the six classes, and may be either past, present, future, or not in time, lit., freed from time (k ā l a v i m u t t a). Scientific imagination, and inferences drawn from observation, appear to come under this head.

Under the category of Things Heard, an auditory instead of a visual image of any one of the six classes of objects is formed. If the formation of this image or idea is accompanied by a belief in the possible existence of the corresponding object in an intuition, thought is an exercise of conception. Conception is changed into memory if the belief amounts to a conviction, as in the processes of Things Seen, that the corresponding object had actually existed in a past intuition. If the idea reproduced is not clear enough, memory becomes reminiscence, and, if it has to be recalled, recollection. An idea may be formed of the future, or of that which is not referred to time. Opinion seems to come under this head. The associated processes under Things Heard are similar to those in the first category. Belief, hypothesis, and scientific theories, seem to come under a combination of the two categories which are confined to experiences in this present life; hence the Experientialist dictum that nothing can be in the intellect that has not been in sense. But apparently *a priori* ideas of all the six classes of sensory objects *may* come intuitively, so to speak, from one's former experiences in past lives, or from the telepathic suggestions of other contemporary beings. The intuitions of the processes under the third category (Things Cogitated and associated processes), however, are not restricted to the past and the present, but may extend to the future and the timeless as well.

Each internally intuitive or reflective process is also invariably followed by its sequels, as in the case of cognition on occasion of sense.

Importance of distinguishing between factors and concrete procedure.

Lay readers may well be wearied with these details of the different forms of consciousness, however much I have been at pains to present them as concisely as possible. A slight acquaintance with them, however, will reveal that it is a mistake to look for *all* higher forms of thought, such as memory, conception, judgment, reasoning, in which a comparison or discrimination is involved, in presentative consciousness; much less in the single states of consciousness that take part in each process, presentative or representative; still less in the bare elements of consciousness (the cetasika's).

Confusions in terminology.

I allude to the various renderings adopted by different Occidental scholars of Buddhist technical terms. To select a few out of many: The much-abused term 'thought' has been made by some to stand for cetanā, by others for vitakka; again, by others for vicāra. Saññā (perception in the widest sense of the term) used to be rendered by 'memory,' as also was sati (presence of mind). The former term is, of course, nearer the mark; and yet to render saññā by 'memory' is to confuse it with the higher process of memory, in which saññā may play a more prominent part than in any other process, but of which it (saññā) is *only an element or factor*. Even in a single stage of a concrete process, saññā would be more predominant in that of delimitation (voṭṭhabbana), apperception, and identification, just as another *element*, attention (manasikāra), is more active when mind adverts to sense-stimuli. For the same reason, the *element* of registering or identification (tad-ārammaṇa) should not be mistaken for a *concrete* process like memory.

Vitakka[1] may operate more actively in the processes of imagination or conception than in any other processes, but to render it by imagination or conception is to confuse it with the processes themselves. Again, adhimokkha[2] may be the more conspicuous *element* in the process of judgment.

The rendering of vicāra[3] by 'reason' is even worse than rendering paññā by the same term. Vicāra may largely operate in the stage of investigation (santīraṇa) and other processes, and would strongly operate in all processes of comparison or discrimination. Paññā (or paññindriya, as it is termed in Part II. of the Manual) is the intellectual *element* which enters into the composition of the classes of consciousness described as

1 Application or direction of mind.

2 Deciding, choosing.

3 Sustained application.

'connected with knowledge,' which take part in such processes of thought as involve comparison and discrimination, notably in the reasoning processes (takkavīthi). The scholastic distinction between paññā and ñāṇa, which is useful in a philological study, does not hold good in philosophy. These two terms and amoha have been used, at least in the Manual, to signify one and the same idea. Just as ekaggatā may be developed into samādhi, so may the bare intellectual element be developed by culture into secular knowledge (lokiya-paññā) on the one hand, ranging from the ordinary reasoning power exercised in most trivial matters, through all phases of logical reason in scientific matters, to the abhiññā's, or supernormal exercise of thought and will; and into higher knowledge (lokuttarā-paññā) on the other, ranging from Path-knowledge, preceded by the 'Modes of Thought,' to omniscience. Therefore, if paññā and ñāṇa be rendered by 'reason,' it must be understood as a power or faculty of understanding as distinguished from the concrete reasoning process. It is the underlying *principle* of all forms of knowledge.

Accordingly the cetasika's, named in Part II. of the Manual with respect to their functions as psychological units, or ultimates, are, in Part VII., largely re-named to suit the special context. Language is an instrument of thought, but there is a danger of dealing with words, instead of with ideas, if a too rigid consistency be observed respecting form. This remark applies with even greater force when writers on Buddhism use the same word for two or more different ideas. We may compare the elements of mental processes known as cetasika's to letter-types of fifty-two different classes. Letter-types of the same class may enter into the composition of this or that word, which word may take its place in this or that sentence. The words into the composition of which the types enter are comparable to the states of consciousness, and the sentences may be likened to the processes of thought. As long as the letter-types of each class remain in their respective compartments, they are similar to one another; but when they enter into the composition of different classes of consciousness, they then have different values—*e.g.*, vitakka has one value as a Jhāna-factor in the First Jhāna, another value as a factor of the Eightfold Path (maggaṅga), when it receives the dignified name of 'perfect aspiration' (sammāsankappa).

Memory and changing personality.

From the discussion of these terms we pass on to consider the question: How is memory possible, if the subject be not the same for any two consecutive moments in life? How is it possible for a person who hears the last word in a sentence to know the meaning of the entire sentence if he be a different being from the one who heard the first word in that sentence?

We must look to the Paṭṭhāna for an answer. We cannot enter here into the detailed consideration of the subject; all we can here point out is this:—Each mental state is related to the next in at least four different modes of relation (paccaya):—Proximity (anantara), Contiguity (samanantara), Absence (n'atthi), and Abeyance (avigata).[1] This fourfold correlation is understood to mean that each expired state renders service (upakāra) to the next. In other words, each, on passing away, gives up the whole of its energy (paccaya-satti) to its successor. Each successor, therefore, has all the potentialities of its predecessors, and more. This being so, the mental element or principle of recognition or perception (saññā), in each of the mental states that take part in a memory-process, with all its heritage of the past, is a *recognizing*, under favourable circumstances, in the image reproduced or the idea revived, of the original object by the very marks which were observed by its predecessors in a certain intuition or reflection. Thus the subject has come to regard the image as the copy, and the idea as the counterpart, of the original object intuited or reflected upon.

The ethical aspect of javana.

So far we have postponed the consideration of the ethical aspect of apperception, which is no less important

[1] See Manual, Part VIII., § 7.

to Buddhists. The stage of apperception pertains to the active side of an existence (k a m m a - b h ă v a), which determines the passive side (u p a p a t t i - b h ă v a) of the next existence. The apperceptional act is thus a *free*, determining, causal act of thought, as distinguished from the mental states, which are fixed, determined, resultant acts of mind. This difference is expressed in Buddhism by seeing in the former a *mode* of k a m m a, and in the latter a *resultant* (v i p ā k a) of k a m m a.

The word l a d d h a - p a c c a y a—meaning the circumstances and conditions which obtain[1]—as applied to apperception in the Manual, would settle the question of the absolute freedom of the will. But I use the word *free* in the sense of 'free by reason of the balance of motives or conditions'—*i.e.*, of h e t u ' s. (H e t u ' s are those special conditions described in Part III., § 4, of the Manual.)[2]

Volition, emerging into action (n ā n a k k h a ṇ i k a - c e t a n ā)[3] at this apperceptional stage, has scope for free play or choice by reason of its freedom from the compulsion of those special motives, and therefore acts with greater force. As determined by the past k a m m a and other causes, and as conditioned by all sorts of circumstances other than the restraint of motives, it is then still free to adapt itself to environment or not, because it is now *equally influenced* by the two different sets of good and bad special motives, but is *not compelled* by either. Freedom understood in this restricted sense has apparently given rise to the idea of the free will of the West, in that, between the two courses of conduct open to a moral agent, he is free to make his choice. And if he chooses, of his so-called free will, the good course, then good thoughts, now accompanied and conditioned by the three good motives, arise; otherwise, bad thoughts arise, accompanied and conditioned by the three bad motives. He is therefore morally responsible for his choice or for his act. Moral

The balance of hetu's.

[1] Lit., 'obtained-relation' (l a b h a t i, to obtain).—Ed.

[2] Three bad: greed, hate, illusion; three good, or the opposite.

[3] See above, p. 16: 'asynchronous volition.'

responsibility, therefore, attaches itself to the apperceptional act of thought—in other words, it is only in this apperceptional stage that the character of an average person (puthujjănă), as distinguished from the noble or elect, is ethically modified one way or the other.

Kamma.

We have said that volition (cetanā), under favourable circumstances, is transformed into kamma. But volition in apperception on occasion of sense (pañcadvārika-javana), which, as we have seen under the theory of the Ludicrous, could not even affect laughter, cannot possibly become kamma. Hence we must look to the volition involved in reflective or representative apperception (manodvārika-javana) for kamma.

Apperceptional moments, as a process, are represented as rising and falling in a thought-wave, the intensest being on the crest of the wave. Thus, of the seven moments of volition involved in each reflective process, the fourth is regarded as the strongest. The first is the weakest of the lot, because it lacks the cumulative conditionedness yielded by the preceding state of consciousness, which is of a different class. The initial moment of volition, if preceded by a sufficiently strong effort, would work out its effects in the very same existence in which it is exercised. It is then termed 'kamma-to-be-experienced-in-this-life.' If not, it becomes inoperative for ever, because it is devoid of reproductive power (janaka-satti). The last of the seven volitional moments is a little stronger than the initial, because it stands in the relation called 'succession' or 'recurrence' (āsevana-paccaya),[1] but at the same time it is weaker than the rest, because it is in the last stage of disappearance. If sufficiently strong, it would work out its effects in the next existence through its reproductive function (janaka-kicca). It is then termed 'kamma-to-be-experienced-in-the-next-birth,' but, if weak, it would fail to effect the next rebirth, and thus would be inoperative for ever. The five intermediate volitional moments are termed 'kamma-to-be-experienced-

Diṭṭha-dhamma-vedaniya-kamma.

Upapajja-vedaniya-kamma.

Aparā-pariya-vedaniya-kamma.

[1] See Manual, Part VIII., § 7.

in-after-lives,' because they are capable of operating (whenever circumstances are favourable) from the second next rebirth onwards till Nibbāna is attained. They are able not only to effect rebirth, but to work out effects during the course of any life, whenever favourable opportunities occur. But each volition can effect only a single rebirth, though its effects in life are not limited.

Ineffectual volition. All ineffectual volitions, by reason of their inherent weakness, and all time-barred kamma's, by reason of their inhibition by more powerful kamma, are termed 'have-not-been's' (ahosika).[1] Volition of the distracted (uddhacca) class of thought cannot effect a rebirth, but only after-effects in any life. Volition in apperception before death (maranāsanna-javana) is too weak to effect a rebirth; its action is merely regulative of the next existence. Volition involved in supernormal consciousness (abhiññā-cetanā) cannot effect a rebirth, because its force is spent in working phenomena; nor can the volition of one graduating in the Paths (magga-cetanā) do so, because it is immediately followed by its Fruit (phala).

These remarks on the ethical aspect of apperception do not apply to those inoperative apperceptions (kiriyā-javana's) which are characteristic of the Buddha and his Arahants, who are neither moral nor immoral. Their acts of thought consist merely in the exercise of such, without their being transformed into kamma, because their volition is now subject only to good hetu's, and is free from evil tendencies (anusayā).

Phala-javana. The apperception of Fruition is of a double character. As 'fruit,' it is merely the resultant of each stage of the Path. But as apperception, it partakes of the character of an inoperative thought (kiriyā).[2]

[1] Ahosi, aorist of atthi, 'is,'+ika.—Ed.

[2] A brief account of kamma will be found in Part V. of the Manual. For fuller details readers are referred to my article entitled 'The Forces of Character,' which appeared in *Buddhism*, vol. ii., No. 1.

Dream-consciousness. Before we proceed to supernormal consciousness, we may discuss dream-consciousness, thereby completing our survey of consciousness as experienced in the forms of existence known as kāma.

Dream has been defined by Nāgasena, as an image (nimitta) coming into the field of consciousness.[1] This definition is incomplete, as it does not distinguish a dream from a waking hallucination. But as the word sŭpĭna (a dream), is derived from the root *sup*, 'to sleep,' Nāgasena undoubtedly meant 'consciousness in sleep.'

Interesting as is the phenomena of dream, it is conspicuous in the Manual only by its absence. References are, however, found scattered here and there in Buddhist works, although it is no easy task to collect them. No attempt at anything like a systematic explanation of dream-phenomena appears to have been made in Burma till nearly a century ago, when one Ariyavaŋsa-Ādiccaraŋsī propounded seven questions relating to dreams.

The forms of dream-thought. The first question: whether dreams are perceived by the senses, or by thought? opens up a line of inquiry into the forms of dream-thought. When scenes are reproduced automatically in a dream with our eyes closed, the obvious inference is that we see them by way of the door of mind. Even in the case of peripheral stimulations, as when a light, brought near a sleeping man's eye, is mistaken for a bonfire, it is this exaggerated light that is perceived in a dream by the mind-door. The possibility of the presentation of all the six classes of objects to the mind has been referred to. But the dream *generally* takes the form of a

[1] *Milindapañha*, p. 298: 'Nimittametaŋ, mahārāja, supinaŋnāma yaŋ cittassa āpātham upagacchati.' In Rhys Davids' translation (*Questions of King Milinda*, ii. 157): 'It is a suggestion, O King, coming across the path of the mind which is what is called a dream.' The Sinh : Cy paraphrases nimittaŋ by aramunuwa = ārammaṇaŋ, translated in this essay as 'object.'—Ed.

vision. Hence the phrase supinaŋ passati, to see a dream.

If these presentations do not come from without, they must come from within, from the 'inner' activities of mind. That is to say, if peripheral stimulations are absent, we must look to the automatic activity of mind itself for the source of these presentations; or, to speak in terms of physiology, we must look to the central activity of the cerebrum, which is now generally admitted to be the physical counterpart of the mind-door, the afferent sensory nerves being the physical counterpart of the five-doors in an 'organized sentient existence' (pañcavokāra-bhava). Substituting these physiological terms for their psychological counterparts, cerebrum is the instrument by which we dream, and it is with the same that we go to sleep or wake up.[1]

Now, when a dream-image is not clear, we experience the thought-forms of the class of indistinct presentations already described (avibhūta), in which the stream of being, after the usual vibration, is arrested by representative cognition (manodvārāvajjana). This reflects on the image for two or three thought-moments, after which the dream-consciousness lapses again into the stream.

Some authorities are of opinion that apperception never obtains in a dream-process. But this view is now generally regarded as untenable. The author of the *Sāratṭha-dipanī-Ṭīkā* holds that, with a clear image, even retention can follow the apperception. In fact, the mental processes in a dream and in waking life are held to be alike, with this distinction only, that there is but a suspension of volitional control over the current of a dream-thought. We shall advert to this later. This may be the reason why dream-processes are not separately described by the author of our Manual.

'All consciousness ending in the function of apperception occurs by the agency of representative cognition, or mind-door faculty, not by the agency of five-door cognition; so

[1] So the *Terasakaṇḍa-Ṭīkā* (part of the *Sārattha-dīpanī-Ṭīkā*).

also our visions in dreaming.'[1] When a bright light is brought near a sleeping man's eye before waking him up, the stream of being is cut off by representative cognition, followed by seven moments of apperception, before consciousness lapses back into the stream. That is to say, he wakes up and reflects on something that has aroused him, but he has not as yet seen the actual, or objective, light. Once more the stream is arrested by the visual process, followed by its sequels, already described under external perception. This time he sees the light. Similarly with a sound, smell, taste, or touch. If, on the other hand, during the transitional period from sleep to waking, he sees a bonfire, he is said to dream through peripheral stimulations.

Dreams classified.

Dhātuk-khobbha. Anubhūta-pubba. Devatopa-saṃhāra. Pubba-nimitta.

The second question relates to the classification of dreams. Dreams are classified under (1) dreams due to organic and muscular disturbances, generally seen, according to Nāgasena, by the flatulent, the phlegmatic, or the bilious;[2] (2) recurrence of the previous dreams, due to previous experiences; (3) spirit-influence, dreams due to suggestions from spiritualistic agents; and (4) foregoing signs, prophetic dreams, due to the force of character of clairvoyant dreamers. The first category includes the dreams of a fall over a precipice, flying into the sky, etc., and what is called 'nightmare'; the second consists of the 'echoes of past waking experiences'; the third may include dream coincidences; and the fourth is of a clairvoyant character.

Theories of Dreams.

Now this question opens up another line of inquiry, namely, into the causes of dreams. We have thus four different theories of dreams corresponding to the four classes. The first of these is clearly the physiological theory, which recognizes a source of dreams in the pathological conditions of the body. Native physicians have long known that organic disturbances in the regions of the stomach, etc.,

[1] From the *Sārattha-sangaha-aṭṭhakathā*, by Siddhattha Thera, compiled from earlier Commentaries at Anurādhapura in Ceylon.

[2] *Milinda*, *loc. cit.*

give rise to dreams, so that they have not failed to diagnose some diseases also from the nature of dreams attending them. The theory of the induction of dreams by peripheral nerve-stimulation, due either to the action of external objects on sense-organs, or to disturbances in the peripheral regions of the nerves, is but a branch of the physiological theory. The second may be called the psychological theory. It recognizes the induction of dreams by central stimulation due to the automatic activities of the mind. The third will, no doubt, be stigmatized in the West as the superstitious theory. But as the deva's, or mythical beings as they would be termed in the West, are, according to Buddhism, but different grades of sentient beings in the thirty-one stages of existence described in Part V. of the Manual, the theory in question merely recognizes the suggestive action of mind on mind, and may therefore be aptly called the telepathic, or telepsychic theory. The last may be called the clairvoyant theory.

The third question relates to the correspondence of dreams with external events. The first two classes of dreams are never true in the sense of correspondence with present or future events. Coincident dreams correspond with present events, and prophetic dreams correspond with the future. The latter are always true. The third class is sometimes true, and sometimes not, according as the telepathic agent sends a true or a false message.

The fourth question concerns itself with the classes of beings who dream. Now Buddhism distinguishes altogether twelve classes of intelligent beings (puggălā), namely, four of the average ordinary class (puthujjanā), and eight of the noble or elect class (ariyā). As it is of some importance to know this classification for the purpose of understanding the process of higher consciousness, to be described later, it is just as well that we should consider them here.

Ordinary beings are living either a woeful life without [good] conditions (duggati-a-hetuka) — *i.e.*, in purgatory, or as Peta, Asura or animal—none of the

Puthujjana's.
1. Duggatiahetuka's.

three good motives (disinterestedness, love, reason) attending their consciousness-at-rebirth (p a ṭ i s a n d h i - c i t t a); (2) a happy life without [good] conditions (s u g a t i - a - h e t u k a)—*i.e.*, in the happier realms of the K ā m a l o k a, but, as in (1), without the attendant good motives (those born blind and deformed belonging to this class); (3) attended by two [good] conditions (d v i h e t u k a)—viz., disinterestedness and love—or (4) attended by the three [good] conditions. Those of the fourth class may be dwellers in the R ū p a and A r ū p a l o k a's as well as in that of K ā m a, and all of these four classes may be dreamers.

2. Sugati-ahetuka.

3. Dvihetuka.

4. Tihetuka.

Ariya's.

Of the eight classes of elect beings—viz., those in the 'stations' of the Four Paths and the Four Fruits—the former (m a g g a ṭ ṭ h ā n ā) cannot dream, because they occupy—*i.e.*, attain to—the consciousness of each Path only for a single thought-moment before they invariably pass on to the corresponding fruitional stations. And of the latter four (p h a l a ṭ ṭ h ā n ā), the first three classes still dream, but the Arahant who is in the final stage is not accredited with dreaming, as he is no longer subject to hallucination (c i t t a v i p a l l ā s a).

Relation of Dream to Sleep.

The fifth question: When does a dream occur, in sleep or in waking? is of great interest to our latter-day dream-theorists, with whom it is still an open question. Dream has been defined by a Western writer as a hallucination in sleep.[1] This definition is as inaccurate as N ā g a s e n a's was incomplete. The much-disputed question regarding the relation of dreams to sleep dated with us as far back as twenty centuries ago. Dreams, according to N ā g a s e n a, occur neither in sleep nor in waking, but in the transitional stage from the latter to the former. The dreamy state, he says, is preceded by fatigue and ended by sleep. Thus he does not take into account the transitional stage from sleep to waking. He adduces the following arguments from analogy to prove his contention: As a mirror in a dark room cannot reflect any image, so a sleeping man cannot see dreams. Neither does a waking man dream, because

[1] The author was quoted anonymously.

he who seeks a secluded spot cannot find it in open public places.[1]

By a different line of reasoning, the same conclusion was arrived at by Buddhaghosa[2] from arguments drawn from our Scriptures, as follows :

To say that dreams occur during sleep would be opposed to the spirit of the Abhidhamma-Piṭaka, where it is laid down that a man sleeps during sub-consciousness (when the stream of being is not perturbed by any thought-wave); and to say that dreams occur in waking hours would be equally opposed to the spirit of the Vinaya-Piṭaka, where it is held that a bhikkhu who commits offences in dreams is not sinful—*i.e.*, not morally responsible for his dream-acts.[3] Avoiding the two extremes, the Buddhists hold that dreams occur during the transitional period (citta-vokiṇṇa), comparable to the sleep of a monkey (kapika-middha)[4], which in sleep quickly changes from one state to another.

I have understood that, in the West, this important question is not yet settled, some authorities holding that dream is but an occasional accompaniment of sleep, while others think that the transitional stage is the most favourable time for dreaming; others, again, go so far as to say that there is no sleep without dreaming, and that dreaming is continuous. The last view, apparently the most favourable received in the West, appears to us to be a gratuitous assumption. Some people indeed betray their dreams by expressions and utterances. They do so not necessarily in the course of a sound sleep, but maybe in the course of a dreamy state. It is also true, from the Buddhist point of view, that dream-thought is very rapid, and that a dream, apparently long to a dreamer, in reality occupies but a few seconds, as in the case of a man who

[1] *Milinda*, 299, 300 ; Translation, ii., 159-161.

[2] In the *Sammoha-Vinodanī*, Commentary on the *Vibhanga*, second book in the *Abhidhamma-Piṭaka*.

[3] *Cf. Vin. Pit.*, iii., p. 112 (transl.) ; *Vin. Texts*, i., 7.—Ed.

[4] *Milinda*, *loc. cit.*

dreamt a long dream when he fell asleep after hearing the first word of a sentence, but woke up before that sentence was finished. But the error of observation, in the case of the symptoms of a long dream during sleep, seems to lie in the assumption that there is only one transitional stage of a few seconds before waking, as in the last case cited, just as Nāgasena assumed only one transitional stage before going to sleep.[1] If several transitional stages, with hardly a break during the course of a long sleep, be assumed as a possible exception, the occasional symptoms of a long dream observed may be satisfactorily explained without assuming that there is no sleep without dreaming.

Are dreams followed by effects? If so, are dreamers morally responsible?

The sixth question: Whether a dream-thought or a dream-act is moral (kusala), immoral (akusala), or unmoral (abyākata)? and the seventh question: Are dreams effective? must be dealt with together. The goodness or badness of a dream pertains to the stage of apperception, and its neutral state to the stages of mind-door (representative) cognition and retention, in one and the same process. If dreams are held to be ethically good or bad, the question arises, How far do dream-thoughts enter into the formation of a man's character (kamma)?

We have seen that the suspension of volitional control over the current of a dream-thought absolves a bhikkhu from sins committed in a dream. Therefore it is said, in the Pārājikaṇḍa-Aṭṭhakathā, that the power of will in dreams is not sufficiently strong to effect a rebirth; but that, at the same time, it may have after-effects in this very life, if only supported by previous waking experiences.

Aristotle held a similar view that many of our actions had their originals in dreams.[2] A stammerer is said to get worse after dreaming of stammering. Unpleasant dreams sometimes put even enlightened minds out of humour the next day. Some dreams may profoundly affect the whole

[1] *Milinda, loc. cit.*: 'A man still watchful, not fallen into sleep, but dozing in a monkey-sleep, will dream a dream.'—Ed.

[2] *De Sensu*, quoted in Siebeck's *Geschichte der Psychologie*, ii., 84.

of one's life. A case is recorded of a man abandoning home under the influence of a dream. Some people reform their character in consequence of certain dreams. Apart from somnambulistic actions, the famous dreams of Condorcet, Condillac, and Coleridge, may be cited as belonging to the effective class of dreams. Condorcet, however, would not have seen the final step of solution in the dream, had he not been at the problem during his previous waking hours.

I have permitted myself to discuss the Buddhist Theory of dreams at rather too great a length, with a view to show how far the West is in advance of the East on the subject. Herewith ends the survey of that section of the Manual which deals with K ā m a-consciousness. And the length of the discussion forces me to consider in briefer detail the forms of higher consciousness.

Adikammika-vithi. thought-transition of a beginner.

Before we deal with those forms of consciousness, known as R ū p a - c i t t a,[1] we have as yet to consider the 'way of the beginner,' *i.e.*, the process of thought-transition from the normal to the super-normal.

Sīla-visuddhi and preliminaries.

'Purity of virtue' or morals is an essential qualification in a beginner, who must be of any one of the four classes of the beings called 'thrice-conditioned' (t i h e t u k ā), described under dreams (p. 50). After cutting off the ten worldly cares (p a l i b o d h ā), he should repair to an adept or expert, replete with the sevenfold qualification, for instruction in the art of meditation. He should have implicit faith in his teacher, and give himself up entirely, body and mind, to him, and act exactly as instructed.

After having carefully selected an object of meditation suited to his character, he should avoid unsuitable places (there are eighteen kinds of them) and repair to a secluded spot which has the five necessary conditions. After going through the usual threefold preliminary function (p u b b a - k i c c a), he should practise meditation with all the effort

[1] See Manual, Part I., § 8.

he can. For all such details there is here no scope, and readers are referred to the Visuddhi-magga.

Kasiṇa-object.

The kasiṇa-object[1] selected and meditated upon is termed 'the mark for preparation' (parikamma-nimitta). When, after being contemplated, it is depicted to the imagination, the image, which is the exact copy of the original with all its original faults (kasiṇa-dosa's), and is represented to the mind as a vivid reality, as if it were seen by the eye, is termed 'the mark for upholding.'[2]

Uggaha-nimitta.

Pari-kamma-samādhi.

The concentration of thought practised on both these classes of nimitta's, percept and image, is termed 'preliminary concentration'; and we have seen that concentration is the power of individualizing (ekaggatā) developed by practice.

Paṭibhāga-nimitta.

By this preliminary concentration, the image, when it is turned into a concept (paññatti), is divested of its reality and its faults, and becomes a sublimated copy, an abstract, yet still an individual. This conceptualized image, or after-image, which can no longer be depicted to sense or imagination as a concrete individual, is now termed 'mark-equivalent' (paṭibhāga-nimitta).

Upacāra-samādhi.

On the realization of this last class of nimitta, the five Hindrances to progress (nīvaraṇā) are inhibited, whereupon the preliminary develops into concentration, 'intermediate concentration.' We shall revert to the inhibition of the Hindrances when we come to deal with jhāna.[3]

After a course of intermediate concentration of thought on the after-image, the stream of being, which is composed, as we have seen, of one or other of the four 'thrice-conditioned' vital continua, begins to vibrate for two moments as usual. When it is arrested by representative cognition, there follow ordinarily four moments of apperception. In other words, if the subject be an ordinary

[1] On the Kasiṇa-object, see *Bud. Psy.*, 48, *n.* 4, 57, *n.* 2.

[2] In its secondary sense uggaha is anything learnt or acquired.

[3] The standard Piṭaka account of the Five Hindrances may be read in *Dīgha Nikāya*, i., 71; *Dialogues of the Buddha*, i., 82.—Ed.

person, his consciousness is that of the automatic or volitional 'great' types of moral consciousness, 'accompanied by joy and connected with knowledge' (Part I., § 6, of the Manual). Or, if he be of the elect who have nevertheless not practised jhāna, his consciousness is now of the corresponding type described under the classes called inoperative. For it must be borne in mind that jhāna is not absolutely necessary to Arahantship, as, *e.g.*, in the case of Arahants termed 'dry-visioned' (sukkhavipassakā).[1]

Parikamma-moment of preliminary preparation.

The first of these four moments of apperception during the transitional stage from normal consciousness to the supernormal is termed 'preparation,' the preliminary moment, namely, of preparation of the mind for the state of jhāna. This moment does not obtain in the case of a person of quick attainment (tikkhapuggala), who therefore at once begins with the moment of 'access,' during which normal thought *approximates* to the supernormal. The moment of access is followed by 'adaptation,' the moment during which the mind equips, fits, or qualifies itself for jhāna. After the last moment of 'adoption,'[2] normal consciousness is cut off by the supernormal. In other words, the subject, as adopted or regenerate, cuts off the heritage of Kāma-consciousness, and evolves the lineage of the Rūpa-class of exalted (mahaggata) consciousness. The concentration of thought exercised during this transitional period is still of the class known as 'access-concentration' (upacāra-samādhi).

Upacāra-moment of approximation. Anuloma-moment of qualification Gotrabhu. Transitional Stage.

Jhāna.

The transitional stage is now superseded by the supernormal consciousness, known as the First jhāna. This, if the subject be an ordinary person, is of the good or moral class; if of the elect, it is of the inoperative class. For one thought-moment he experiences ecstasy (appanā), after which consciousness subsides into the subconscious stream of being. The practice for the attainment of jhāna *with ecstasy* is, in the majority of cases, attended

Appanā-jhāna.

[1] See p. 75.

[2] Lit., 'becoming one of the clan;' regeneration.

with the greatest difficulties, and is known as the Distressful Path (dukkha-paṭipadā).

Jhānanga's and nīvaraṇa's.

The first jhānic thought of the Rūpaloka has, among others, five constituent parts or factors (anga's), corresponding to the Five Hindrances respectively inhibited. Vitakka, by which sloth-and-torpor (thina-middha)[1] is inhibited, directs, as I have said, its concomitant properties towards the 'equivalent mark' (paṭibhāganimitta). Vicāra next permits the continued exercise of the thought on the same, and doubt (vīcikicchā) is thereby inhibited. Pīti, whereby aversion (byāpāda) is inhibited, creates an interest in the same object. There was, of course, at first a dull or slight sense of interest (khuddaka-pīti), growing keener and keener through oscillating interest (okkantika-pīti)[2] into an intense interest amounting to thrilling emotion (ubbegā-pīti), followed finally by interest amounting to rapture (pharaṇā-pīti). This diffused rapture is invariably followed by pleasurable, easeful, happy feeling (sukha), by which distraction and worry (uddhacca-kukkucca) are inhibited.

Five grades of pīti.

Pīti and sukha.

The difference between pīti and sukha is usually illustrated by the simile of a thirsty traveller in the desert. The former is compared to the feeling of thrilled attention excited by the sight of an oasis at a distance, and the latter to the feeling derived from drinking the water found in that oasis. Pīti, then, speaking generally, is the precursor of sukha.

In the practice of jhāna this indescribable pleasure derived from intense interest develops the element of individualization (ekaggatā) into ecstatic concentration, (appanā-samādhi) or state of being *en rapport* with the after-image, by which sensuous desire (kāma-chanda) is inhibited.

Appanā.

Jhāna-ecstasy (appanā) is defined as that which

[1] Burmese Pali reads a short i in thīna, a long i in vicikicchā. —Ed.

[2] Lit., descending; pharana is radiating.—Ed.

carries (or rather thrusts) its concomitants into an object. Primarily, the term is applied to the developed element of mental application (vitakka). Ordinary vitakka merely throws its concomitants on to the surface, so to speak, of an object—*i.e.*, it is the initiative element in cognition of a superficial kind. But appanā-vitakka is mind penetrating into the inwardness or import of its object, and it has come to be applied to samādhi, 'concentration' or developed individualization of thought. Ecstasy is generally compared to a solid body, which sinks to the bottom of water and remains where it is as long as it is not taken out; while the undeveloped, and therefore superficial, individualizing of Kāma-consciousness is comparable to a hollow case which is kept under water by pressure, but is buoyed up to the surface as soon as that pressure is removed.

Thus concentration is the *Alpha* and *Omega* of the practice of spiritual culture, termed collectively 'tranquillization' or 'calm' (sămătha). Samatha is so called because it puts to sleep, as it were, or lulls, the Five Hindrances for the time being. Access (upacāra) and ecstatic concentration (appanā-samādhi) are two aspects of 'purity of thought,' so called because the mind is now free from the Hindrances. Samatha-culture. Citta-visuddhi.

The above is, of course, but a bald and bare statement of the psychology of jhāna. Nevertheless, attainment in jhāna is a very important psychological moment, marking an epoch in his mental experience for the person who succeeds in commanding it. He has for the first time in his life tasted something unlike anything he has ever experienced before. The feeling is simply indescribable. He felt an entirely changed person, purged from the Hindrances. He was living a new, higher life, the life of a god of the heavens called Rūpa; experiencing the consciousness believed to be habitual to those dwelling there. A new life opened up.

The same form of thought-transition holds good for transition from Kāma-consciousness to the higher stages of jhāna, with this distinction, that, in the second Higher jhānas.

jhānic thought, the services of vitakka are dispensed with; in the third, both vitakka and vicāra are absent; in the fourth, pīti is got rid of; in the fifth, sukha is replaced by upekkhā, or hedonic indifference to the pleasure derived from the five grades of interest. This hedonic indifference, or neutrality of emotion is brought about by the continued voluntary exercise of the mind on the after-image to which it has been directed. And by it ecstatic concentration reaches its full development in the fifth stage of jhāna. In attaining to it, apperception of the two 'great' types, which are 'accompanied by joy,' is superseded by one of the types which are 'accompanied by indifference.'[1]

Jhāna is often divided into four classes, instead of five, in which classification the second and the third are combined into one.[2]

The object of consciousness, in the transitional stage, may be the after-image of any one of the ten 'circles'; or, again, it may be the after-image of one of the ten 'foul things' (asubha), or of the living body, or only of the breath. The assumption is that it ceases when the jhāna thought itself ceases.

Dual post-jhānic Habit.

After each initiatory process of thought-transition, repeated several times by way of practice, the beginner has to cultivate two supplementary jhāna-habits, namely, 'the habit of reflecting' (āvajjana-vasitā)—*i.e.*, on the jhānic thought just induced, or on one of its constituent factors—and 'the habit of reviewing' the same (paccavekkhanā-vasitā). These two habits occur in a single supplementary process of retrospection (paccavekkhanā-vīthi), the form of which is as follows:

When a person wishes to review the past jhāna, or

[1] See Manual, I., §§ 6-8.

[2] The Sutta Piṭaka knew apparently nothing of this fivefold and probably somewhat later elaboration. But in the Abhidhamma Piṭaka the fivefold is given as supplementary to the fourfold. See *Dh. S.*, §§ 160-175: 'Catukkanayo, Pañcakanayo.' On the 'foul things,' see Manual, IX., § 2.—Ed.

its constituent factors, the stream of his being, after the usual vibration, is arrested by representative cognition (manodvārāvajjana), after which follow four moments of retrospection (or five, according as a person is quick or slow of attainment). These moments of retrospective apperception belong, in the case of an ordinary being, to one of the eight great classes of 'moral consciousness,' or, in the case of one of the elect, to one of the eight great classes of inoperative consciousness.[1] Thereupon the stream resumes its normal flow. The number of intervening moments of vital continuum (bhavanga's) between any two retrospective processes depends upon the degree to which the dual habit in question has been cultivated.

Thus there are six classes of reaction after the first jhāna; five of these has each of its constituent factors as object, and one has the jhānic thought itself as a whole for its object. After the second jhāna there are five modes of reaction; four after the third, three after the fourth, three after the fifth.

Samāpatti-process of induction of, and emergence from jhāna at will.

The method for attaining to sustained or prolonged jhāna (jhāna-samāpatti-vīthi, or samāpajjana-vīthi) is the same as that for attaining the transitional form. The only distinction is that here the number of moments of jhāna induced at will is unlimited, their number depending only upon the degree of certain previous exercises. These are, first, the cultivation of 'predetermining' the duration of the jhāna that is to be induced (adhiṭṭhāna-vasitā); secondly, the cultivation of prolonging jhāna at will while under its influence (samāpajjana-vasitā); and thirdly, the cultivation of waking or rousing one's self punctually on the expiry of the interval pre-determined (vuṭṭhāna-vasitā).

As in the case of the transitional process, each inductive process is followed by the retrospective processes already described.

Progressive Steps to Higher jhāna.

If a person wishes to rise to higher jhāna, he should

[1] See Manual, *loc. cit.*

first enter into the next lower j h ā n a. On waking therefrom he should reflect on the relatively gross nature of the j h ā n a just induced. In this reflection he should consider the particular constituent factor to be got rid of, as being gross by reason of its liability to be counteracted by the inimical influences of the Hindrances respectively inhibited by each factor (p. 56). Reflecting on the consequent liability of that j h ā n a to loss, and with a strong desire for the next higher j h ā n a, he should make great efforts until he succeeds in attaining it.

Preliminary course of mental training

If now an adept in the Fifth j h ā n a wishes to attain super-intellectual powers (a b h i ñ ñ ā), it will be necessary for him to go through a course of mental training in fourteen processes, described in the V i s u d d h i - m a g g a. This course is intended to enable will to gain a complete mastery over intellect and feeling.

Iddhipāda's.

Adhipati's.

Supernormal powers of will, known in Buddhism by the technical term i d d h i - v i d h ā, may then be developed by means of the so-called four bases of i d d h i (c a t t ā r o i d d h i p ā d ā). These involve respectively the development of Four dominant or predominant principles of purpose, effort, knowledge, and wisdom, as described in the Manual, VII., § 6, as well as the cultivation of sixteen fundamental principles for acquiring such power, and for satisfying the eight conditions for acquiring it. Readers are referred to the V i s u d d h i - M a g g a for details.

Classes of iddhi.

There are ten classes of i d d h i known to Buddhism :[1]

[1] The oldest version of these ten classes known as yet occurs in the P a ṭ i s a m b h i d ā m a g g a (ii., 205), of the S u t t a P i ṭ a k a. Two versions at least of the ten are given by B u d d h a g h o s a (*Vis. Magga*, xii., and *Atthasālinī*, p. 91). The former tallies exactly with the P i ṭ a k a list. The list in this essay differs slightly from both:—(1) The order is quite different. (2) In the older versions, 3. is k a m m a v i p ā k a j ā i d d h i ; 4. is p u ñ ñ ā v a t o i d d h i. (In *Asl.* b h ā v a n ā m a y ā i d d h i replaces 6). (3) Good done in former births is not mentioned in the canonical description of 4. (4) I d d h i is, in the canon, described as 'n e k k h a m m e n a k ā m a c c h a n d a s s a p a h ā n a ṭ ṭ h o i j j h a t ī t i'—*i.e.*, the kind of i d d h i so named is that which is a result of resigning all sensuous,

1. Tattha-tattha-sammāpayoga-paccayiddhi (lit., 'iddhi conditioned by perfect usage in this and that') is the ordinary power exercised by men in ordinary walks of life.

2. Vijjāmayiddhi (lit., '*i.* consisting of knowledge') is the power acquired by knowledge (science, art, hypnotism, etc.).

3. Kammajiddhi (lit., '*i.* born of kamma') is the inherent or inborn power due to the force of kamma—*e.g.*, the flying power of birds, the power of spirits, and of gods.

4. Puññiddhi (lit., *i.* of merit) is a form of the last-mentioned, but appearing later in life as the fruition of the good kamma of some previous existence.

5. Ariyiddhi (lit., *i.* of the Ariyas or elect ones) is the power of looking upon agreeable objects as disagreeable or *vice versa.*

6. Samādhivipphāriddhi (lit., *i.* of radiating through concentration) is the power, induced by samādhi, of resisting pain, death, etc.

7. Ñāṇavipphāriddhi (lit., *i.* of radiating through insight) is the power, induced by knowledge, of resisting pain, death, etc.

8. Adhiṭṭhāniddhi (lit., *i.* of resolve or will-fixing) is the power of creating phenomena outside of one's body.

9. Vikkubbaniddhi (lit., *i.* of transforming) is the power of transforming one's body into different personalities.

10. Manomayiddhi (lit., *i.* composed of mind) is the power of creating phenomena connected with one's body.[1]

The last three constitute the iddhividhā,[2] of which Iddhi-vidhā.

---

all worldly desires. Apart from these few details, the fact of the relatively intact tradition is very remarkable.—Ed.

[1] Described in the Paṭisambhidā as the power of creating one's own double.—Ed.

[2] Vidha is simply 'kind,' the German -*Art*.'—Ed.

they are but three different aspects. The agent hereupon enters into the Fifth jhāna, which is now termed adhiṭṭhāna-pādaka-jhāna, that is jhāna as base for fixation of will, because it is used as a basis for the 'willing' process. He now *wills* the desired phenomenon in the process so called. The form of it is as follows:

Adhiṭṭhāna-vīthi

The stream of being, after the usual vibration, is arrested by representative cognition, followed by the usual seven moments of apperception before consciousness lapses again into the vital continuum. In this process those seven moments of volitional apperception (adhiṭṭhāna-javana) are, in the case of ordinary beings, of the main types of good consciousness, but in the case of Arahants, they are of the inoperative class.[1]

Padaka-jhānas.

Once more he enters the Fifth jhāna, which is now termed 'jhāna as base for super-normal thought' (abhiññāpādaka-jhāna), because it is used as a basis for abhiññā. Both these basic jhāna's may be induced by any one of the ten circles.

Abhiññā-vīthi.

Lastly, in the abhiññā-vīthi (process of super-intellectual thought), the particular phenomenon willed sets up the usual vibration in the stream of being, which is then arrested by the same transitional stage as in the thought-transition already described. This transitional stage is followed by a single thought-moment of super-normal apperception (abhiññā-javana), during and by which the desired phenomenon is effected, and after which consciousness subsides into the vital continuum. This super-normal apperception is no other than the Fifth stage of so-called Rūpa jhāna, specially developed in the above way for producing the desired phenomenon. As like classes are followed by like classes, it may be of either the moral (kusala), or the inoperative (kiriyā) class according as it is preceded, in the transitional stage, by the fifth or sixth of the eight great classes of moral consciousness, or, in the case of an Arahant, of inoperative consciousness.

The same four processes obtain in the case of each of the

[1] *Cf.* p. 20.

four other kinds of secular (or worldly) super-normal thought, with slight differences as regards the procedure thus:

1. Dibba-cakkhu.

In the case of hyperæsthesia or telepathy of sight (dibba-cakkhu-abhiññā),[1] the 'basic' jhāna's are induced by one of three circles—namely, heat (tejo), white colour (odāta), or light (āloka), and the adept in the willing process wills to see the desired thing beyond the sensory range. It is said that light has to be created where darkness is, in order to enable the celestial eye to observe and discern things in the dark. The four processes of celestial vision may be followed by a process termed 'super-normal insight concerning event-according-to-deed' (yathākammupaga-abhiññā), by which a particular event in the *past* history of a particular individual is discerned; or by that of insight concerning the future (anāgataŋsa-abhiññā), by which a particular event in his *future* history is discerned. The power of prophecy, however (anāgataŋsa-ñāṇa), is the privilege of the Buddha, for, when a future event is foretold, every possible condition must be taken into account.

2. Dibba-sota.

In the case of the super-normal insight called the Celestial Ear, or hyperæsthesia of hearing (dibba-sota), the adept wills that he may hear sounds beyond the normal sensory range.

3. Ceto-pariya-ñāṇa.

By the four processes of the super-normal thought called 'discerning the thought of another' (cetopariya-ñāna, or paracitta-vijānāna), another man's thought is read. These 'thought-reading' processes of thought-transference or telepathy must necessarily be preceded by those of the Celestial Eye.

The lower grades of the elect cannot possibly read the thoughts of the higher grades. The thoughts discerned may be past, present, or future, and the question arises, when present thought is read, what particular states of consciousness in the thought-process of a person are discerned? The Mahā-Aṭṭhakathā holds that the particular

[1] Lit., 'celestial, or divine eye-super-knowledge.'—Ed.

state of consciousness, which comes into being at the same 'nascent' instant as that of the thought-reader's representative cognition discerning it, is read throughout the thought-process of the reader. The Mūlaṭīkā (or sub-commentary), on the other hand, holds that each particular state in the thought-process of the person read is attended to by that particular state of the thought-reader, which corresponds in time to the state read.

4. Pubbenivāsānussati. By the insight known as remembrance of previous circumstances the past history of one's self, or of another can be read. The limit to this improved memory or hypermnesia is of course different in different individuals.

Jhāna and the body. Before I conclude this subject I might as well observe that ecstatic apperception (appanā-javana) is capable of maintaining the bodily postures of standing, sitting, and lying for an indefinite period of time without allowing fatigue to set in. In other words, the cataleptic condition of body may be induced by jhāna.[1]

Arūpa-jhānas. With a slight difference in procedure in mental attitudes and mood of thought, the same forms of the transitional, inductive, or sustained and retrospective processes of the Fifth Rūpa-jhāna obtain in the case of the four Arūpa-jhānas, with the distinction that the respective objects of jhāna here are: (1) The concept 'infinity of space,' in the case of the first Aruppa; (2) the conception of the first Arūpa-consciousness as infinite, in the case of the second; (3) the concept 'nothingness,'[2] in the case of the third; and (4) the conception of the third Arūpa-consciousness as calm and serene, in the case of the fourth.

How to rise to Arūpa-jhāna. When an adept in the Fifth Rūpa-jhāna, who has repeatedly induced the same through any one of the ten circles, with the exception of space, erroneously believes that all physical pain and misery are due to the existence

[1] On the Abhidhamma-Piṭaka catechism respecting these more abstract exercises, see *Dhamma-Sangaṇi*, §§ 265 *ff.*, and *Buddh. Psychology*, pp. 71 *ff.*—Ed.

[2] According to the Tīkā's, 'The concept of the *first* concept regarded as nothing.' *Cf.* p. 90, *n.* 2.—Ed.

of the body, he then shrinks from the idea of having this physical frame in future, and he feels disgusted with, and detests, even the after-image of the circle, which has induced the fifth r ū p a - j h ā n a, because of its similarity to his physical frame, in so far as its materiality is concerned. Reflecting on the relative grossness of this j h ā n a, he wishes to attain the first a r ū p a - j h ā n a, which he considers to be very calm and serene. With this frame of mind he concentrates his mind on the concept, 'the infinity of space,' as divested of all material objects used for 'circles.'

Diṭṭhi-visuddhi.

A person who wishes to transcend the experience of this conditioned world must first of all cultivate 'purity of views' (d i ṭ ṭ h i - v i s u d d h i), so called because it is the correct view of the universe, freed from the idea of an identical *substance* of mind, or matter. This he must do by a study of the characteristic marks, functions or properties, phenomenal effects, and immediate causes of each of the material qualities of body and the mental properties, after drawing a preliminary distinction between mind and matter (n ā m a - r ū p a - p a r i c c h e d a - ñ ā ṇ a).

Kankhā-vitaraṇa-visuddhi.

Next he must cultivate the 'purity of transcending doubt' (k a n k h ā - v i t a r a ṇ a - v i s u d d h i), by which all the sixteen classes of doubt with reference to the past, present, or future are transcended. The discipline for this is a careful study of the Buddhist doctrine of evolution, or p a ṭ i c c a - s a m u p p ā d a - d h a m m a.

Ten vipassanā's. 1. Sammasana-ñāṇa.

Then he cultivates the Ten Modes of Insight (v i p a s - s a n ā - ñ ā ṇ a 's) in the following order:—He contemplates the conditioned as impermanent, evil, or unsubstantial. In other words, he cultivates that contemplative insight (lit., 'handling'), in which he contemplates those three salient marks of things.

2. Udayabbaya-ñāṇa.

And when he develops the insight into flux (lit., rising and waning), by which he observes the growth and the decay of things, or being and non-being in the process of becoming, there may be an emission of human aura from the body, and nine other inimical influences may operate against further progress, known as the ten 'corrupters of insight' (vippasanupakkilesā).

Maggā-magga-ñāṇa-dassana-visuddhi. The Meditator is now apt to mistake these ten 'defilements' for the Path; if not, he is said to attain the Purity of insight by which the actual Path is distinguished from that which is not Path (maggāmagga-ñāṇa-dassana-visuddhi).

3. Bhanga-ñāṇa. Next he cultivates 'insight into disruption' (bhanga-ñāṇa), by which he confines his attention merely to the decay of things, as it is less discernible than their growth, growth being, as a rule, more marked.

4. Bhaya-ñāṇa. **5. Ādīnava-ñāṇa.** **6. Nibbidā-ñāṇa.** **7. Muccitukamyatā-ñāṇa.** **8. Paṭisankhā-ñāṇa.** **9. Sankhārupekkhā-ñāṇa.** By 'insight into what is to be feared' he sees the danger in the decay of things; by 'insight into evil' he realizes the evil nature of this danger; by the 'insight of repulsion' he gets disgusted with the evil nature of that danger; by the 'insight associated with the desire to be set free' he aspires to be emancipated from all evils; by the 'insight of *re*-contemplation' he re-contemplates the conditioned with reference to the Three Salient Marks (Impermanence, Ill, No-soul); by the 'insight of indifference to the activities of this life' he is now indifferent to the world. In other words, he is no longer affected by the good and the bad in this world. This feeling of indifference (upekkhā) is fostered by the balance of the mind, or equanimity (tatramajjhattatā), which must not be confounded with upekkhā, the neutral aspect of feeling, or zero-point between pain and pleasure, joy and sorrow. The former is a higher mental attitude, which may eventually be raised to the dignity of a bojjhanga (an indispensable condition or factor of knowledge or wisdom). The two may exist side by side, as in the 'consciousness accompanied by indifference' of the eight classes of moral consciousness (Man. I., § 6).

10. Anuloma-ñāṇa. And when the last-mentioned kind of insight matures, it changes itself into the 'insight of adaptation' (anuloma-ñāṇa), by which the meditator *fits* himself with mental equipments and qualifications for the Path.

All these Insights, from the 'insight into disruption' upward, are collectively termed 'purity of insight during the progress of the practice of discernment,' or more simply 'purity of intellectual culture.' Paṭipadā-ñāṇa-dassana-visuddhi.

The matured insight of equanimity which has reached the climax of discernment in the stage of adaptation, receives the special designation of 'insight of discernment leading to uprising' (vuṭṭhāna-gāminī-vipassanā-ñāṇa), because it invariably leads to the Path, conceived as a 'Rising-out-of.' It is also styled 'the mouth or gate of Emancipation' (vimokkha-mukha), because the Path is reached immediately after one more moment of 'adoption' (gotrabhu). Vuṭṭhāna-gāminī-vipassanā-ñāṇa. Vimokkha-mukha.

This 'gate of emancipation' has a triple designation. It is termed the 'Signless' (animitta) when the meditator contemplates things as impermanent by ridding his mind of the signs of the three delusions—namely, of the hallucination of perception, thought, and views (saññā-vipallāsa, citta-vipallāsa, and diṭṭhi-vipallāsa), which have led mankind to believe that impermanent things are permanent. It is termed 'the Undesired' (appaṇihita) when he contemplates things as evil by ridding his mind of the craving which has led mankind to covet things as if they were good. It is termed 'the Void,' or 'Emptiness' (suññatā), when he contemplates things as unsubstantial by ridding his mind of the idea of an ego, or soul. Animitta. Three vipallāsas. Appaṇihita. Suññatā.

Emancipation itself, whether of the Path, the Fruit, or Nibbāna, also receives the same triad of names, according as it is preceded by the contemplation of things by 'uprising discernment' (see above) as either impermanent, or evil, or unsubstantial. Vimokkha and its triple designation.

The mental element of intelligence (paññindriya-cetasika), which has developed itself through various stages or phases into the Perfected View (sammā-diṭṭhi) of the lowest class in the Path-consciousness, with which we are about to deal, is called 'purity of insight' or simply 'Path-insight' (magga-ñāṇa). Ñāṇa-dassana-visuddhi

The process of thought-transition to Path-consciousness

Magga-vithi. is similar to the form of mental transition to the consciousness known as Rūpa-citta, or that known as Arūpa-citta. That is to say, the stream of being, after the usual vibration, is arrested by representative cognition, followed by the usual transitional stage of four moments, or three only, according as the person is slow or quick of attainment.

The evolution of 'adoption' (gotrabhu), which follows 'the adaptation' (anuloma) already described, cuts off the heritage of the ordinary average person (puthujjana), and evolves the lineage of the Transcendental. It is followed by a single moment of Path-consciousness, by which the first of the four Noble Truths is clearly discerned. Error and doubt are got rid of, Nibbāna is intuited, and the Ariyan Eightfold Path-Constituents are cultivated.

Fourfold function of the Path-thought corresponding to the Four Noble Truths.

These four simultaneous functions correspond to the Four Noble Truths.

The Path-thought is immediately followed by two or three moments of its Fruition (according as the individual is slow or quick of attainment) before consciousness lapses again into the stream.

One of the Three Salient Marks of things forms the object of consciousness prior to adoption (gotra-bhu). But adoption implies an evolution which transcends the conditioned, and has for its object (as in the case of the Path-thought and the consciousness of Fruition) Nibbāna.

In the Three Higher Paths, adoption (gotrabhu) receives the special name of the moment of purification

Vodāna. (vodāna), each of the Three Higher Paths being possible

The Four Paths. 1. Sotāpanna. only to a being who has attained the next lower. The sotāpanna (Winner of the Stream, or Attainer of the First Path) will have as yet to undergo seven more rebirths at the outside, in the kāma-loka, or universe of full sensuous experience.

The attenuation to which all sensual passion and ill-will have been brought by one attaining the Second Path, has this result, that only one more such rebirth remains.

2. Sakadāgāmi. Such an one is called Once-Returner.

But the complete destruction of the last two mentioned defilements (kilesa's) does not permit of another such rebirth in the case of the Never-Returner of the Third Path. He would be reborn in the Pure Abodes (suddhāvāsā) of the Brahma-loka if he has practised the Fifth jhāna, or in one of the lower Brahma-lokas if he has only practised the lower jhānas. 3. Anāgāmi.

The wisdom of the Highest or Supreme Path (arahatta-magga-ñāṇa), by which all the kilesa's have been destroyed, root and branch, and the Four Noble Truths completely realized, is the same mental element of intelligence (paññindriya-cetasika) developed into the Perfected View (sammā-diṭṭhi) of the highest order, and is the last stage of the purity of insight already referred to. 4. Arahant. Sammā-diṭṭhi.

And it is the complete destruction of the kilesa's that has qualified the Arahant to be a WORTHY—*i.e.*, one who is 'fit for gifts,' worthy of all kinds of offerings that the world can make him (dakkhineyya).

The transitional process in the case of the Three Lower Paths is followed by five processes of review or retrospect, in which (1) the Path attained, (2) the Fruit enjoyed, (3) the Nibbāna intuited, (4) the kilesa's already got rid of, and (5) the kilesa's as yet to be got rid of, are respectively reflected upon. In the case of the Highest Path, only four of these so-to-speak post-graduate processes obtain, because there are no more kilesa's to be got rid of. The form of these retrospective processes is as follows: Paccavekkhanā-vithi.

The stream of being, after the usual vibration, is arrested by representative cognition, followed by seven moments of apperception before the stream resumes its flow. If the subject have attained any but the Highest Path, his consciousness is of Nos. 1, 3, 5, or 7 of the eight great moral types 'connected with knowledge'; or of the corresponding numbers of the eight great 'inoperative' types, if he have reached the Highest (Man. I., § 6), except in the case of the two processes in which the kilesa's are reflected upon, when any one of the former eight classes, in the case of the Three Lower Paths, or any one of the latter eight classes in the case of the Highest Path, performs the function of apperception.

Phala-samāpatti.

Each being who has attained a lower Path spends his time in enjoying the Fruit of that Path, before he attains the next higher. The process of enjoying the Fruit for an indefinitely prolonged time is termed 'sustained fruition' (p h a l a - s a m ā p a t t i), which corresponds to sustained j h ā n a (p. 59). The form is as follows:

When such a person makes all possible modes of discernment converge on 'things as conditioned' (s a n - k h ā r a d h a m m ā), and contemplates them as Impermanent, Ill, or Unsubstantial, the stream of being, after the usual vibration, is arrested by representative cognition, followed by four moments, or three, of the stage of 'adaptation,' according as the person is slow or quick of attainment. During these, one of the four numbers named above of the eight moral classes in the case of the three lower Paths, or one of the corresponding four of the inoperative classes, in the case of the highest Path, contemplates the three Characteristic Marks of things. Again, of these four, in each case, only the first two, 'accompanied by joy,' can take part in the case of four lower j h ā n a 's, and only two 'accompanied by indifference,' in the case of the fifth j h ā n a. This stage of adaptation is followed by an unlimited number of apperceptive moments of Fruition of the respective Paths, having as their object N i b b ā n a.

Nirodhasamāpatti.

The 'Never-Returner' (a n ā g ā m i), or the Arahant, who has achieved all the previous r ū p a- and a r ū p a - j h ā n a s, may enjoy what is called Nibbāna-under-present-conditions (d i ṭ ṭ h a - d h a m m a - n i b b ā n a), if he be not satisfied with the mere intuition of N i b b ā n a in the sustained consciousness of fruition (p h a l a - s a m ā p a t t i).

First of all he enters into the First R ū p a - j h ā n a (Man. I., § 8). Waking therefrom he reflects on the three Characteristic Marks of things as experienced in First j h ā n a, by means of the ten modes of Insight (v i p a s -

sanā's) up to the last already described; next he enters into the Second jhāna, then into the Third, and so on, in the upward order, up to the concept of Nothingness (ākiñcaññāyatana), the third Arūpa-jhāna alternating the induction of each preceding jhāna with the contemplation of that jhāna by the ten modes.

On waking from the Third Arūpa-jhāna, however, he, instead of exercising the Modes of Insight, performs the four preliminary functions of willing: (1) that such necessaries of life as are not connected with his body may not be destroyed by fire, etc.; (2) that he may wake up when his services are required by the Order; (3) that he may wake up when he is called by the Buddha; and (4) that he may ascertain whether he will live within the next seven days.

Four Preliminary Functions.

After this he enters into the Fourth Arūpa-jhāna in the transitional stage to sustained cessation (nirodha-samāpatti) or total suspension of mind, mental properties and material qualities born of mind. The process is as follows:

After the above-mentioned functions, the third form of arūpa consciousness enters his field of presentation, sets up the usual vibration in the stream of being, which is then arrested by representative cognition, followed by the usual transitional stages of preparation, access, adaptation, adoption (*cf.* p. 55). During this stage one of the two classes of moral consciousness 'accompanied by indifference' and 'insight' (Man. I., 6), performs the function of apperception in the case of the Non-Returner, and one of the corresponding inoperative classes, in the case of the Arahant, after which the Fourth Arūpa-jhāna occurs for two thought-moments before all activities of the mind cease.

On waking from trance, apperception of the Fruition of the respective Paths invariably occurs for one thought-moment, with Nibbāna as its object, before the resumption of the stream. The difference between the consciousness of sustained fruition and that in the process just described is that Nibbāna is merely intuited in the former, but partially enjoyed in the latter, when the person is entirely immune from pain. The process is followed by one of review, in which one of the first two of the eight great moral classes in the case of the Non-Returner, or of the eight inoperative classes in the case of the Arahant, follows representative cognition before the stream resumes its flow. And it is evidently in this post-cataleptic meditation that the Nibbāna-under-present-conditions, enjoyed erewhile, is remembered.[1]

I have described all the possible varieties of mental experience in life, and now come to life's last episode.

Philosophy of death.

Four causes of death.

The philosophy of death is no less important to the Buddhist than the philosophy of life. In that philosophy Death is assigned to one of four causes: (1) The exhaustion of the force of the reproductive (janaka) kamma that has given rise to the existence in question; (2) the expiry of the maximum life-term possible to this particular generation;[2] (3) the combination of both these causes; (4) the action of a stronger arresting kamma that suddenly cuts off the reproductive kamma before the latter's force is spent, or before the expiry of the life-term.

Janaka-kamma presented to the dying man.

I have said that either the kamma, or a symbol of it, or a sign of its tendency, *i.e.*, his destiny, is presented to the dying man (p. 26). By kamma here is meant the past efficient action, or reproductive kamma which is about to effect the next rebirth. It may be either very impressive kamma (garuka-kamma); or, if experience have afforded nothing impressive, it may be action proximate to death (āsanna-kamma); or, failing that, it may be habitual conduct (ācinna-kamma); or, if that fail to act, it may be one of the cumulative reserves of the endless past (kaṭatta-kamma).

Classes of reproductive kamma.

By āsanna-kamma is meant the thought of the

[1] See Man. IX., § 12.

[2] On ancient Indian beliefs respecting life-terms in different æons, see *Dīgha Nikāya*, ii., pp. 3, 4.—Ed.

Āsanna-kamma.

dying man in a process immediately before the dying consciousness to be described. Hence, if kamma is presented to the dying man, it must necessarily be of the past, and can therefore be presented only to the mind as a concrete *represented* object. If this kamma fails to present itself, a symbol of its more impressive phase may be presented.

Kamma-nimitta.

By a kamma-symbol is meant any sight, sound, smell, taste, touch, or idea which obtained at the time of the commission of that kamma. The kamma being past, its accompaniments are, for the most part, also *past*, in which case the symbol can only be presented to the mind either as an image, or as an idea. It is possible that this symbol of the past is presented to the mind as a vivid reality. But on certain occasions, as when a man dies in the immediate presence of the objects accompanying this proximate kamma, which is about to effect the next rebirth, the symbol may be *present*, in which case it may be intuited in presentative consciousness. In such cases the dying consciousness of the present life, the rebirth-consciousness of the next, and a few subsequent vital moments, may have a *present* object. With this exception, the presentation in the next life always partakes of the character of the past.

Gati-nimitta.

If neither of these two classes of presentations make their appearance, then the sign of destiny enters the field of presentation. This indicates the next existence to be affected by the reproductive or efficient kamma.

According to certain authorities—*e.g.*, the Aṭṭhakathā—this last symbol is of the nature of a presentative vision before the mind's eye. According to the Ledi School, it may be of the six classes of objects respectively presentable to the six senses, including mind as the sixth sense, and it may be either present or past. If past, it can only be represented to mind.

These indications of the immediate future may occur some time before death-consciousness actually sets in, in which case a careful observer beside the death-bed should take steps to alter the nature of the indications from bad to good. This he may do by influencing the thoughts of the dying man, so that his good thoughts may now act as the proximate kamma, and counteract the influence of the reproductive kamma which is about to effect the next rebirth.

The forms of consciousness prior to death are similar to those already described under cognition presentative and representative (pp. 27-39), with the distinction that apperception here occurs only for five thought-moments, by reason of its weakness, instead of for the usual seven. For this reason it lacks all reproductive power, its action being merely regulative of the new existence.

Physical Basis of Thought near Death. The physical basis of dying consciousness is the material qualities born of kamma at the seventeenth moment reckoned backward from the moment of death. No renewal of physical functioning occurs after that seventeenth moment.

Consciousness of decease (cuticitta) may occur after the retentive phase (tadārammaṇa), or after apperception, in presentative or representative process; or death may occur after mere vital unconscious process following either of those two phases, as the case may be.

Change of Existence. In the case of those beings who are about to be reborn in the Kāma-loka, the presentation is necessarily of the classes of Kāma-object. And the apperception may be one or other of the twenty-nine Kāma-classes. If this apperception be of the twelve classes of immoral or bad consciousness, the person is bound to be reborn in one of the four planes of miserable existence.[1]

In the case of Kāma-beings about to be reborn in the Rūpa-loka, the dying consciousness is of the representative kind, inasmuch as the kamma symbol is a concept (paññatti), to wit, the conceptualized after-image of the circle, etc.

Final Death. I omit all further allusion to the traditional Buddhist beliefs respecting the correlation between the different stages of attainment in jhāna and different forms of

[1] See Man. I., § 2; V., §§ 2, 4.

consequent rebirth, and will conclude with a word on the decease of an Arahant, which is final death.

If the Arahant be of the class known as 'dry-visioned' (sukkha-vipassaka),[1] who does not practise jhāna, his final death, which takes place on the Kāma-plane, occurs after apperception or retention of impressions. And, as for dying Arahants in general, moments of mere vital continuum or 'stream' (bhavangasota) may intervene between consciousness and death. Apperception will be one of the eight main inoperative kinds of consciousness, and the object of his consciousness will be things 'seen as they really are.' If he be proficient in jhāna, final death may occur (*a*) after sustained jhāna;[2] or (*b*) after apperception in subsequent retrospect; or (*c*) after the moment of 'super-intellectual' knowledge (abhiññā),[3] or, finally, (*d*) after retrospection following the attainment of the Topmost Fruit.

Sukkha-vipassaka-Arahant.

Jhāna-lābhi-arahant.

Such is a brief résumé of the inexhaustible teaching conveyed in and built up around the contents of the little Manual which we are presenting to the European reader. It will be seen from the above survey that Buddhist psychology is complicated by the number of distinctions it draws in the *forms* or *elements* of consciousness, and is made still more complex by the variety of the *matter* of consciousness as depending upon the planes of existence, the classes of beings, the classes of conscious states, the classes of objects, and other conditions. Into the ancient traditions respecting the first two of these last four classes of material, it has been impossible to enter here, nor would it be advisable.

Conclusion.

The investigation of the circumstances under which each

[1] See above, p. 55. Childers wrote (*Dictionary*, *s.v.* Samatho): Vijesinha told him, the Arahant of this class 'is so called because he attains sanctification by contemplating the "dry" facts of physical and moral phenomena, such as impermanence,' etc.—Ed.

[2] P. 59. [3] P. 62.

class of consciousness takes part in this or that experience, and of the related modes in which the several states of consciousness stand to the object and its surroundings, and of the related modes in which the several concomitant mental elements in any state of consciousness stand to one another, presents a very wide field of study. I have indicated, as far as I could, the classes of consciousness that can take part in a process of human thought; but the rules of sequence of states or classes of consciousness cannot be too carefully studied.[1]

SHWE ZAN AUNG.

RANGOON,
July, 1910.

[1] We have excised from this essay several paragraphs of matters too technically treated for an introductory essay. A few of these will be found in the Appendix (under javana, Bhavanga, etc.), and on p. 220. —Ed.

ABSTRACT OF CONTENTS

PART I

Compendium of Consciousness

§ 1. The Four Ultimate Categories.

(1) Consciousness as experienced in K ā m a l o k a.

§ 2. Types of Immoral Consciousness - - - - - 12

§ 4. Resultant Consciousness (from past ill deeds) - - 7
Resultant Consciousness (from past good deeds) - - 8
Inoperative Consciousness (as to future result) - - 3

18

§ 5. Consciousness of the Beautiful :

§ 6. Great Types of Moral Consciousness - - - 8
Great Types of Moral Consciousness, resultants - - 8
Great Types of Inoperative Consciousness - - 8

(2) Consciousness as experienced in R ū p a l o k a.

§ 8. Moral Consciousness in j h ā n a ' s - - - - 5
Moral Consciousness resultants of j h ā n a - - - 5
Inoperative Consciousness in j h ā n a ' s - - - 5

(3) Consciousness as experienced in A r ū p a l o k a.

§ 10. Moral Consciousness in a r ū p a - j h ā n a ' s - - 4
Moral Consciousness resultants of a r ū p a - j h ā n a ' s - 4
Inoperative Consciousness in a r ū p a - j h ā n a ' s - - 4

(4) Transcendental Consciousness.

§ 12. Path-Consciousness - - - - - - - 4
Fruition-Consciousness - - - - - - 4

59

(12 + 18 + 59 = 89)

PART II

Compendium of the Mental Properties

(Concomitants or Adjuncts in Consciousness)

§ 2.	I. Common Unmoral Properties	7
	II. Particular Unmoral Properties	6
	III. Immoral Properties	14
	IV. Common Moral Properties	19
	V. Abstinences	3
	VI. Illimitables	2
	VII. Reason or Intelligence	1
		52

§ 4. Distribution of each Property.

§ 11. Syntheses of Properties.

PART III

Compendium of Particular Concomitants in Consciousness

§ 2. Feeling.

§ 4. The Six Special Conditions, or H e t u ' s.

§ 6. Function.

§ 8. Doors.

§ 10. Objects.

§ 12. Bases.

PART IV

Compendium of the Process of Cognition

§ 2. The 'Sixfold Six' involved in Process.

§ 3. Duration and Intensity of Sense-Impressions.

§ 5. Mind-door Procedure.

§ 7. Ecstasy in Apperception.

§ 9. Retention.

§ 11. Duration in Apperception.

§ 13. Kinds of Apperceiving Individuals.

§ 15. Consciousness and Grades of Existence.

PART V

Compendium of Consciousness not Subject to Process

PART VI

Compendium of Matter. Nibbana

PART VII

Compendium of Categories

PART VIII

Compendium of Relations

PART IX

Compendium of the Stations of Religious Exercise

NOTE

In Pali pronounce the vowels as in Italian, but the unaccented *a* like *u* in *nut*. *All* unaccented *a*'s and *i*'s are short. Thus, the vowels, and cadence, in such a term as manodvāravīthi, are such as we should use in saying: *Hullo, father sweetie!*

Pronounce consonants as in English except *c*, which *always* equals *ch* in *church*, and *g*, which is *always* hard. Dotted dentals as palatal, like our own *t* and *d*; when undotted, they are genuine dentals, as in Italian. In a doubled consonant detach the pair, as in Italian *gat-to*, *dam-mi*. In aspirated consonants, let the aspirate be heard—*e.g.*, *th* in attha like *t-h* in *at home*. Ṇ = ng.

References to Pali books where the initial only of title is given, are to be read as follows:

> *D.* = *Dīgha Nikāya* (transl. in *Dialogues of the Buddha*);
> *M.* = *Majjhima Nikāya*;
> *S.* = *Saŋyutta Nikāya*;
> *A.* = *Anguttara Nikāya*;

quoted by vol. and page of the P.T.S. editions. In the *Milinda* the pages of the *text* are quoted in the *translation*.

A COMPENDIUM
OF BUDDHIST PHILOSOPHY

HONOUR TO THE EXALTED ONE, THE ARAHANT BUDDHA SUPREME!

PART I

COMPENDIUM OF CONSCIOUSNESS

§ 1. *Introductory.*

The peerless very Buddha, with the Law
Of Righteousness and the Fraternity
Of worth supreme, with reverence I salute.
Now will I speak in summaries concise
Of things in Abhidhamma-lore contained.

These things are set forth, in their ultimate sense,[1]
As Categories Four—first, Consciousness;
Next, Mental Properties; then Qualities
Material, Bodily; Nibbana last.

Of these, first, Consciousness is fourfold, to wit:

1. Consciousness as experienced in Kāmaloka.[2]
2. Consciousness as experienced in Rūpaloka.

[1] Paramatthato is explained by the Ceylon Commentator as sammutiŋ thapetvā, nibbattita-paramatthavasena: —'in the ultimate sense of things (springing into being as facts), as abstracted from [or divested of] names.'

[2] Kāmāvacaraŋ cittaŋ, etc. The first compound is derived from kāme avacaratīti:—'that which moves about in, haunts,

3. Consciousness as experienced in Arūpaloka.
4. Transcendental (supramundane) Consciousness.

1. OF CONSCIOUSNESS AS EXPERIENCED IN KĀMALOKA.

Of these four, what is consciousness as experienced in Kāmaloka?

§ 2. *Types of Immoral Consciousness.*

There are eight classes of consciousness rooted in appetite[1] to wit:

1. Automatic[2] consciousness, accompanied by joy[3] and connected with error.[4]

2. Volitional consciousness, accompanied by joy and connected with error.

3. Automatic consciousness, accompanied by joy and disconnected from error.

---

frequents the kāmaloka,' and is applied to all classes of kāma-consciousness, whether of experience on occasion of sense-stimulation, or of representative cognition, volition, etc. Now kāma is either (1) that which desires (kāmetīti kāmo), or that which is desired (kāmiyatīti kāmo). The latter may refer to the pleasures derived from sense, or to the eleven grades of Kāmaloka life, where such pleasures prevail. And these eleven consist in four infra-human forms of existence—purgatory, the animal world, etc.,—in birth as man, and in the six lower heavens of devas. Hence there is in Western languages no one adequate word for kāmāvacara or kāmaloka, and we have decided to retain this and, for equivalent reasons, the names of the other loka's.

[1] Lit., 'accompanied by.' In ethical treatment, lobha is more usually rendered by greed or lust. See below p. 4, *n.* 2. On these classes, see *Dh. S.*, §§ 365 *ff.*—Ed.

[2] In *Dh. S.*, §§ 1, 146, etc., only the alternative classes are explicitly distinguished as sasankhārena. The fact that consciousness may be determined by another person, and against the will of the conscious subject, renders the term 'voluntary,' as usually opposed to 'automatic,' inaccurate or, at best, misleading.—Ed.

[3] Somanassa is here of psychological import, meaning simply 'pleasurable feeling *plus* excitement.'

[4] Diṭṭhi, often rendered by 'opinion,' which may be and often is erroneous. *Cf. B. Psy.*, 83, *n.* 1. Micchādiṭṭhi is here implied. —Ed.

4. Volitional consciousness, accompanied by joy and disconnected from error.

5. Automatic consciousness, accompanied by hedonic indifference[1] and connected with error.

6. Volitional consciousness, accompanied by hedonic indifference and connected with error.

7. Automatic consciousness, accompanied by hedonic indifference and disconnected from error.

8. Volitional consciousness, accompanied by hedonic indifference and disconnected from error.

Next, there are two classes of consciousness rooted in aversion,[2] to wit:

9. Automatic consciousness, accompanied by grief and connected with aversion.

10. Volitional consciousness, accompanied by grief and connected with aversion.

Next, there are two classes of consciousness rooted in nescience,[3] to wit:

11. Consciousness accompanied by hedonic indifference and conjoined with perplexity.[4]

12. Consciousness accompanied by hedonic indifference and conjoined with distraction.[5]

[1] Upekkhā, here implying simply absence of felt pleasure or pain, is to be distinguished from the more complex intellectual and ethical upekkhā, which=tatramajjhattatā, balance of mind, equanimity. Introd. Essay, p. 14. Appendix, Upekkhā.

[2] Paṭigha, repugnance, a form of dosa, or hate. See *B. Psy.*, p. 109, *n.* 2.—Ed.

[3] Momūhacittāni, confused or muddled consciousness. 'Moha' is used by Buddhist authors as a synonym of avijjā (ignorance). 'Momūha' is derived from the intensive form of the verb muyhati, to be stupefied. The reduplication, as in the case of 'devadevo,' indicates that moha, in these two classes, acts with greater force than the moha present in the foregoing ten classes of consciousness.

[4] Or doubt. On this rendering, see *B. Psy.*, 115 *n.*—Ed.

[5] Uddhacca, the state of being distrait, the opposite of concentration; rendered also by 'flurry' (*Dialogues of the Buddha*, i., p. 82) and 'excitement' (*B. Psy.*, p. 119, *n.*).—Ed.

These summed up amount in all to twelve classes of immoral[1] consciousness.

§ 3. *Mnemonic.*

Eight kinds of thought in Appetite are rooted, two in Hate,
And two in Nescience:—twelve immoral classes here we state.

§ 4. *Of Consciousness without Hetu's.*[2]

There are seven classes of consciousness which are the results of evil [done in a former birth], to wit:

1. Consciousness by way of sight, accompanied by hedonic indifference.

2-4. Consciousness by way of hearing, smell, or taste, similarly accompanied.

5. Consciousness by way of touch, accompanied by pain.[3]

6. Recipient[4] consciousness, accompanied by hedonic indifference.

7. Investigating[5] consciousness, accompanied by hedonic indifference.

[1] In this translation, kusala and akusala, where not rendered by the more usual 'good' and 'bad,' are rendered by 'moral' and 'immoral.' *Cf. B. Psy.*, lxxxii. *f.*—Ed.

[2] Ahetukāni cittāni:—unconditioned by one or more of those six radical conditions (hetu's)—greed, hate, ignorance, and their opposites—which prompted that conduct in a former birth, the result whereof is now consciously experienced. In these seven classes of consciousness only the first three hetu's are taken. On the term hetu, and on our decision to retain it untranslated, see Appendix, Hetu; *cf. Dh. S.*, § 1073; *B. Psy.*, 285 *n.* (*dele* there th in ahetukā, l. 3); *Duka-paṭṭhāna*, i., p. xii.—Ed.

[3] On the positively hedonic nature of the feeling accompanying tactile cognition, as compared with the neutral feeling in other sensations, see *B. Psy.*, 127, *n.* 1. *Cf.* below, part iii., § 2; and see also Introd. Essay, p. 14 *f.* Appendix, Upekkhā.—Ed.

[4] On these, *I believe*, post-piṭakan developments in the Buddhist theory of Cognition, see Introd. Essay; *Cf. B. Psy.*, lxxxi.—Ed.

[5] Santīraṇa is derived from 'tīreti,' 'to decide,' which, accord-

Next, there are eight classes of consciousness which are the results of good [done in a former birth], and are without h e t u ' s, to wit:

8. Consciousness by way of sight, accompanied by hedonic indifference.

9-11. Consciousness by way of hearing, smell, or taste, similarly accompanied.

12. Consciousssness by way of touch, accompanied by joy.[1]

13. Recipient consciousness, accompanied by hedonic indifference.

14. Investigating consciousness, accompanied by joy.

15. Investigating consciousness, accompanied by hedonic indifference.

Next, there are three classes of consciousness without h e t u ' s and inoperative,[2] to wit:

16. Consciousness turning to[3] impressions at the five doors,[4] accompanied by hedonic indifference.

---

ing to the Ceylon Cy., is used in the sense of 'v ī m a ṁ s a t i,' 'to investigate'; for judgment is not formed till we come to the v i n i c c h a y a -process, in which, however, s a n t ī r a ṇ a has no place. See Introd. Essay.

[1] See note 3, p. 82.

[2] K r i y ā (or k i r i y ā), effecting no k a r m a. See Appendix, K r i y ā.

[3] Ā v a j j a n a is derived by Commentators from ā v a ṭ ṭ e t i, to 'turn towards,' and 'reflection' is its nearest etymological equivalent. This, however, is not adequate, for p a ñ c a d v ā r ā v a j j a n a is never a phase of representative cognition, nor is m a n o d v ā r ā v a j j a n a confined to purely representative cognition. Anger is felt directly as a mental presentation. Hence the phrase 'turning to' has been adopted to cover all cases. At this stage the object is not yet *perceived*. There is only awareness: 'What is this?' See Appendix, Ā v a j j a n a.

[4] The picturesque analogy of the 'door,' to indicate sense-impression, found an unconscious plagiarist in John Bunyan and his 'five gates of Mansoul' (*cf. B. Psy.*, liv. *n.* 1). The translator opines that a theory of doors or windows, 'through which someone looks out,' is more compatible with animistic belief, and hence that the metaphor is probably pre-Buddhistic. There are, indeed, five d v ā r a's in the old *Chāndogya Upanishad* (iii., 18), but they are 'doors' of the heart and modes

17. Consciousness turning to impressions at the mind-door, similarly accompanied.

18. Consciousness of the genesis of æsthetic pleasure,[1] accompanied by joy.

These summed up amount in all to eighteen classes of consciousness without h e t u ' s.

Mnemonic.

From past wrong deeds seven kinds of thoughts are seen,
And eight, where deeds have meritorious been,
Three bringing no result:—in all eighteen.

§ 5. *Of Thoughts of Things Beautiful.*

Some thoughts we have from evil free, and free
From presence of the root[2] that gave them growth,
These are our thoughts of things as Beautiful.
They number fifty-nine, or ninety-one.

§ 6. *The Great*[3] *Types of Moral Consciousness.*

There are eight classes of consciousness of a moral kind arising in K ā m a l o k a experience, to wit:

---

of respiration. (Ś a n k a r a, centuries later than the P i t a k a s, called 'the gate-keeping d e v a s' the senses). As a metaphor for the avenues of sense, the term often occurs in the P i t a k a s—g u t t a d v ā r o (*e.g.*, *D.*, i., 70)—and in the canonical theory of sense d v ā r a is quoted (*as a* S u t t a n t a *metaphor*, *S.* iv., 194), *Dh. S.*, § 597 *f.* But there is no positive evidence to show that 'door' had become a technical psychological term before Buddhaghosa's time. The discussions on sense in the *Milinda* and the *Nettippakaraṇa* do not even allude to the term. Our own term 'organ' may be said to have undergone a similar development. On the 'mind-door,' see Appendix D h ā t u.—Ed.

[1] Lit., of mirth, or laughter; *cf.* Part III., § 2; Part IV., § 15. On the Buddhist theory of the Beautiful and the Ludicrous, see Introd. Essay, pp. 20 *ff.*

[2] H e t u. 'Some thoughts' are the remaining fifty-nine classes of consciousness, excepting the twelve immoral and the eighteen classes without h e t u ' s referred to in the foregoing sections.

[3] *Dh. S.*, §§ 1-159. The word 'm a h ā' is usually prefixed to higher classes of K ā m a l o k a consciousness to indicate a more extensive field of action

1. Automatic consciousness, accompanied by joy and connected with knowledge.[1]

2. Volitional consciousness, accompanied by joy and connected with knowledge.

3. Automatic consciousness, accompanied by joy and disconnected from knowledge.

4. Volitional consciousness, accompanied by joy and disconnected from knowledge.

5. Automatic consciousness, accompanied by hedonic indifference and connected with knowledge.

6. Volitional consciousness, accompanied by hedonic indifference and connected with knowledge.

7. Automatic consciousness, accompanied by hedonic indifference and disconnected from knowledge.

8. Volitional consciousness, accompanied by hedonic indifference and disconnected from knowledge.

9-16.[2] Next, there are eight classes of consciousness, similar to the foregoing, which are results of action done in a former birth in Kāmaloka, and which are accompanied by their hetu's.

17-24.[3] Next, there are eight classes of consciousness arising in Kāmaloka, which are accompanied by their hetu's, but are inoperative.

These, again, are similar to the first eight.

These, summed up, amount in all to twenty-four classes of consciousness of moral, resultant, and inoperative[2] kinds which arise in Kāmaloka, and are accompanied by their hetu's.

[1] Ñāṇa-sampayuttaṃ. Into this class of consciousness the cetasika (property or element, see Part II.) called faculty of reason (paññindriya) enters (*cf.* Part II., § 2 [vii.]), giving the class its specific character. Ñāṇa and paññindriya are used as interchangeable terms in this work. *Cf.* Introd. Essay, pp. 40 *ff.*, 67.

[2] *Dh. S.*, § 498.

[3] *Dh. S.*, § 566 *f.*

§ 7. *Mnemonic.*

In Kāmaloka consciousness we see
Together with their hetu's[1] classes three.
First there is one which merit brings, and then
One brought by previous merit, then again
A class wherefrom results can never be.
Divide these three according as they show
Feeling, and knowledge, and volition[2]—now
Eight modes appear in each. Thus there are found
Twenty-four classes to their 'hetu's' bound.

(*Summary of Kāmaloka consciousness.*)

'Resultants'[3]: *three and twenty* kinds; a *score*
Of kinds that good or ill desert entail;
Eleven kinds that no desert bring. *Four*
And fifty make the Kāmaloka tale.

---

2. Consciousness as experienced in Rūpaloka.

§ 8. *Of Moral Consciousness.*

There are five classes of consciousness which are moral and arise as Rūpa-mind, to wit:

1. Moral consciousness of the first stage of jhāna.[4]

[1] Sahetu, for sahetuka; see note on a-hetukāni cittāni, p. 4, the opposite kind of consciousness in this respect. Of this so-called sahetuka consciousness, the twelve classes 'unconnected with knowledge' (*i.e.*, in the twenty-four above, classes 2, 4, 6, 8, 10, 12, 14, 16, and so on), are said to be accompanied by *two* of the six hetu's—viz., disinterestedness (alobha) and love or amity (adosa). The corresponding twelve 'connected with knowledge' (1, 3, 5, 7, and so on) are said to be accompanied by *three* hetu's—viz., the two named, and knowledge or intelligence (amoha).

[2] Sankhāra—*i.e.*, according to Ledi Sadaw (p. 26), pubbābhisankhāro, or 'previous volitional effort on the part of self or another.' See Appendix, Sankhārā.

[3] Pākāni, effects or resultant consciousness.—Ed.

[4] Rapt systematized meditation. 'Jhāna' is another term we have agreed to naturalize, as easy to pronounce and cumbrous to translate. *Dh. S.*, § 167 *f.* On Rūpaloka, see Introd. Essay, 12, 57.—Ed.

This occurs together with initial application, sustained application,[1] pleasurable interest,[2] pleasure,[3] and individualization.[4]

2. Moral consciousness of the second stage of jhāna. This occurs together with sustained application, pleasurable interest, pleasure, and individualization.

3. Moral consciousness of the third stage of jhāna. This occurs together with pleasurable interest, pleasure, and individualization.

4. Moral consciousness of the fourth stage of jhāna. This occurs together with pleasure and individualization.

5. Moral consciousness of the fifth stage of jhāna. This occurs together with hedonic indifference and individualization.

Next, there are five classes of Rūpaloka consciousness which are the results of jhānas, to wit:

6-10. Resultant[5] consciousness of each of the five stages of jhāna characterized as above.

Next, there are five classes of Rūpaloka consciousness which are inoperative,[6] to wit:

11-15. Inoperative consciousness of each of the five stages of jhāna characterized as above.

[1] Vitakka and vicāra. See Introd. Essay, pp. 17, 56, and Appendix, Cetasika.

[2] Pīti. On the five phases of pīti, see Introd. Essay, p. 56.

[3] The psychological, and not the ethical, sukha. On the difference between pīti and sukha, see Introd. Essay, p. 56; also Appendix, Cetasika, Vedanā. *Cf. B. Psy.*, 13, *n.* 3. Other passages illustrative of sukha may be found at *A.*, i., 81, 216; *Nettipk.*, 12.—Ed.

[4] Ekaggatā. This is the element, in consciousness, of awareness of one object and one only, because, by the selective act, the mind is not distracted by several different objects. Lit., 'one-pointedness' as to object of attention (Ledi Sadaw, p. 79). Buddhists, equally with Mansel (*Metaphysics*, p. 35), see in 'an individual' the ultimate object of all consciousness. On the mutual relation of the factors of jhāna and how this develops into samādhi, see Appendix, Cetasika.

[5] *I.e.*, consciousness caused by the effect of jhāna practised in the immediately preceding life. *Dh. S.*, § 499.

[6] *Dh. S.*, § 577.

These, summed up, amount in all to fifteen classes of Rūpaloka consciousness, moral, resultant, and inoperative.

§ 9. *Mnemonic.*

Fivefold our thought on Rūpaloka's plane,
E'en as fivefold of jhāna is the chain.
As *making merit*, or as just *effect*,
Or *bringing none*, gives fifteen as correct.

3. CONSCIOUSNESS AS EXPERIENCED IN ARŪPALOKA.[1]

§ 10. *Of Arūpa-jhāna.*

There are four classes of consciousness which are moral and arise as Arūpa-mind, to wit:

1. Moral consciousness dwelling on the infinity of space.[2]

2. Moral consciousness dwelling on the infinity of consciousness.

3. Moral consciousness dwelling on nothingness.

4. Moral consciousness wherein perception neither is nor is not.[2]

Next, there are four classes of consciousness which are

[1] *Dh. S.*, §§ 265-8.

[2] Āyatana, in the Mnemonic below ālambana (= ārammaṇa), 'object of thought.' According to the Ṭīkā's, the citta has as its object the infinity of space; the second citta has as its object the *first* citta or viññāṇa; the third citta has as its object the *first* citta regarded as 'nothing.' The object of the fourth citta is consciousness of any kind—saññā being a symbolical or representative term—wherein complete hypnosis is all but attained. Perception can, therefore, be taken in its older wider sense as 'that act whereby the mind becomes conscious of anything' (Johnson's Dictionary). Buddhaghosa, commenting on the term in the *Mahā-nidāna-suttanta* (D. ii., xv. 71), remarks: '[one might say] neither viññāṇa nor not viññāṇa, as well as neither saññā, etc., so subtle and delicate is the consciousness.' See Introd. Essay, p. 64; Appendix: Āyatana, and *B. Psy.*, 74, *n.* 2. The use by myself and others of 'sphere' for āyatana is shown by the Ṭīkā's to be misleading.—Ed.

results of jhāna of similar kinds practised in the life immediately previous, to wit:

5-8.[1] Resultant consciousness of each of the four objects of thought characterized as above.

Next, there are four classes of consciousness which bring no result and belong to Arūpaloka, to wit:

9-12.[2] Inoperative consciousness of each of the four objects of thought characterized as above.

These, summed up, amount in all to twelve classes of Arūpaloka consciousness, moral, resultant, or inoperative.

§ 11. *Mnemonic.*

Four kinds of *mental object* may be sought
In mind rapt in Arūpaloka thought,
Classed as to *merit*, or as just *effect*,
Or *bringing none*, twelvefold will be correct.

---

4. Transcendental (Supramundane) Consciousness.[3]

§ 12. *Of Consciousness in the Paths and Fruition.*

There are four classes of consciousness which are transcendental and moral, to wit:

1. Consciousness belonging to the path of Stream-attainment.
2. Consciousness belonging to the path of Once-returning.
3. Consciousness belonging to the path of Never-Returning.
4. Consciousness belonging to the path of Arahantship.

[1] *Dh. S.*, § 501. [2] *Dh. S.*, § 579.

[3] **Lokuttara**, lit., 'beyond the worlds,' *i.e.*, beyond earth and heaven, or having nothing to do with getting well-reborn, except incidentally, in that such thoughts tend to expel the causes of rebirth. See *Dh. S.*, § 277 *f.*; *B. Psy.*, pp. 82-97, where, to avoid the European implications in 'transcendental,' I have used the phrase 'Thought engaged upon the Higher Ideal.'—Ed.

Next, there are four classes of transcendental resultant consciousness, to wit:

5-8.[1] Consciousness belonging to the fruition of each of the above-named four paths.

These, summed up, amount in all to eight classes of consciousness, both moral and resultant, arising in transcendental thought.

§ 13. *Mnemonic.*

Four are the Paths, hence, four *good* kinds of thought,
Four Fruits, hence four *resultant* kinds, we're taught.
Eight states in all, when highest things[2] are sought.

Concluding Remarks.

There are but classes *twelve* of consciousness
Known as immoral; classes *twenty-one*
Of moral consciousness, and *thirty-six*
Resultant kinds; inoperative kinds
A *score*: [so have I shown above.]
In Kāmaloka, consciousness is *four-*
And-fifty fold; *fifteen* alone are told
For Rūpaloka; for Arūpa *twelve*;
Eight in the Highest thought. Thus *eighty-nine*,
Or else *six score and one* we find to be
Classes of consciousness by seers discerned.

---

14. How can consciousness that is analyzed into eighty-nine come to have one hundred and twenty-one classes?

[By resolving *each* of the eight kinds of transcendental consciousness into *five*, thus obtaining forty kinds in place of eight]:

In the path of Stream-attainment there is a class of consciousness for each of the five stages of jhāna.

In the path of Once-Returning there is a class of consciousness for each of the five stages of jhāna.

[1] *Dh. S.*, § 505 *f.*

[2] Anuttaraŋ, 'without beyond.'—Ed.

So for the paths of Never-Returning and of Arahantship, making twenty classes of Path-consciousness in all.

Similarly there are twenty classes of Fruition-consciousness; and these together make forty classes of transcendental consciousness.

§ 15. *Summary.*

Distinguishing the j h ā n a of each Path,
As well as stage, we multiply by five;
And thus the thought that's Highest called becomes
Increased to forty kinds of consciousness.
Whereas the R ū p a l o k a consciousness
And thought called Highest may be classed 'neath one
And all five modes of j h ā n a, to the Fifth
Alone belong A r ū p a l o k a thoughts.
Hence are revealed eleven modes of thought
'Neath every j h ā n a till the last, and that
Yields three and twenty; add the thirty-seven
Kinds meritorious, and fifty-two
Resultant kinds, and thus six score and one
Classes of consciousness have Sages taught.

Thus ends Part I. in the Compendium of Philosophy, entitled The Chapter on the Compendium of Consciousness.

PART II

COMPENDIUM OF THE MENTAL PROPERTIES

§ 1. *Of kinds of Mental Properties.*

Allied to thought are two and fifty states
Called Mental Properties.[1] They rise and cease
With it, and share its object and its base.

§ 2. *How (are they distinguished)?*

I. There are seven Mental Properties which are common to every act of consciousness, to wit:

(1) contact (phassa);
(2) feeling (vedanā);
(3) perception (saññā);
(4) volition[2] (cetanā);
(5) individuality[3] of object (ekaggatā);

[1] Cetasʼikā, the adjectival form of ceto or citta, which is translated by consciousness, or in the verses sometimes by 'thought.' In any section of conscious experience the Buddhist distinguishes citta from its concomitants—*i.e.*, all other mental factors or elements distinguishable in the fact of conscious or subjective experience. We shall first consider these cetasikas as logically distinguishable. On how citta=viññāṇa=mano comes to be *logically* distinguished from the several mental factors which combine to constitute a *state* of consciousness (cittuppāda), see Introd. Essay, pp. 12 *ff.*; 39; 41; *Dh. S.*, §§ 1, 365, etc.

[2] Cetanā is derived from the causal verb ceteti, lit., to cause to think. On the twofold functions of this causal principle in thought, see Introd. Essay, p. 16, and Appendix: Cetanā.

[3] Why this and 'contact' should be regarded as mental properties, see Introd. Essay, p. 14 *f.*

(6) psychic life (j ī v i t i n d r i y a);
(7) attention (m a n a s i k ā r a).[1]

II. Next, there are six Mental Properties termed *Particular*[2] (not invariably present in consciousness), to wit:
(1) initial application (v i t a k k a);
(2) sustained application (v i c ā r a);
(3) deciding (a d h i m o k k h a);
(4) effort (v i r i y a);
(5) pleasurable interest (p ī t i);
(6) conation, desire-to-do (c h a n d a).[3]

Now these thirteen mental properties are to be considered as being either one or the other.[4]

III. Next, there are fourteen immoral mental properties, to wit:
(1) dulness (m o h a);
(2) impudence (a h i r i k a);

[1] The translator, in his luminous and valuable discussion of the position and function of c e t a s i k a ' s in Buddhist psychology (see Essay and Appendix), wished to extend the use of 'attention' by applying it also as 'initial' and 'sustained' to properties II. (1) and (2). Our 'attention' exactly corresponds to the Buddhist c e t a s i k a as an *element* in consciousness. The only flaw in its coming under the second list is that it is hard to conceive consciousness *without* some sort of initial attention. Buddhaghosa defines I., 7 as follows: M a n a s i - k ā r a means acting (k i r i y ā k ā r o), making with respect to consciousness (m a n o), making consciousness one's field as if it were a previous consciousness. M a n a s i k ā r a has three modes, according as it is concerned with object, sense-procedure, or apperception. In the last two it is synonymous with the mind 'turning towards' sensation or idea respectively (above, p. 28). Here only the first mode is meant, and here it means movement of mind confronting its object and *passing it on like a driver, to whatever it is connected withal*' (*Asl.*, 133). Hence we may say that Buddhist analysis resolves attention into the *constant* element of selective, co-ordinating consciousness I. (7), and the *variable* element of mental strain or tension, consciously felt, and connoted by II. (1), (2).—Ed.

[2] P a k i ṇ ṇ a k ā, lit., scattered about.

[3] K a t t u k a m y a t ā - c h a n d a is here intended.

[4] A ñ ñ a s a m ā n ā. That is to say they are purely psychological terms of un-moral import, but become moral or immoral, according as they combine in a moral or immoral thought.

(3) recklessness of consequences (a n o t t a p p a);
(4) distraction (u d d h a c c a);
(5) greed (l o b h a);
(6) error (d i ṭ ṭ h i);
(7) conceit (m ā n a);
(8) hate (d o s a);
(9) envy (i s s ā);
(10) selfishness (m a c c h a r i y a);
(11) worry (k u k k u c c a);
(12) sloth (t h i n a);[1]
(13) torpor (m i d d h a);
(14) perplexity (v i c i k i c c h ā).

IV. Next, there are nineteen mental properties which are common to all that is [morally] beautiful,[2] to wit:

(1) faith (s a d d h ā);
(2) mindfulness (s a t i);
(3) prudence (h i r i);
(4) discretion (o t t a p p a);
(5) disinterestedness (a l o b h a);
(6) amity (a d o s a);
(7) balance of mind (t a t r a m a j j h a t t a t ā);
(8) composure of mental properties[3] (k ā y a p a s s a d d h i);
(9) composure of mind (c i t t a p a s s a d d h i);
(10) buoyancy of mental properties (l a h u t ā);
(11) buoyancy of mind;
(12) pliancy of mental properties (m u d u t ā);

[1] Burmese manuscripts read t h i n a; Sinhalese, t h ī n a.—Ed.

[2] S o b h a ṇ a s ā d h ā r a ṇ a. See § 8.

[3] That 'k ā y a' here, meaning aggregate, refers to the n ā m a - k ā y a as opposed to the r ū p a k ā y a, can be seen from the following comment: K ā y o ' t t i c ' e t t h a v e d a n ā d i k h a n d h a t t a - y a s s a g a h a ṇ a m. S. Z. A. This agrees with Buddhaghosa (*Asl.*, 150): '[In *Dh. S.*, §§ 40 *ff.*] k ā y a means the three k h a n d h a s, v e d a n ā, etc.' Hence 'the distinction appears to be, not so much between sense and thought (*B. Psy.*, p. 23), as between factors of consciousness and consciousness as a whole.—Ed.

(13) pliancy of mind;
(14) fitness of work of mental properties (kammaññatā);
(15) fitness of work of mind;
(16) proficiency of mental properties (pāguññatā);
(17) proficiency of mind;
(18) rectitude[1] of mental properties (ujukatā);
(19) rectitude of mind.

V. Next, there are three Abstinences,[2] to wit:
right speech,
right action,
right livelihood.

VI. Next, there are the Illimitables,[3] to wit:
pity,
appreciation.[4]

These, together with (VII.) reason,[5] in all manner of division are to be considered as the twenty-five morally beautiful mental properties.

§ 3. *Mnemonic.*

So far we have:

[Of co-efficients] fifty-two; thirteen
As such *nor good nor bad*, but *bad*, fourteen,
And five and twenty *lovely* in act are seen.

---

[1] *Cf. B. Psy.*, 25, *n.* 1.

[2] Virati-yo, lit., dispassion-s. The term is probably derived from the formula of the Five Precepts (sīla), 'finding no pleasure in taking life' (pāṇātipātā veramaṇī sikkhāpadaŋ, or paṭivirato hoti), etc. (*B. Psy.*, 83, *n.* 3). On the presence of these as 'properties' among the cetasika's, see Appendix: Cetasika.—Ed.

[3] *I.e.*, two of the four Brahmavihāra's. The other two are represented by IV. (6) amity, for mettā; love, or ἀγαπή; and IV. (7) equanimity, impartiality, for upekkhā. See Pt. IX., § 2 (IV., 4).—Ed.

[4] Muditā is joy felt over a better than one's self, or over good work done; the congratulatory or benevolent attitude.

[5] Paññindriya as cetasika is not confined to the lokuttara-citta's.

Of these thought-adjuncts,[1] as they cluster round
Thoughts that arise in us, each in its turn,
The distribution henceforth shall be told.

Mnemonic.

First *seven*, linked with every phase of thought;
The *six*, in this or that phase must be sought;
The *fourteen* only with our bad thoughts mate;
The *beautiful* on none but fair thoughts wait.

§ 4. *In what Way?*

In the first place, those seven universally common concomitants obtain in all the eighty-nine modes of consciousness.[2]

Next, among the particular concomitants:

1. *Application* arises in fifty-five kinds of consciousness, to wit:

(i.) In all kinds of Kāmaloka consciousness, with the exception of the twice fivefold sense-impressions themselves.[3]

(ii.) It also arises in the eleven kinds of consciousness connected with the first stage of jhāna.[4]

2. *Application* arises in sixty-six kinds of consciousness, to wit: In all the above-named fifty-five, and also in the eleven kinds of consciousness connected with the second stage of jhāna.

3. *Deciding* arises in all kinds of consciousness, with the exception of the twice fivefold sense-consciousness, and of consciousness accompanied by perplexity.

[1] Cittāviyuttānaŋ, *i.e.*, Cetasika's.

[2] Cituppāda is literally a genesis or state of citta (consciousness), considered as constituting this or that process of mind, but the term here may be taken as representing a class, kind, or mode of citta.

[3] *Twice* fivefold, as accounting for the sensations being pleasurable or painful. Vitakka, *i.e.*, is absent from the initial momentary flash of visual or other sense impressions, but present in the rest of the process of sense-cognition.

[4] See Pt. I., § 15. Appendix: Cetasika (Vitakka).

4. *Effort* arises in all kinds of consciousness with the exception of—

(i.) Consciousness *turning to* impressions at the five gates of sense.
(ii.) The twice fivefold sense-cognitions themselves.
(iii.) The act of mental reception.[1]
(iv.) The act of investigation.[2]

5. *Pleasurable interest* arises in all kinds of consciousness with the exception of—

(i.) Consciousness accompanied by grief or hedonic indifference.
(ii.) Tactile impressions.[3]
(iii.) Consciousness connected with the fourth jhāna.

6. *Desire-to-do* arises in all kinds of consciousness, with the exception of such as are not accompanied by their hetu's *and* of muddle-headed consciousness.[4]

Taking these particular concomitants in the order described, the numbers of (kinds of) consciousness are as follows :

§ 5. *Mnemonic.*

Lacking these six adjuncts, in order given,
Sixty-six, fifty-five, eleven,
Sixteen, seventy, and twenty kinds we rate.[5]
But fifty-five, and sixty-six, and eight,
And seventy, seventy-three, and fifty-one,
And sixty-nine :—so do the numbers run
Of all those classes of our thought
Into the which these six adjuncts are wrought.

[1] and [2] Sampaṭicchana and santīraṇa respectively. See above, Part I., § 4. The act of investigation here is confined to the object *presented to* the mind, and is therefore more or less of a passive nature. See Introd. Essay, p. 28.

[3] On the theory of Touch, see Appendix : Upekkhā.

[4] Chanda (conation, or desire to do) is akin to intention or purposive volition, and a muddle-headed and foolish man has no volition deserving the name of purposive.

[5] *I.e.*, classes of consciousness.

§ 6. *Of Immoral Concomitants.*

The four called 'mental properties common to all immoral consciousness' obtain in all the twelve classes of immoral consciousness, to wit:

(1) dulness;
(2) impudence;
(3) recklessness [of consequences];
(4) distraction.

Greed obtains only in the eight kinds of consciousness given over to appetite.

Error obtains in the four kinds of consciousness connected with erroneous views.

Conceit obtains in the four kinds of consciousness disconnected from erroneous views.[1]

Hate, envy, selfishness, and *worry*—these four obtain in the two kinds of consciousness connected with aversion.

Sloth and *torpor* obtain in the five kinds of [immoral] consciousness which are volitional.[2]

Perplexity obtains only in the kind of consciousness that is 'accompanied by perplexity.'[3]

§ 7. *Mnemonic.*

In *all* demeritorious thoughts are Four
Adjuncts. In greed-h e t u there are but Three;
Four, in the hate-h e t u. Again, Two more
In thoughts volitional. Dubiety,
In thought allied with doubt. And thus we see
Fourteen Bad Adjuncts in Five ways are bound
To the Twelve thoughts that are immoral found.

[1] In commenting on this to us somewhat paradoxical statement, the teachers refer to the *inconstant* association of conceit or pride with such views, which is made explicit only in the Mnemonic, § 10:—'Pride sometimes;' *i.e.*, when a real superiority over others is the cause of self-advertisement and complacency. A similar reminder is made in the case of 'sloth and torpor' occurring in volitional consciousness. They so occur when the mind is unfit for work. On m ā n a see *B. Psy.*, 298 *f.*, *n.* 8.—Ed.

[2] See above, Part I., § 2.

[3] *Ibid.*, class 11.

§ 8. *Of [Morally] Beautiful Concomitants.*[1]

Now among the concomitants called [morally] beautiful, in the first place, there are the nineteen mental properties common to [morally] beautiful consciousness. These are present in every one of the fifty-nine classes of beautiful consciousness.

Next, the three *abstinences* obtain, always and all at once, in all cases of transcendental consciousness. But in mundane[2] [morally] beautiful consciousness, it is only in the [eight kinds of] Kāmaloka moral consciousness[3] that the three are sometimes and severally apparent.

Next, the two *illimitables* spring up, sometimes and mutually exclusive, in twenty-eight kinds of sublime[4] consciousness, excluding the fifth jhāna, in the eight kinds of Kāmaloka moral consciousness,[5] and in the eight classes of consciousness arising in the Kāmaloka-mind, which are accompanied by their respective hetu's, but which are inoperative.[6]

[1] Sobhaṇā. My interpolated word in brackets is perhaps supererogatory. But the manual contains hints at a psychological theory of æsthetic consciousness indicated by words meaning literally 'mirth,' and not 'beauty.' And sobhanā is literally beautiful. *Cf.* Jāt. ii., 346, where a courtesan is called nagara-sobhaṇā, 'town beauty.' I do not know of any passage as old as the Piṭakas, where the word is explicitly opposed to pāpa, 'evil,' as it is in Childers's reference to Gogerly, *s.v.* Sobhaṇo.—Ed. See Introd. Essay, p. 20.

[2] Lokiya, the contradictory of lokuttara 'transcendental,' and meaning 'of the three loka's.'—Ed.

[3] See above, Part I., § 6.

[4] Mahaggatacittesu. The Ceylon Commentaries explain this term to mean those classes of consciousness that have grown great, or become exalted or sublime, because of the absence of the Hindrances, etc. (Vinīvaranāditāya mahattaŋ gatāni), or by reason of the excellent jhāna's (mahantehi jhāyīhi gatāni). S. Z. A. *B. Psy.*, 265, § 1019, *n.* 2. According to Buddhaghosa, so termed because of the ability (of such thinking) to resist vice, of abundance of good result, of wide extension, of attainment to a high pitch of volition, energy, thought wisdom. *Asl.* 44.—Ed.

[5] See above, Part I., § 6 (1-8). [6] *Ibid.* (17-24).

Some teachers, however, say that 'pity' and 'appreciation' are not in such consciousness as is accompanied by hedonic indifference.

Next, *reason*[1] enters into combination with forty-seven classes of consciousness, to wit, with twelve kinds of consciousness arising in the Kāmaloka that are 'connected with knowledge,' and also with all the thirty-five kinds of sublime and of transcendental consciousness.

§ 9. *Mnemonic.*

In nine and fifty kinds of thought, nineteen
Adjuncts spring into birth, three in sixteen,
And two in twenty-eight. But reason shines
In seven and forty forms. And so the lines
Binding the adjuncts 'beautiful' in thought
In these four groups of classes must be sought.

§ 10. *Of Concomitants as Essential and as Accidental.*

Sometimes and sev'rally appearing see
Envy, and selfishness, and worry; three
Path-factors 'Abstinences' called; beside
These, pity and appreciation; pride
Sometimes; so sloth and torpor too. The rest,
If the foregoing thou rememberest,
Are NECESSARY adjuncts of our thought,
[Not now and then into our thinking wrought.]

Now all these several parts I'll try to fit
Into a synthesis where they permit.

[1] Paññā. The Protean significance of this term, however it be rendered in English, can be seen from this passage. The factor here combining with these forty-seven is, according to circumstances, knowledge (*i.e.*, knowing, not product of knowing), intellect, understanding, intelligence, insight, right view or wisdom factor (bojjhanga).

§ 10A. *Of Classes of Consciousness in Synthesis.*

Into our highest thought come thirty-six,
And five and thirty into thoughts sublime,
And into Kāmaloka consciousness
Of loveliness and beauty thirty-eight.
In thoughts demeritorious thirty-seven,
And twelve in thoughts that rise without hetu.
Fivefold the synthesis of adjuncts stands,
Duly assorted as they come to pass.

---

§ 11. *How (is it so)?*

First of all, in transcendental consciousness there are thirty-six concomitant states which enter into combination with any one of the eight classes of consciousness arising in the first jhāna, to wit, the thirteen immoral concomitants, and twenty-three [of the twenty-five] beautiful concomitants, omitting only the two illimitables.[1]

Similarly, thirty-five concomitant states, [initial] application being now excluded, enter into combination with any one of the eight classes of consciousness arising in the second jhāna.

Similarly, thirty-four and thirty-three concomitant states, application and pleasurable interest being successively excluded, enter into combination with any one of the eight classes of consciousness arising in the third and fourth jhānas respectively.

And thirty-three concomitant states, hedonic indifference replacing pleasure, enter into combination with any one of the eight classes of consciousness arising in the fifth jhāna.

Thus, under all circumstances, there is only a fivefold

[1] The two *illimitables* are excluded because their object, which is satta-paññatti (the concept 'mankind') is totally different from that of transcendental consciousness—namely, Nibbana.

Cf. on this *B. Psy.*, 83, *n.* 3.—Ed.

synthesis of concomitants with the eight kinds of transcendental consciousness corresponding to the five stages of jhāna.

§ 12. *Mnemonic.*

Fivefold the synthesis that comes in highest plane of thought—
From thirty-six to thirty-three, the last ta'en twice—is taught.

§ 13. *Of 'Sublime' Consciousness.*

Next, in sublime consciousness, there are thirty-five factors which enter into combination with any one of those three[1] classes of consciousness that belong to the first stage of jhāna, to wit, thirteen un-moral concomitants, and twenty-two morally beautiful concomitants, the three 'abstinences' being excluded.[2]

Here be it noted that 'pity' and 'appreciation' combine severally only.

Again, the same concomitants, with the exception of initial application, enter into combination with any one of the [same] three classes of consciousness that belong to the second stage of jhāna, and also to the third and fourth stages, dropping in succession application, both initial and sustained, at the third stage, and then these two and pleasurable interest at the fourth stage.

But in the fifteen classes of consciousness that belong to the fifth stage of jhāna, the two illimitables do not obtain.

Thus, reckoning every possible way, the combinations of concomitants with the twenty-seven kinds of sublime consciousness by way of fivefold jhāna may be summarized under five heads.

[1] Part I., § 8. Moral, resultant, and inoperative consciousness.

[2] Because they do not bear on the object of jhāna practice, and they are totally different in function from jhāna. The function of the three 'abstinences' is to purify act and word either temporarily or permanently, whilst the function of jhāna is to purify the mind of one who has already had his act and word purified.

§ 14. *Mnemonic.*

Groups of adjuncts in thoughts sublime we find
As it may hap, on fivefold wise combined :—
First thirty-five the factors ; thirty-four ;
One less ; one less ; last, thirty and no more.

---

§ 15. *Of Morally Beautiful*[1] *Consciousness in Kāmaloka.*

Next, in morally beautiful consciousness in **Kāmaloka**, in the first place, there are thirty-eight states, which enter into combination in any one of the *first two* classes of moral consciousness,[2] to wit, the thirteen un-moral concomitants and the twenty-five morally beautiful concomitants.

Here it should be noted that the two 'illimitables' and the three 'abstinences' combine separately.

Similarly, these thirty-eight enter into combination in any one of the *second* two, 'knowledge' only being excluded; in any one of the *third* two, 'knowledge' being included, but 'pleasurable interest' being excluded; and in any one of the *fourth* two, both 'knowledge' and 'pleasurable interest' being excluded.

Again, taking [the eight kinds of **Kāmaloka**] inoperative consciousness,[3] and excluding the three 'abstinences,' those thirty-eight—now thirty-five—concomitant states are to be reckoned as similarly combining in four different ways, in four pairs of inoperative classes of consciousness.

And again, taking the eight kinds of **Kāmaloka** resultant consciousness, and excluding both the two illimitables and the three abstinences, those thirty-eight—now thirty-three—concomitant states are to be reckoned

[1] See above, § 8, *n.* 1.

[2] *I.e.*, of the eight moral classes, Part I., § 6. By the '*first* two,' the '*second* two,' etc., is to be understood both the automatic and the volitional of each pair.

[3] Part I., § 6.

as similarly combining in four different ways in four pairs of resultant kinds of consciousness.

Thus, reckoning every possible way, the combinations of morally beautiful concomitants in pairs with the twenty-four morally beautiful classes of Kāmaloka consciousness may be summarized under twelve heads.

§ 16. *Mnemonic.*

In Kāmaloka, when to hetu's bound
Thought rises, if to merit it redound,
Or is resultant, or works nothing, aye
The adjuncts rise with it in many a way :—
On thoughts of *moral beauty* thirty-eight,
Twice thirty-seven, and thirty-six await.

In thought inoperative joined we see
Of adjuncts thirty-five, twice thirty-four,
And thirty-three. In thoughts resultant, three
And thirty, and twice thirty-two, once more,
Thirty-one adjuncts may commingled be.

In thoughts inoperative, and exalted thought
The adjuncts three called abstinence may ne'er be sought.
The four illimitables come not into mind
Transcendent ; neither them nor the three former find
In thought-resultants of the Kāmaloka kind.

In highest consciousness the jhāna stages show
Distinctive, and where thoughts at medium[1] level flow.
Here too th' illimitables, and on lower plane,[2]
With threefold abstinence and knowledge they again,
With pleasurable interest,[3] distinction gain.

[1] The J.P.T.S. text has majjhime for mahaggate, a term used in such comparisons in *Dhs.*, *e.g.*, §§ 1025-7.—Ed.

Majjhime, however, is the correct reading both according to the Burmese Text, and according to metre.—S. Z. A.

[2] Referring to the twenty-four beautiful classes of consciousness in Kāmaloka.

[3] See Part II., § 2.

§ 17. *Of Immoral Consciousness.*

Now, in immoral consciousness, in the first place, there are nineteen concomitant states which enter into combination with any one of the first automatic class in the eight kinds of consciousness called appetitives,[1] to wit, the thirteen unmoral concomitants, and the four common immoral concomitants, making seventeen, to which add greed and error.

In like manner with the second automatic class, the same seventeen concomitants combine, together with greed and conceit.

In like manner with the third automatic class, the same seventeen concomitants combine with the exception of pleasurable interest, but together with greed and error, giving eighteen in all.

In like manner with the fourth automatic class, omitting pleasurable interest, but adding greed and conceit.

But with the fifth automatic class which is connected with aversion, to the seventeen foregoing concomitants [of the first class] add hate, envy, selfishness, and worry, and from them omit pleasurable interest, thus making twenty concomitants combining with that fifth class.

But of those four, envy, selfishness, and worry can only combine separately.

In like manner with the five corresponding *volitional* classes of the twelve kinds of immoral cognition, the foregoing combinations of concomitants obtain, with this difference, that sloth and torpor must be included.

Excluding desire-to-do and pleasurable interest, eleven unmoral and the four common immoral concomitants, fifteen states in all, are associated with that class of consciousness which is accompanied by distraction.[2]

[1] Literally, in the greed-rooted (kinds of consciousness). See Part I., § 2.—Ed.

[2] See Part I., § 2 (12).

In like manner with that class of consciousness accompanied by perplexity, fifteen concomitants, deprived of the element of 'deciding,' but accompanied by perplexity, combine well.

Thus, all being reckoned up, there is a sevenfold synthesis of concomitants, numerically considered, combining in the twelve kinds of immoral consciousness.

§ 18. *Mnemonic.*

With evil thoughts of classes manifold
The blend of adjuncts 'neath seven heads is told:—
Nineteen, eighteen, and twenty—one to three;
Then twenty-one and twenty [as you see];
And twenty-two and fifteen:—these the seven.
Only to fourteen adjuncts is it given
With every thought of wrong to be in-wrought.
These are the four common to all bad thought,
And ten[1] besides—[these must above be sought].

§ 19. *Of Unmoral Consciousness.*

Lastly, in consciousness not accompanied by hetu's, there are twelve of the thirteen unmoral concomitants, desire-to-do being excluded, which enter into combination, in the consciousness of æsthetic pleasure.

They combine also in the consciousness of determining,[2] pleasurable interest being excluded as well as desire-to-do; and again with the consciousness of investigation with pleasure, effort being excluded as well as desire-to-do.

They combine also with the triple faculty of *apprehension*,[3] and with the dual process of 'rebirth-conscious-

[1] *I.e.*, with the exception of chanda, pīti and adhimokkha from the thirteen unmoral concomitants.

[2] Voṭṭhabbane, (Sinh. MSS.: voṭṭhappane), fixing, assigning impressions, the stage before 'apperception.' See below, Part III., § 4, and also Introd. Essay, p. 28.—Ed.

[3] The triple faculty of apprehension (manodhātu) comprises the mind 'turning towards' stimuli (pañcadvārāvajjana), and

ness,'[1] which is not accompanied by its h e t u ' s. Here desire-to-do, pleasurable interest and effort are excluded.

Lastly, they combine with the twice five[2] groups of sense-cognitions; here, however, all the 'particular' concomitants must be excluded.

Thus, all being reckoned up, the synthesis of concomitants numerically considered, combining with the eighteen classes of consciousness not accompanied by their h e t u ' s, consists of four groups.

§ 20. *Mnemonic.*

Adjuncts, that blend with eighteen kinds of thought
Not bound to the six h e t u ' s we have brought
Under four heads, thus: Twelve, eleven, and ten,
And seven—such is the synthesis. Again,
The seven adjuncts that are common mix
With all those eighteen. As conditions fix,
Combine the others. Now in detail you see
Adjuncts in summaries of thirty-three.[3]

---

the two recipient elements (s a m p a ṭ i c c h a n a ' s), capable of taking part only in a presentative (but never in a representative) cognition with any one of the five sensibles as their object.

[1] The two classes of rebirth-consciousness are the two classes of consciousness, which have been designated in Part I. as u p e k k h ā - s a n t ī r a ṇ a (investigating-consciousness with hedonic indifference). It will always remain a puzzle to Occidentals, why this particular class should be active at rebirth. It will be seen from Part III. that it is capable of performing five different functions, and is therefore entitled to five different designations corresponding to each function. As an individual person may be at once a poet, a philosopher, and a politician, even so, says the Buddhist, one class of consciousness may function on different occasions.

[2] See above, § 4, *n.* 3.

[3] Namely, in § 12, 5; in § 14, 5; in § 16, 12; in § 18, 7; in § 20, 4=33.

Thus have we come to know the summary
And methods of the mind's concomitants.
Thence have we found it easier to explain
How to divide and classify our thought.

Thus ends the Second Part in the Compendium of Philosophy, entitled the Chapter on the Compendium of the Mental Properties of Consciousness.

PART III

COMPENDIUM OF PARTICULAR (CONCOMITANTS OF CONSCIOUSNESS).

§ 1. *Introductory.*

IN thought and its concomitants we may
Distinguish three and fifty states of mind,
Combined this way and that as is their law.
Hereof, let us now make the summary
By way of thoughts only *as they arise*,
Treating of feeling, and of h e t u 's six,
Of thought as having 'function,' sprung from 'doors,'
As having 'objects,' and material 'base,'
And as is fit[1] bear all in memory.

---

§ 2. *Of Feeling.*

Summarizing feeling, in the first place, feeling is threefold—it is pleasant, painful, and neither [or neutral]. Or, again, it may be divided into five[2]—pleasure, pain, joy, grief, and hedonic indifference.

[1] Y a t h ā r a h a ŋ. This term, often rendered below as 'according to circumstances,' means that the learner should study, summarize, and commit to memory (1) h e t u 's, with reference to s a h e t u k a consciousness; (2) 'doors,' with reference to those classes of consciousness arising through them; (3) 'bases,' with reference to those classes other than A r ū p a l o k a thoughts which are without 'bases'; (4) feeling, function, and objects, with reference to all classes.

[2] Spoken of as the i n d r i y a - divisions, i n d r i y a meaning controlling power or faculty. *Saŋyutta-Nikāya:* v., 207 *f.* (I n d r i y a - S a ŋ y u t t a). *Cf. B. Psy.*, lvii., lviii.

Here, among sense-impressions, which are the result of moral deeds [done in a former birth], there is only one kind that is accompanied by pleasurable feeling, and that is tactile impressions.[1] Likewise there is only one kind of those sense-impressions, due to immoral deeds [done in a former birth], that is accompanied by painful feeling, and that again is tactile impressions.

Now there are sixty-two kinds of consciousness which are accompanied by joy, to wit:

(*a*) The [eighteen classes of kāmaloka] consciousness which are 'accompanied by joy'—*i.e.*:

four of the eight appetitives;[2]
twelve of the Kāmaloka morally beautiful kinds of consciousness;[3]
the *two*:—pleasurable investigation and æsthetic pleasure.[4]

(*b*) The forty-four classes of 'sublime' and transcendental consciousness,[5] termed first, second, third, and fourth jhāna.

But the thoughts accompanied by grief are the only two classes of consciousness 'connected with aversion.'[6]

All the remaining fifty-five kinds of consciousness are accompanied by hedonic indifference.

[1] See above, Part I., § 4. Kāyika-sukha, bodily pleasure and Kāyika-dukkha, bodily pain, are here intended. The remaining modes of psychical sukha and dukkha are cetasika or mānasika (mental pleasure and pain).

[2] Part I., § 2 (the first four).

[3] Part I., § 6.

[4] Part I., § 4. Somanassa, 'joy,' is sukha, 'pleasure,' plus excitement. The ethical sukha, 'happiness,' and dukkha, misery or 'ill,' are not meant here.

[5] Part I., §§ 8-12.

[6] Part I., § 2.

§ 3. *Mnemonic.*

Pleasure, pain, and neutral feeling—aspects of sensation[1]
three,
Fivefold, if in these distinguished [two more]—joy and
sorrow—be ;
Pleasure in one thought is known,
Pain lies too in one alone,
Grief in twain, but glad emotion mated is to sixty-two,
And indifference[2] may itself in five and fifty thoughts
renew.

§ 4. *Of the Six Conditions called Hetu's.*

Summarizing the hetu's: these appear as six, to wit, greed, hate, ignorance [or dulness], disinterestedness, amity and intelligence.[3]

Now, there are eighteen kinds of consciousness which are not conditioned by any of these six—namely, five-door apprehending,[4] the twice fivefold sense-impressions, receiving, investigating, determining, and æsthetic pleasure.

All the remaining seventy-one kinds of consciousness are conditioned by those six hetu's.[5]

Of these, again, the two classes of ignorant [or dull] consciousness[6] are conditioned by one only of the hetu's.

The remaining ten classes of immoral consciousness, and twelve of the Kāmaloka morally beautiful classes of con-

[1] Spoken of as anubhavana-division, anubhavana meaning 'feeling,' 'enjoying.'

[2] The hedonic upekkhā, and not the intellectual tatramajjhattatupekkhā, balance of mind, mental equipoise, is here meant.

[3] Amoha is another term used by Buddhist writers as a synonym of paññā, the paññindriya-cetasika being here intended, or constant element in all intellectual functioning.

[4] Part I., § 4, Class 16.

[5] That is, appear in consciousness together with one or more of the six.—Ed.

[6] Part I., § 2.

sciousness, which are disconnected with knowledge, together make twenty-two kinds, conditioned by two of the hetu's.[1]

Again, forty-seven classes of consciousness are bound up each with three[2] of the hetu's, to wit, twelve classes of Kāmaloka morally beautiful consciousness which are connected with knowledge,[3] and thirty-five sublime and transcendental kinds of consciousness.

§ 5. *Mnemonic.*

Greed, hate, dulness—these of acts immoral are the hetu's three;
Their opposites, of acts both good and indeterminate, hetu's be.
Not bound to these are eighteen thoughts; two thoughts by one alone are driven;
Two hetu's govern twenty-two; from hetu's three spring forty-seven.

§ 6. *Of Function.*

In summarizing functions (we find) fourteen of these, to wit:

(1) rebirth;[4] (3) apprehending;[6]
(2) life-continuum;[5] (4) seeing;

[1] The eight appetitive classes are bound up with, or conditioned by, the *two* hetu's, greed and ignorance; the two classes of consciousness connected with aversion are bound up with the *two* hetu's, hate and ignorance; and the twelve classes of Kāmaloka morally beautiful classes disconnected with knowledge, are conditioned by the *two* hetu's, disinterestedness and amity. *Cf.* pp. 91 and 92.

[2] Namely, disinterestedness, amity, and intelligence.

[3] That amoha, of which the paññindriya-cetasika is the psychical ultimate, should be found in classes connected with knowledge shows that amoha, paññā, and ñāṇa, refer to one and the same adjunct of consciousness.

[4] Paṭisandhi is, philosophically speaking, confined to the momentary mental function at the initial moment of *re*conception. In popular language it includes reconception, embryonic growth, and rebirth.

[5] Bhavanga. Unconscious life comparable to Leibniz's "state of obscure perception,' not amounting to consciousness, in dreamless sleep. See Introd. Essay, p. 9.

[6] Āvajjana. See p. 5, *n.* 4.

(5) hearing; (10) investigating;
(6) smelling; (11) determining;
(7) tasting; (12) apperceiving;[1]
(8) touching; (13) retention;[2]
(9) receiving; (14) re-decease.[3]

But if we classify these fourteen functions by way of 'stage' (ṭhāna), then the category of stages must be considered as tenfold.[4]

[Regarding consciousness under the aspect of function, we may distinguish]:

(*a*) Nineteen classes of consciousness functioning at rebirth, during life-continuum and at re-decease, to wit:

(i.) *two* classes of investigation-consciousness accompanied by hedonic indifference.
(ii.) *eight* great classes of resultants.[5]
(iii.) *nine* resultants in Rūpaloka and Arūpaloka.[6]

(*b*) Two classes of consciousness functioning by way of the impressions called 'turning towards' [the sense-stimulus].

[1] On (8)-(12) see Introd. Essay, p. 28 *f*.

[2] Tad-ārammaṇa, or tad-àlambana (both forms occur in the manual), meaning, literally, '*that*-object' is the curious scholastic term—apparently not found prior to Buddhaghosa—for the final phase in the registration of impression by way of sense. *That* object *which has been just apperceived*, if vivid enough, reaches this stage. —Ed.

[3] Cuti, lit., 'falling,' co-incident etymologically with the English rendering.—Ed.

[4] Ṭhāna, lit., 'place' or 'occasion.' It is pretty clear, from the fact that the only difference between kicca (function), and ṭhāna (stage) lies in five senses, or a fivefold sense, that the meaning is:—the five senses having the same mental status form only one distinctive class. Only one at a time can take part in a process of presentative cognition.

[5] See p. 87 (9-16).

[6] *Dhs.*, §§ 499-504.

(*c*) Two classes of consciousness functioning in each of the five senses and in [the mental] reception of impressions.

(*d*) Three classes of consciousness functioning by way of investigation.

'Mind-door' cognition[1] alone performs the function of determining [or fixing] the sense-impression at the 'five-doors.'

(*e*) Fifty-five classes of consciousness functioning in apperception, to wit, fifty-five[2] modes of moral, immoral, fruitional,[3] and inoperative consciousness, not counting the two in (*b*).

(*f*) Eleven classes of consciousness in the retentive function, to wit, the eight great resultants,[4] and the three modes of investigation.

[Now a class of consciousness may perform one or more functions:]

(i.) [What is ordinarily called] 'investigation-consciousness accompanied by hedonic indifference' may perform five functions—*i.e.*, it may be active at rebirth,[5] during the life-continuum, at re-decease, in retention and in investigation itself.

(ii.) The Eight main resultants may perform four functions—*i.e.*, they may be active at rebirth, during the life-continuum, at re-decease, and in retention.

[1] The manodvārāvajjana, Class 17 in Part I., § 4. This class receives the name of voṭṭhabbana, when it takes part in a presentative cognition, and *determines* the sense-impression (already investigated) for apperception.

[2] Namely, 21, 12. 4, and 18=55.

[3] Phala, not vipāka.

[4] *Dhs.*, § 498.

[5] It must not be supposed that investigation-consciousness investigates its object at rebirth. See p. 109, *n.* 1. This particular class of consciousness is simply active as rebirth-consciousness connecting the two consecutive existences. None of the classes of consciousness can perform more than one function at a unit of time.

(iii.) The Nine resultant sublime classes may perform three functions—*i.e.*, they may be active at rebirth, during the life-continuum, and at re-decease.

(iv.) [What is called] 'investigation-consciousness accompanied by joy' may perform two functions—*i.e.*, it may be active both in investigation and in retention; and again determining consciousness may be active in determining and by way of 'turning to' impressions.

(v.) All the remaining kinds of consciousness can perform only a single function. They are the [fifty-five] apperceptions, the triple element of apprehension,[1] and the twice five kinds of sense-cognition, each cognition functioning simply, as it comes to pass.

§ 7. *Mnemonic.*

If thoughts uprising 'neath aspect of function be divided,—
Rebirth, life-process, and the rest,—fourteen we find provided.
Or ten,[2] if 'sense, in rank, to count as one' shall be decided.
[As functional,[3] each class of thought has various work to do :—]
Single, double, triple function, fourfold, fivefold, too.
Eight and sixty single, double *two*, and triple *nine*.
Quadruple *eight*, quintuple *two* :—the functions thus assign.

---

§ 8. *Of Doors (or Organs).*

In the summary of doors, 'door' is the name given to six organs, to wit, eye-door, ear-door, nose-door, tongue-door, body-door, and mind-door.

[1] Manodhātu, includes five-door cognition, and the two modes of reception in (*c*) § 6, latter clause. See p. 108, *n*. 3, and see p. 122.

[2] *I.e.*, ten ṭhāna's or stages.

[3] The Commentaries, in discussing the latter of the two summaries in § 6, use the term kiccavantāni, functionaries or functionals, to denote cittāni considered as functioning, or having kicca.

Here the eye is just the eye-door; and so for the ear-door and the next three. But the life-continuum itself may be described as the mind-door.[1]

Of these organs, through the first, the door of sight, forty-six classes of consciousness take their rise, according to fitness [in subject and object],[2] to wit:

(*a*) five-door cognition;
(*b*) visual cognition;
(*c*) reception;
(*d*) investigating;
(*e*) determining;
(*f*) Kāmaloka apperception;
(*g*) retention.[3]

So for the next four 'doors.'

And when all are reckoned, there are fifty-four kinds of Kamaloka consciousness which take their rise through the five 'doors.'

But, by way of the mind-door, sixty-seven kinds of consciousness come to pass, to wit, mind-door consciousness,[4] the fifty-five kinds of apperception, and retention.

There are nineteen kinds of consciousness, which are free, in functioning, from any 'door';[5] those, namely, which are active at rebirth, during the life-continuum, and at re-decease.

Of those, on the other hand [which take their rise

[1] How and why bhavanga came to be regarded as mind-door, see Introd. Essay, p. 10.

[2] The Ceylon Commentary (Abhidhammattha-Vibhāvanī) explains this yathārahaŋ as follows: 'According as the object is agreeable or not; as that object is properly attended to or not; and as the percipient is an Arahant or not, etc. Ledi Sadaw explains the same by 'According to the object, the plane of existence, the subject, attention,' etc.

[3] Annotators make up the 46 thus:—(*a*), 1; (*b*), 2; (*c*), 2; (*d*), 3; (*e*), 1; (*f*), 29; and (*g*), 8.

[4] Manodvārāvajjana=Class 17, Part I., § 4.

[5] Lit., 'door-freed.' See Introd. Essay, pp. 9, 25.

through doors], thirty-six kinds of consciousness come to pass through *one* door, according as there is mutual fitness, to wit, the [twice] five classes of sense-consciousness, sublime, and transcendental[1] apperceptions.

The triple element of apprehension comes to pass through [any one of] five doors.

Investigation accompanied by pleasure, determining consciousness and K ā m a l o k a apperceptions are cognitions happening through six doors.[1]

Investigation, which is accompanied by hedonic indifference, and the main resultant classes of consciousness happen either by way of the six doors, or are independent of any door.[2] Resultant sublime cognitions are always independent of any door.

§ 9. *Mnemonic.*

Thoughts that arise through *one* sense-door are thirty-six in kind;
Three classes through *five* doors; through *six* doors thirty-one we find.
Ten kinds arise now through *six* doors, now *without* doors of sense,
And nine are *wholly free* from doors:—five heads of difference.

§ 10. *Of Object of Consciousness.*

In the summary of objects, that which is called object is of six kinds, to wit, visible object, audible object, odorous object, sapid object, tangible object, and cognoscible object. Here only visible form[3] is visible object; again, only sound is audible object, and so forth.

[1] See Part I., § 12.

[2] According to the Commentators, the former is the case in our investigation and retaining; the latter, at rebirth, during unconscious life, and at re-decease. See p. 118, and p. 116, *n.* 5.

[3] R ū p a here seems to be confined to the v a ṇ ṇ ā y a t a n a, or sense of colour, the only strictly visible object (s a n i d a s s a n a-r ū p a ŋ), the form, the figure, the shape (s a ṇ ṭ h ā n a) being

But cognoscible object is classified under six groups, to wit, the sensitive [parts of] organs, subtle forms,[1] cognitions, mental concomitants, Nibbana, and name-and-notion.[2] Here, of all cognitions arising through the organ of sight, visible form only is the object, and such visible form as is *present*. Again, of all cognitions arising through the organs of hearing, smell, taste, and touch, the corresponding sense-objects only are the objects, and they are *present* objects.

But the object of mind-door cognitions is a sixfold *present*, or *past*, or *future* object, or one *out of time*, according to its capacities.

Further, the objects of those 'door-freed' classes of consciousness which are called rebirth, life-continuum, and re-decease cognitions, are also of six kinds according to circumstances. They have usually been grasped [as object] in the immediately preceding existence by way of the six doors;[3] they are objects of things either present or past, or they are concepts.[4] And they are [technically] known as 'karma,' 'sign of 'karma,' or 'sign of destiny.'[5]

Of those [classes of consciousness, which have this or

---

known inferentially in one of the 'sequels' of sense-cognition described in the Introd. Essay, p. 82 *f.*

[1] 'Gross' and 'subtle' is one division of all rūpa, or non-mental 'forms' (*i.e.*, material qualities). The former comprises all sense-organs and sense-objects; the latter, the principles, or states, of the two sexes; the vital principle, the two media of communication (viññatti), space, certain properties of matter, and the nutritive principle in foods. See Manual, Part VII., § 8. *B. Psy.*, pp. 207 *ff*, 172 *ff*.

[2] Paññatti includes nāma-paññatti (name or term), and attha-paññatti (notion, or idea, or concept). See Part VIII., §§ 14, 15, and Introd. Essay, p. 4 *f.*

[3] And that at the time of approaching death.

[4] Paññattibhūtāni vā. The attha-paññatti, 'the idea,' 'the notion,' or 'the concept,' is here intended. See below, Part VIII., § 14.

[5] Gati-nimittaŋ, lit., 'sign of going,' or of the 'objective' of one's going, *i.e.*, of one's destiny. See farther, Part V.—Ed.

that object], visual cognition has visible form only as its object; similarly in the case of the other four [special] senses. But the objects of the triple element of apprehension[1] are fivefold, being the five sense-objects.

The remaining kinds of Kāmaloka resultant consciousness, as well as æsthetic pleasure, have in all cases only Kāmaloka objects.

Immoral consciousness, as well as such Kāmaloka apperceptions as are 'disconnected from knowledge,'[2] may have all kinds of objects except transcendental objects.[3]

Those classes of Kāmaloka moral consciousness which are connected with knowledge, as well as those belonging to super-intellection,[4] which is reckoned as of fifth jhāna moral consciousness, may have all kinds of objects except the Path and the Fruit of Arahantship.

Inoperative Kāmaloka consciousness, which is connected with knowledge, as well as inoperative super-intellection and determining cognition, may have all kinds of objects under any conditions.

In purely Arūpaloka consciousness the second and the fourth class have only 'sublime' objects.[5] All the remaining kinds of 'sublime' consciousness have objects which are concepts.[6]

Transcendental consciousness has Nibbana as its object.

[1] Manodhātuttikaŋ. See p. 108, *n*. 3, above.

[2] Part I., § 6.

[3] The Commentators number these as nine: The four 'Paths,' the four 'Fruits,' and Nibbana.

[4] Abhiññākusalaŋ. See Part IX., end of § 4, and Introd. Essay, p. 62 *f*. Appendix: Abhiññā.

[5] *I.e.*, the first and the third Āruppas (Arūpaloka jhāna's) respectively.

[6] Paññattālambanāni. Aṭṭhapaññatti is here intended. All the five stages of jhāna, in the fifteen classes of Rūpa-consciousness, are induced by the paṭibhāga-nimitta or the transformed after-image (*i.e.*, the image *conceptualized*) of one or other of the ten kasiṇa-circles, or by the after-image arising in the breathing exercise. But the after-image of any one of the ten asubhas (impurities, Part IX., § 2), or of the living body, is capable of inducing the first stage only of jhāna. The first four stages of

§ 11. *Mnemonic.*

To different kinds of consciousness seven kinds of objects fix:—
Lower objects to twenty-five; exalted thoughts to six.
Notion, concept,[1] to twenty-one; to eight, Nibbana's field,
To twenty kinds those objects which *naught transcendental* yield.
Five kinds *all sorts of objects* have, *save Highest, Path, and Fruit;*
Of thoughts six classes, lastly, which *all sorts of objects* suit.

---

§ 12. *Of Bases.*

In the summary of bases, what are called 'bases' are of six kinds, to wit, the bases: eye, ear, nose, tongue, body, and heart. In the Kāmaloka all these obtain. In the world of Rūpa there exists no basis of smell, taste, or touch. In the world of Arūpa none of the bases exist.

Now, the five elements of sense-cognition proceed wholly and solely in dependence on the five sense-organs as their respective bases. But the elements of mind[2]—that is to say, adverting,[3] and reception of the five-door impres-

---

jhāna, induced by the exercise of amity (or love), pity, and appreciation, are worked on the *concept* 'mankind'; but the fifth stage, induced by the exercise of 'equanimity,' is also concerned with that *concept*, not as an object of love, pity, or appreciation, but as an object of relative indifference. The first exercise in the Arūpa-jhāna is on the *concept* 'space'; the third Arūpa-jhāna is exercised on the *concept* 'nothingness.' Thus the fifteen Rūpa- and the six Arūpa-jhāna's, twenty-one in all, work by *concepts*.

[1] Vohāre, a synonym for paññatti in *Dhs.*, § 1308. See previous *n.*—Ed.

[2] Manodhātu. Rendered before by 'the element of apprehension.' See p. 117, *n.* 1.

[3] Lit., 'turning to.' See p. 85, *n.* 3.

sions, proceed solely in dependence on the heart.[1] The element of mind-consciousness,[2] comprising investigation-cognitions, the main classes of resultant consciousness, the two 'aversive' kinds of consciousness, the consciousness of the first path, æsthetic pleasure and Rūpaloka consciousness, proceed in dependence on the heart.

But all other classes of consciousness, when they are moral or immoral, inoperative or transcendental, are either dependent on, or independent of, the heart-basis; when they are Arūpaloka resultants, they are independent of the heart-basis.

§ 13. *Mnemonic.*

In Kāmaloka seven[3] kinds of thought dependent see
On bases six; in Rūpaloka, four, on bases three.
But in Arūpaloka, one, mind-element,[4] upsprings
Baseless, alone. Forty-three kinds need base to come to birth.
Forty-two kinds now rise on base, now baseless issue forth.
Resultants in Arūpaloka thoughts are baseless things.

Thus ends the Third Part, in the Compendium of Philosophy, entitled the Chapter on the Compendium of Particular (Concomitants of Consciousness).

[1] *Cf. B. Psy.*, lxxviii. *ff.* It is interesting to note that in this medieval work, there is as yet no indication of substituting a brain-vatthu for the heart. See, however, Appendix. Hadayavatthu. —Ed.

[2] Manoviññāṇa-dhātu, literally rendered so as to cover the seventy-six classes of consciousness named, which are capable of taking part in both presentative and representative cognition. In the Introd. Essay it is called 'element of comprehension,' to distinguish it from manodhātu, 'element of apprehension.'

[3] *I.e.*, 5 pañcaviññāna-dhātu's + 1 manodhātu + 1 manoviññāṇadhātu = 7. See Part VII., end of § 8.

[4] Dhātvekā = dhātu + ekā. Manoviññāṇadhātu, but not manodhātu, is here intended.

PART IV

COMPENDIUM OF THE PROCESS OF COGNITION

§ 1. *Introductory.*

THIS further summary of geneses
Of thought now having made, I will go on
To speak concisely, summing up again
Processes of the mind, in birth and life,
By order due, the 'after,' the 'before,'
Distinguishing both person and life-plane.

---

§ 2. *Of the Vehicles in Procedure.*

In a summary of thought-procedure,[1] six classes of six kinds each must be understood, to wit:

(1) six bases;
(2) six doors;
(3) six objects;
(4) six modes of cognition;
(5) six processes;[1]
(6) sixfoḍ phenomenon of presentation[2] of objects.

[1] Vīthi. For explanation of the term, see Introd. Essay, p. 25. It will there be seen that 'form of consciousness,' used approximately in the Mansellian sense, is a useful term to indicate the *constant* element in the processes of thought. When we distinguish these processes *logically*, they are better spoken of as 'forms.'* When we speak of them as *psychological* facts or happenings, then 'process' or 'vīthi' is the appropriate term.

[2] Visaya-pavatti. The C.C. (Saya Pye's Edition, p. 115) defines this term as 'the presentation of objects of consciousness

Now, the [sixth and last of these, namely the] phenomenon of the presentation of objects, is threefold in the case when consciousness is set free from processes of sense and thought, to wit, k a r m a, k a r m a - signs, destiny-signs.[1]

Of the foregoing classes, (1) 'base,' (2) 'door,' and (3) 'object,' have been already dealt with. Next (4) the six modes of cognition are consciousness by way of sight, hearing, smell, taste, touch, and thought.

Next (5), the six 'processes' are the processes by way of the eye-door, ear-door, nose-door, tongue-door, body-door, mind-door, under the aspect of 'door.' Or [they may be called] processes of consciousness by way of sight, etc., under the aspect of consciousness, thus connecting mental procedure with procedure of door [or organ].

(3) Finally[2] (6), the sixfold phenomenon of presentation of objects is to be understood as follows :

The intensity of object, at the five sense-doors, is either very great, great, slight, or very slight ; at the mind-door the impression is either clear or obscure.[3]

§ 3. *Of Processes of Sense-Cognition.*

How (must processes of sense-cognition be understood) ?

[A single unit of mental activity], termed one thought-moment, consists of three time- [phases], to wit, nascent, static, and arrested.[4] Seventeen of such thought-moments constitute the duration of material phenomena.[5] One of

---

at the doors,' and, again, 'the genesis of thoughts on the presentation of such objects.' I have used 'presentation' to cover both meanings.

[1] See Introd. Essay, p. 26 *f.*

[2] This sentence, paragraphed under § 3 in the P.T.S. Text, belongs more properly to § 2.—Ed.

[3] V i b h ū t a ŋ, a v i b h ū t a ŋ. *Cf.* this term in *Mil.*, 308 (transl. by Rhys Davids, S. B. E., XXXVI., p. 174).—Ed.

[4] B h a ṅ g a, lit., 'broken.' Misprinted b h a v a n g a in P.T.S. Edition.—Ed.

[5] See Introd. Essay, p. 25 *f.* Buddhist philosophy has hit upon a thought-moment of three instants as the ultimate standard of the

several thought-moments must have passed when the five kinds of sense-objects, at the static stage, enter the avenue[1] of the five doors of sense.

Hence the process is thus:—*When*, say, a visible object, after one thought-moment has passed, enters the avenue of sight and, the life-continuum vibrating twice, the stream of that continuum is interrupted; *then* consciousness of the kind which apprehends sensations, apprehending that visible object, rises and ceases (1).

Immediately after this, there rise and cease in order—

visual consciousness, seeing just that visible object (2);
recipient consciousness receiving it (3)[2];
investigating consciousness investigating it (4);
determining consciousness determining it (5).

After that, among the twenty-nine modes of Kāma-loka apperception, any one apperception, determined by the conditions evoking it, apperceives,[3] normally, for seven thought-moments (6-12).

And, as immediate consequences of the apperception, two resultant thought-moments of retention take place (13, 14).

After that comes subsidence into the life-continuum.[4]

---

measurement of time which, after all, in its last analysis, is reducible to a succession of mental states. This thought-moment is computed by them as between a billionth and two billionth part of the time occupied by the snapping of one's finger, or a wink of one's eye (Ledi Sadaw's Comy., p. 130). It is for modern scientists accurately to determine the number of thought-oscillations in any given period of time. From their own standard Buddhists apparently deduce the life-term of material things, for the purpose of measuring the duration of an object in consciousness.

[1] Āpātho.

[2] *I.e.*, assenting to, acquiescing in it. Sampaṭicchana implies all this.—Ed.

[3] Javanaŋ javati.

[4] Bhavanga-pāto. The subject of the whole process is more fully dealt with in the Introd. Essay, pp. 27-30.

Thus far are now complete the seventeen thought-moments (mentioned above), to wit:

fourteen in the process of the genesis of cognition;[1]
two vibrations of the life-continuum;
one thought-moment at inception.[2]

After that [the mental object] ceases.

Such an object is, in the scale of intensity, termed 'very great.'[3] An object with an intensity that is simply 'great,' is not able, after entering the sense-avenue, to survive till the two moments of retention (13, 14). In that case subsidence into the life-continuum occurs at the end of the apperceptive moments (6-12); no retention takes place. Again, an object, with a 'slight' intensity is not able, after entering the sense-avenue, to survive till the genesis of the [usual seven] apperceptive moments. In that case, apperception not arising, there is only a [process of] determining for two or three moments, after which comes subsidence.

Lastly, an object with a 'very slight' intensity enters the avenue of sense already about to cease, and is not able to reach the stage of determining. In that case there is only the vibration of the life-continuum, but no genetic process of consciousness takes place.

As in the sight-door, so in the other four (special) senses: procedure in the field of sense of that which has become, at one of the five doors, an 'object' is, under all conditions, to be understood as fourfold, in the four grades respectively known as—

(1) the grade [ending with] retention;
(2) the grade [ending with] apperception only;

[1] See the numbers attached to each factor in the process.—Ed.

[2] Literally, which has passed before.—Ed.

[3] See § 8. The several processes summarized here are developed in Introd. Essay, p. 81 *f*.

(3) the grade [ending with] determination only;
(4) the futile grade.[1]

§ 4. *Mnemonic.*

Fourteen thought-moments in cognition's act one finds,
And in that process stages seven we see.
And of our consciousness the four and fifty kinds
Can share in five-doored sense, if fit they be.[2]

Thus far the method of how cognition proceeds on occasion of sense.

§ 5. *Of Procedure by way of the Mind-door.*

In the case of the mind-door, when a clear object enters the avenue of that door, then, at the termination of the vibration of the life-continuum, of mind-door apprehension and of apperception, the resultant retentive (moments) take place. After that comes subsidence into the life-continuum. But when the object is obscure, then the subsidence occurs at the termination of apperception; no retention takes place.

§ 6. *Mnemonic.*

Threefold the process in the mind-door's act,
And moments ten therein we're told;
But forty-one[3] the kinds of thought implied,
If we in full detail unfold.

Thus far the section on minor acts of apperception.

[1] Moghavārasaṅkhāto; muyhanti sattā etenāti mogho, tuccho-mogho, 'the futile' (or vague) is that by which persons are stupefied, are muddled; it means empty, vain.

[2] Yathārahaṃ; as circumstances permit. See summary under § 7, in Part I.: 'four and fifty make the Kāmaloka tale.' These are capable of taking part in the five-door process of cognition on occasion of sense.

[3] The 'forty-one' is obtained by excluding, from the fifty-four classes of Kāmaloka consciousness, the twice fivefold sense-cognitions

§ 7. *Of Ecstatic Apperceptional Procedure.*

But in treating of ecstatic apperception,[1] no distinction is made between 'clear' and 'obscure.' Nor is there any retentive activity. For in this case [consider the stage when apperception is reached :—] a certain apperception—one of the eight Kāmaloka apperceptions associated with knowledge—has arisen for four or three successive moments. These moments, in this procedure, are termed preparation, approximation, qualification,[2] adoption.[3] As they cease, at the fourth, or the fifth moment, that kind of apperception, in the twenty-six kinds of sublime and transcendental apperceptions which fits the case of the apperceiver, descends into the process of ecstatic apperception. After that, at the end of the ecstasy, subsidence into the life-continuum occurs.

Here, after an apperception accompanied by joy, ecstasy, also accompanied by joy, may be expected; and after apperception accompanied by hedonic indifference, ecstasy

---

and the triple element of apprehension. See Introd. Essay (p. 86) for the full treatment of the processes of thought by way of the mind-door; also Appendix, Dhātu and Āyatana, on Manodhātu.

[1] Appanā javanaṃ. Appanā is a term primarily intended for the vitakka-factor of jhāna, because vitakka (or application), as a jhāna-factor sinks the mind, so to speak, into the inside of its object, whilst ordinary vitakka merely throws the mind on to the surface of its object. But the term is secondarily applied to samādhi. See Introd. Essay, pp. 55-7.

On appanā, *cf. Yogāvacara's Manual.* Introduction by Rhys Davids, P.T.S., 1896. This is another term I have not met with in the earlier scriptures.—Ed.

[2] Anuloma—the stage at which the beginner or ādikammika *fits, equips,* or *qualifies* himself for the higher stage. See Introd. Essay, *ibid.*

[3] Gotrabhū. See Introd. Essay, *ibid.* *Cf.* Part IX., § 8. This term, meaning 'evolving the lineage,' is the name for the stage when, in a moment of spiritual regeneration, the kinship to Kāmaloka is rejected for the communion of the Ariyas—*i.e.*, all who have taken Nibbana as their quest (*cf.* 135, *n.* 2).

accompanied by hedonic indifference. Again, a moral[1] apperception has for its sequel a moral apperception as well as the lowest three of the four fruits; an inoperative apperception has as its sequel inoperative apperception and the fruit which is Arahantship.

§ 8. *Mnemonic.*

After gladsome meritorious thoughts may follow thirty-two,[2]
After thoughts of neutral feeling, twelve kinds may alone be due.
After glad inoperative thoughts but eight may come to be.
After neutral thought inoperative, six kinds possibly.
Ecstasy succeeds e'en worldling's meritorious Kāmā-thought,
And the learner's, and of them who final victory have wrought.
In the first, and second, consciousness with hetu's three is fraught;[3]
In the third no less, but here effect of consciousness is naught.

Thus far the method of the processes of cognition in the mind-door.

§ 9. *Of Retention.*

Under all circumstances, if an object be undesirable, it is the result of past immoral action, taking effect in sense-cognition, reception, investigation, and retention; if an object be desirable, it is the result of past moral action; if an object be extremely desirable, investigation and retention are accompanied by joy. In this case, at the termination

[1] Or good; kusalajavanaŋ.

[2] *I.e.*, classes of consciousness.—Ed.

[3] Tihetuto. The three good hetu's of alobha, adosa, and amoha are here intended. Exigencies of rhyme have expanded 'inoperative' (kriyato) into the last line.—Ed.

of the inoperative apperception, which is also accompanied by joy, there follow retentive moments accompanied by joy; or if the inoperative apperception be accompanied by hedonic indifference, so also are the ensuing retentive moments. Or if the apperception be accompanied by grief, then both the retentive moments and the subsidence into the life-continua[1] become accompanied by hedonic indifference.

Hence, when an individual who has been reborn with a sense of joy,[2] experiences no retentive moments at the termination of an apperception accompanied by grief, then there arises instead [that class of consciousness styled] 'investigation accompanied by hedonic indifference' respecting some merely 'minor' object presented in the past.[3]

Teachers say that the subsidence into the life-continuum comes immediately after that. They also say that reten-

[1] In this instance alone bhavanga is plural. The singular bhavanga has been used as a generic term, either for the whole *series* of the bhavanga moments in process of cognition or for all the *nineteen classes* of bhavanga. The use of the plural here is therefore significant in showing that there is an āgantuka-bhavanga (adventitious element) as opposed to the mūla-bhavanga (normal element). This āgantuka bhavanga is dealt with in the following passage.

[2] *I.e.*, one who is of a joyous nature by birth, without needing always the stimulus of a pleasant experience.—Ed.

[3] Lit., 'formerly stored-up minor object.' The Commentators call all things of Kāmaloka—namely, all the fifty-four classes of Kāma-consciousness, together with all the mental concomitants that enter into combination in these fifty-four, and all the twenty-eight rūpa's,—'paritta.' When a naturally jovial person is offended, his previous apperception, if not ordinarily followed by the retentive moments, cannot lapse directly and abruptly back to the normal life-continuum which is by birth one of joy. It is therefore invariably followed by an adventitious bhavanga, accompanied by *hedonic indifference*, which intervenes as a sort of mediator between two uncompromising aspects of feeling—*grief* and *joy*. It must not be supposed that the santīraṇa which is called upon to do this duty of paving the way for the reappearance of the normal bhavanga, investigates here.

tion is desirable[1] only (i.) at the termination of Kāmaloka apperception; (ii.) for Kāmaloka beings; and (iii.) of Kāmaloka things[2] which have become objects.

§ 10. *Mnemonic.*

If, in activity of 'sense,'[3]
Subject and object and fetch of mind[4]
Combine in process clear, intense,
Retention then we're sure to find.[5]

So far for the law of retention.

---

§ 11. *Of the Law of Apperception.*

Again, among apperceptions, in the process of minor[6] apperception, Kāmaloka apperceptions apperceive for seven moments, or for only six, or, in the case of feeble procedure, in dying, and at other times, for only five moments. They say, also, that when the Exalted One was performing the 'twin miracle,' and the like, the alert procedure of his 're-viewing'[7] mind was such as to require only four or five

[1] The ideals of the teachers here are that the three conditions indicated by (i.), (ii.), and (iii.), must be satisfied, in order that retention may take place in a process.

[2] See p. 131, *n.* 3.

[3] Sense stands here for Kāmaloka consciousness.—Ed.

[4] Javana-sattālambaṇānaŋ. This is the nearest approach in the work to the term 'subject' (satta, lit. 'being'). *Cf.* the orthodox javanāni javanti, in § 8, § 11, etc. On the significance of the term 'subject' in Buddhist psychology, see Introd. Essay, p. 7 *f.*—Ed.

[5] See p. 125 (8). Retention, *as a rule*, takes part only in a sense-door process with a 'very intense' object, or in a mind-door process with a 'clear' object.

[6] See p. 131, *n.* 3.

[7] Paccavekkhana-cittāni, lit., 'consciousness[es] viewing again' (paṭi-ikkhanaŋ). The reviewing apperceptions are confined to processes succeeding the jhāna ecstasies and the spiritual experiences known as the Paths and Fruits. See Introd. Essay, p. 69.

moments. But in the first performances of a novice [in higher thought], sublime and super-intellective apperceptions always occupy but one unit [of thought time]. After that comes subsidence into the continuum.

The four geneses of Path-[consciousness] are of one thought-moment each. After these the cognitions [known as] the Fruits arise, occupying two or three moments each. After that comes subsidence into the continuum.

At the time of attaining cessation [of consciousness in trance], apperception, then apperceiving for two moments, belongs to the fourth stage of Arūpaloka jhāna-cognitions.[1] After that cessation is attained.[2] And at the time of revival from that state, when there has arisen for one [time-]unit the [consciousness which is the] 'Fruit' of the Never-returning Path, or of Arahantship, according to his stage [of evolution], and when [this consciousness] has ceased, then occurs subsidence into the life continuum.

And in every case of the process of the Attainments[3] [we have to] hold that there is no hard and fast[4] limit in the process, even as in the case of the stream of the life-continuum, and that several [moments of apperception] may also obtain.

[1] *I.e.*, the cognition of the sphere of neither consciousness nor unconsciousness. See Part I., § 10.

[2] Phussati, lit., 'touched'— a term wherein Buddhist ecstatic phraseology coincides with the 'desire for contact,' 'striving after conjunction' of Neo-Platonism.—Ed.

[3] Samāpatti—*i.e.*, of the five jhānas and the four Fruits of the Paths. See Part XI., § 12; Introd. Essay, p. 70 *f.*

[4] Niyamo ṅatthi.

§ 12. *Mnemonic.*

Seven moments last the minor apperceptions of the mind;
In Path and Abhiññā,[1] the norm is *one*, so it's divined;
Though sometimes many moments to such acts may be assigned.

So far for the law of apperception.

§ 13. *Of Kinds of Individuals.*

Now inoperative apperceptions and ecstatic apperceptions are not obtained by those [whose rebirth-consciousness is] accompanied by [only] two of the [six] hetu's,[2] or not accompanied by any of the hetu's. Nor do these, when in a happy world, obtain resultant consciousness united with knowledge. But, in a world of misery, they obtain not even the 'great resultant' kinds of consciousness unconnected with knowledge.

Further, among those [whose rebirth consciousness is] accompanied by the three hetu's of good action, Arahants[3] do not obtain apperceptions that are either moral or immoral.[4]

Again, disciples and average worldly persons do not

[1] Supernormal intelligence, touched on in Part IX., § 4, and dealt with in Introd. Essay, p. 62 *f.*, and Appendix: Abhiññā.

[2] According to the C.C. (*Abhidhammattha-Vibhāvanī*) duhetuka-puggala's, *i.e.*, persons of two hetu's, are beings reborn with an innate sense of disinterestedness (alobha) and amity (adosa). Ledi Sadaw of Burma, reiterates the same in different words, by saying that the rebirth-consciousness of such a one, consists of one or other of the four 'great' resultant classes of consciousness unconnected from knowledge. This is, of course, according to Buddhism, due to the past reproductive kamma which was also disconnected from knowledge. *Cf.* with Introd. Essay on dream-consciousness, p. 46 *f.*

[3] Khīṇāsavā: 'Who have the Āsavas extinct'—a frequent Piṭaka synonym.—Ed.

[4] Moral or immoral=making good or bad karma for after-lives. The Arahant 'beyond good and bad' had done with it all. See *B. Psy.*, xcii.-xciv. (on xciv. for 'Yes,' read 'Yet').—Ed.

obtain inoperative apperceptions: disciples do not obtain apperceptions full of doubt, or such as are united to erroneous views; 'never-returning'[1] individuals do not obtain apperceptions full of aversion. But transcendental apperceptions are experienced only by 'Ariyans,'[2] according to the capacities of each.

§ 14. *Mnemonic.*

By classes four and forty apperceives an adept's mind.
Initiates'[3] apperceptions six and fifty are in kind.
And fifty-four experience the remainder of mankind.

So far for [classification of consciousness according to] kinds of individuals.

§ 15. *Of Planes [of Conscious Existence.]*[4]

On the Kāmaloka plane all the foregoing kinds of consciousness by way of process are experienced according to circumstances.

On the Rūpaloka plane the same holds true, with the exclusion of apperceptions [united with] aversion, and of retention-moments.

On the Arūpaloka plane the same holds true, with the exclusion of the [apperception of] the First Path, of consciousness belonging to the Rūpaloka plane, of æsthetic pleasure, and of the lower Arūpaloka cognitions.

[1] Those who will be no more reborn in Kāma-loka.

[2] Used for Buddhas and their disciples who walk in the Four Paths and who enjoy the Four Fruits. The word has usually been rendered 'noble,' especially in the 'Noble Eightfold Path,' and the 'four Noble Truths.' But there are racial implications in it, which commend the retention of the original word. See Rhys Davids, *Early Buddhism*, 1908, pp. 49, 50.—Ed.

[3] Se[k]kha-, lit., 'disciple,' 'learner' (§ 8), a term applied to the seven lower classes of the eight 'Ariyans,' as opposed to 'Ase[k]kha,' adept, a term applied to the Arahant.

[4] Bhūmi, lit., ground, *terrain*.—Ed.

Under all conditions, too, those who are devoid of this or that seat of impressions,[1] do not obtain process-cognitions by way of the corresponding 'doors.'

And for unconscious beings,[2] under no conditions is there any cognitional procedure.

§ 16. *Mnemonic.*

On plane of Kâmaloka eighty kinds of consciousness
Take part, as they may fitted be, in this or that process;
In 'Rūpa' and 'Arūpa,' sixty-four and sixteen less.

So far for the chapter on Planes.

---

§ 17. *Summary.*

And thus, the processes of six-doored cognition proceed, intersected[3] by the life-continuum as it happens to be constituted, and continually as long as one lifetime lasts.

Thus ends the Fourth Part, in the Compendium of Philosophy, entitled the Chapter on the Compendium of Processes.

[1] Pasâda, 'the pleasure-giving part'—*i.e.*, the most sensitive part of a sense-organ.

[2] There is held to be a celestial region peopled by such mindless beings. See next Part, p. 142.—Ed.

[3] Bhavangantaritā is explained by Ledi Sadaw as 'bhavangeantaritā. As a matter of fact, it is the thought-processes that intersect the life-continuum.

PART V

COMPENDIUM OF CONSCIOUSNESS NOT SUBJECT TO PROCESS[1]

§ 1. *Introductory.*

Set forth have been processes of our thought
In natural order. Now let's on to make
Summary of procedure at rebirth.

§ 2. *Of the Realms of Life.*

In summarizing classes of consciousness not subject to process, four sets of four should be understood, to wit:

I. four planes of life;[2]
II. fourfold rebirth;
III. four karmas;
IV. fourfold advent of death.

Of these, the four planes of life are—

(1) 1. the plane of misery;
2. the plane of fortunate sense-experience;
3. the Rūpaloka plane;
4. the Arūpaloka plane.

Among these, again, the first is also fourfold, to wit, purgatory, the animal kingdom, rebirth among Peta's,[3] the host of the Asura-demons.

[1] Vīthi-mutta, lit., 'process-freed.'

[2] Bhūmi-catukkaŋ. See Part IV., § 15, *n.* 4.

[3] Petti-visayo, the Peta's are unhappy ghosts. See p. 24.

(2) Fortunate sense-experience is sevenfold, to wit, the realm of human beings, the realms of the four kings,[1] of the Thirty-three gods, the Yāmā gods,[2] the heaven of Delight, the heavens of the gods who rejoice in [their own] creations, and of the gods who make others' creation serve their own ends.

These, taken together as eleven, are grouped as the *plane of Kāmaloka*.

(3) The Rūpaloka plane is of sixteen grades, comprising:

(*a*) the plane of first jhāna, to wit, the realm of Brahma's retinue, that of Brahma's ministers, that of the great Brahmas;[3]

(*b*) the plane of second jhāna, to wit, the heavens of minor lustre, of infinite lustre, of the radiant gods;[4]

(*c*) the plane of third jhāna, to wit, the gods of minor aura, of infinite aura, and of the gods full of steady aura;[5]

(*d*) the plane of fourth jhāna, to wit, the realm of the gods of the great reward,[6] of the unconscious beings, and of the pure abodes.

[1] Of the four quarters of the firmament.

[2] Lit., 'the misery-freed gods,' according to the Ceylon Cy.; the governing gods, according to Ledi Sadaw. This word should not be confounded with Yama, the mythical King of Death.

[3] There is historical interest in comparing the mythology in this chapter with the earlier mythologies in the *Dīgha* and *Majjhima Nikāyas*, and in the brief list of the *Vibhanga*, pp. 422-6, a passage on which is summarized in § 4 (2).—Ed.

[4] Ābhassarā, from ā $\sqrt{}$bha + $\sqrt{}$sar, the gods from whose bodies the rays of light are emitted like lightning.

[5] Subhakiṇhā. A mass of steady light emitted from a body is termed subhā, lit., 'good light.'

[6] Vehapphala=Vipulaŋ+phalaŋ, 'abundant reward' (of jhāna practice), great, compared with the rewards of the Lower Brahmas.

The last named are fivefold, to wit, the abode of the Immobile, Serene, Beautiful, Clear-sighted,[1] and Supreme Beings.

(4) The Arūpaloka plane is of four grades, comprising:

(*a*) the sphere of the conception of infinite space;
(*b*) the sphere of the conception of infinite consciousness;
(*c*) the sphere of the conception of nothingness;
(*d*) the sphere of neither consciousness nor unconsciousness.[2]

§ 3. *Mnemonic.*

In Pure Abodes there come not anywise to be
Worldlings, or new converts,[3] or those who Once Return,
Nor in th' Unconscious Sphere, or Spheres of Misery
Can come the Ariya folk.[4] To be elsewhere reborn
May be both Ariyas' and non-Ariyas' destiny.

Thus far for the four planes [of life].

---

§ 4. II. *Of Fourfold Rebirth* [*Rebirths* 1 *and* 2].

(1) Fourfold rebirth comprises birth to a state of misfortune, to a state of fortunate sense-experience, to the Rūpaloka, and to the Arūpaloka.

A single rebirth to a state of misfortune is as follows: that class of consciousness [usually styled] 'Investigation accompanied by hedonic indifference and resulting from *immoral* conduct in the past' becomes reconception,[5] at the moment of descent, on the plane of misfortune. There-

[1] These are, more literally rendered, well-looking and well-seeing. —Ed.

[2] On these terms see Part I., § 10.

[3] Sotāpannā.

[4] See above, Part IV., § 18 *n.*

[5] *I.e.*, the very commencement of rebirth. See p. 114, *n.* 4; *cf.* p. 109, *n.* 1, and p. 116, *n.* 5. It would be less embarassing to Occidentals to have this rebirth-consciousness and the next in separate classes from the santīraṇa's (classes of investigation-consciousness).

after it [becomes][1] the life-continuum, and, becoming at the close of life a re-decease-consciousness, is cut off.

But when that class of consciousness [ordinarily called] 'Investigation, accompanied by hedonic indifference' results from *moral*[2] conduct in the past, it proceeds on the plane of *happy* sense-experience by way of rebirth, life-continuum and re-decease, in the case of human beings who are born blind and the like, as well as in the case of the earth-bound degraded A s u r a -demons.[3]

The eight main resultant kinds of consciousness take effect in every case by way of rebirth, life-continuum, and re-decease, on this plane of fortunate sense-experience.

These nine classes are comprised under rebirth on the plane of fortunate sense-experience.

The ten modes in the foregoing are reckoned together as rebirth on the plane of K ā m a l o k a.

---

(2) There is no [fixed] limit to the duration of life in beings reborn to misfortune in the four planes of misery, in human beings and in degraded A s u r a s. The life-term in the case of the gods called the Four Kings is 500 celestial years—that is to say, as men reckon years, 9,000,000. The life-term of the Thirty-three gods is four times this amount.[4] That of the Y ā m ā gods is again

[1] In the J.P.T.S. text, for b h a v a n g a - p a r i y o s ā n e j a v a n a ŋ h u t v ā, I read b h a v a n g a ŋ [h u t v ā] p a r i y o s ā n e c a v a n a ŋ h u t v ā.—Ed.

[2] The logic and justice of this paragraph is in the existence of *indifferently* good conduct, not decidedly bad nor good unalloyed. The immoral leaven in the *moral* conduct of the past accounts for the existence of the congenitally deformed and unhappy creatures on the happy planes.

[3] It was held that, of the degraded A s ŭ r a - demons bound to the earth, only those who are born blind and the like have this class of rebirth consciousness. Some texts read b h u m m i s s i t ā for b h u m m a s s i t ā. J a c c ā d ī n a ŋ is governed by m a n u s s ā n a ŋ as well as by a s u r ā n a ŋ.

[4] C a t u g g u ṇ a ŋ. Strictly speaking, double the life-term of the Four Kings. Both the Singhalese and the Burmese commentaries

four times the life-term of the Thirty-three; and so on for the gods of the heavens of Delight, for those of the gods who rejoice in their own creations, and for those of the gods who make others' creations serve their own ends.

§ 5. *Mnemonic.*

Of millions nine thousand, two hundred and ten,
And yet six millions more, as years go with us here,
Are the years of a god so remote from our ken
As he who resides in the Disposers' sphere.[1]

---

§ 6. *Of Rebirths 3 and 4.*

The resultant (consciousness) of first jhāna (meditations) takes effect on the plane of first jhāna[2] by way of rebirth, life-continuum and re-decease [in those heavens]. In the same way, second jhāna resultants and third jhāna resultants take effect on the plane of second jhāna;[3] fourth jhāna resultants take effect on the plane of third jhāna, and fifth jhāna resultants take effect on the plane of fourth jhāna.[4]

---

explain this curious 'twice double' as (1) *double* the celestial day (measured by 50 human years) as well as (2) *double* the celestial term of life (measured by 500 celestial years). Thus a celestial day in the heaven of the Thirty-three would be equal to 100 human years, and the life-term therein 1,000 celestial years, measured by 36,000,000 human years; and this is exactly four times the 9,000,000 human years of the Four Kings. The celestial day of the Yāmā gods is 200 human years, and their life-term, 2,000 celestial years, measured by 144,000,000 human years, which again are *four times* the 36,000,000 human years of the Thirty-three gods, and so on for the rest. Thus it is clear that 'four times' refers to the human standard of time.

[1] The last two lines represent the one word vasavattīsu (in the original). On this curious mythic fancy, see Paranimmita in Childers's Dictionary.

[2] See above, § 2, (*a*) the Brahmaloka.

[3] *Ibid.*: Among the Radiant, etc., gods.

[4] It should be remembered that the fivefold division of jhāna stages is more recent than the fourfold, and the distinction between

But for beings attaining to the unconscious realm there is rebirth only of material form. And similarly thereafter, during life, and at the time of re-deceasing, it is only material form which, having lived, ceases to be.

These are the six modes of rebirth in the R ū p a l o k a.

Among these the life-term of gods in [the heaven of] Brahmā's retinue is the third of an æon;[1] of gods in that of Brahmā's ministers, half an æon;[1] of the great Brahmās, one æon;[3] of the gods of minor lustre, two (great)[2] æons; of the gods of infinite lustre, four (great) æons; of the radiant gods, eight (great) æons; of the gods of minor aura, sixteen (great) æons; of the gods of infinite aura, thirty-two (great) æons; of the gods full of steady aura, sixty-four (great) æons; of the gods of great reward, and of the unconscious beings, five hundred (great) æons; of the immobile gods, a thousand (great) æons; of the serene gods, two thousand (great) æons; of the beautiful gods, four thousand (great) æons; of the clear-sighted gods, eight thousand (great) æons; of the supreme gods, sixteen thousand (great) æons.

Resultants of the first stage of A r ū p a l o k a j h ā n a meditation, and of the following stages take effect on the

---

stages 1 and 2 in the former scheme is very superficial. Hence we have here, as it were, five j h ā n a grades of preparatory meditation and four j h ā n a grades of rebirth, or planes.—Ed.

[1] By 'k a p p a' is here intended an a s a n k h e y y a - k a p p a (lit., incalculable cycle), equal to one-fourth of a m a h ā k a p p a (great cycle). This exceeds the time required to exhaust an area filled with mustard-seeds, equal to one square y o j a n a, by throwing away a seed in every hundred years. Each a s a n k h e y y a - k a p p a consists of sixty-four a n t a r a - k a p p a's (interim cycles); or twenty, according to some authorities; or eighty, according to others; or fourteen, according to those who were versed in the V e d a s. These are sometimes spoken of as c ū ḷ a - k a p p a's (smaller cycles). An a n t a r a - k a p p a is measured by the time required by the pendulum of the life-term of generations to swing from a ten-year-term to an a s a n k h e y y a-term and back again to the ten-year-term.

[1] By 'k a p p a' here, and in the following cases, is intended the m a h ā - k a p p a. See preceding note.

plane of the four grades[1] of the Arūpaloka plane respectively, by way of rebirth, life-continuum, and re-decease.

These are the four modes of rebirth in the Arūpaloka.

Among these four, the life-term of the gods who have attained to the sphere of infinite space is twenty thousand (great) æons; that of the gods who have attained to the sphere of infinite consciousness is forty thousand (great) æons; that of the gods who have attained to the sphere of nothingness is sixty thousand (great) æons; that of the gods who have attained to the sphere of neither consciousness nor unconsciousness is eighty thousand (great) æons.

§ 7. *Mnemonic.*

In any one rebirth, life, death, the mind
Is one,[2] one to its object, and its kind.

So far for the four kinds of rebirth.

---

§ 8. *Of Karma.*

A. With respect to function,[3] there are four kinds of karma:[4]

[1] See above, § 2 (4).

[2] Ekam eva; the identity being, in Buddhism, similarity in a process of constant becoming.—Ed.

On Identity see also Introd. Essay, pp. 8, 11, 42. The Commentators say that the rebirth consciousness, life continuum, and re-decease consciousness in any one existence are similar to one another in respect of plane (bhūmi), class (jāti), composition (sampayutta-dhamma), cause (sankhāra), and object (visaya or ārammaṇa).

[3] Kiccavasena. Kicca is what ought to be done, translated in this work by 'function.' Kamma (karma), it should never be forgotten, is simply 'doing,' or 'acting.' In S. B. E., x. 116, §§ 60, 61 (*Dhammapada* and *Sutta-Nipāta* Translations), it is rendered by 'work.'—Ed.

[4] These categories may be compared with the earlier less elaborate

1. Karma reproductive [of an after-life].
2. Karma maintaining [the effects of Class 1].
3. Karma unfavourable [to the effects of Class 1, and to the working of Class 2].
4. Karma destructive [to Classes 1 and 2].

B. With respect to function, there are four kinds of karma:

1. Weighty karma.[1]
2. Proximate karma.[2]
3. Chronic karma.[3]
4. [All other] outstanding karma.[4]

C. With respect to time of taking effect there are four kinds of karma:

1. Karma (the fruit of which is) to be experienced in this life.
2. Karma (the fruit of which is) to be experienced in (the next) life.

---

and incidentally introduced classifications of (*a*) the Piṭakas—*e.g.* M. iii., Cūḷa and Mahā kamma-vibhanga suttas; (*b*) the *Milinda*—*e.g.*, 46, 108, 134, and *Nettipak.:* 37.—Ed.

[1] Garukaŋ—*i.e.*, of telling effect. The Commentaries instance *e.g.*, serious crimes.

[2] Āsannaŋ is a contraction of maraṇāsannaŋ—*i.e.*, according to the Commentaries, action or thought just before death.

[3] Āciṇṇakaŋ—*i.e.*, habitually repeated kamma, repeated either in act or thought.

[4] Kaṭattā: in *Asl.* p. 262, where no other kind is distinguished the synonym given is katakaraṇā, 'because done.'—Ed.

Kaṭattā (lit., katassa+bhāvo, 'the state of having been done') is the name applied to residual kamma of the present life which is not of the first three classes, and also to any kamma of anterior lives, which has as yet to work out its effects whenever favourable opportunities occur, when it becomes aparāpariya-kamma, the kamma of Class 3 under the next head of classification. It is the kamma held in reserve.

3. Karma [the fruit of which is] to be experienced in some after-life.

4. Karma 'which has been.'[1]

D. With respect to place for working out its effects there are four kinds of karma:

1. Bad karma [working out its effect] in the Kāmaloka.
2. Good karma [working out its effect] in the Kāmaloka.
3. Good karma [working out its effect] in the Rūpaloka.
4. Good karma [working out its effect] in the Arūpaloka.

Under the first of these four heads, and with respect to the 'door,' bad karma is threefold, to wit, karma of act, speech, and thought.

How [may these be described]?

Karma of body, so called from being done commonly through the 'door' of the body, considered as the medium[2] of bodily expression, is taking life, taking what is not given, and inchastity.

Karma of speech, so called from being done commonly through the 'door' of speech, considered as the medium of vocal expression, is lying, slandering, abusive language, and idle talk.

Karma of thought, so called from being done commonly through the ['door' of the] mind [with or][3] without overt expression, is covetousness, ill-will, and erroneous opinion.

(1) Of the foregoing forms [of bad karma], taking life, abusive language and ill-will spring from the root of hate;

[1] Ahosi-kammaŋ. *Cf.* Vergil's 'fuit Ilium' . . . (*Æn.*, II., 325)—karma which has lapsed in potential force.—Ed.

[2] Viññatti. See Part VI. 'Kāya' (body) here connotes 'act.'

[3] The Commentators explain the force of 'api' as showing that the karma of thought is not always confined to the mind door alone, but it very often takes effect at the other two 'doors,' accompanied by overt expression.

inchastity, covetousness, and erroneous opinion,[1] spring from the root of greed. The other four come to pass from [these] two 'roots' also.[2]

Analyzed with respect to classes of consciousness,[3] there are altogether twelve kinds of bad[4] karma.

(2) Next, taking good karma, with respect to the 'door,' it also is threefold, to wit, karma of body, proceeding at the 'door' of the body; karma of speech, proceeding at the 'door' of speech; karma of thought, proceeding at the 'door' of mind.

Threefold also with respect to charity (lit., giving), virtue, and mental culture, it is eightfold with respect to classes of consciousness. Or again, tenfold taking into account charity, virtue, mental culture, reverence, service, transference of merit,[5] rejoicing in [others'] merit, hearing the doctrine, teaching the doctrine, and forming correct views.[6]

It is these twenty kinds[7] that are counted as karma in Kāmaloka.

(3) Good Rūpaloka karma is only mental action (karma of thought). It consists in mental culture and involves the attaining of ecstasy. It is fivefold, corresponding to the stages of jhāna.

(4) Good Arūpaloka karma is also only mental

[1] This, belonging at first sight more properly to the third 'root,' suggests the proverb of 'the wish (lobha) being father to the thought' (diṭṭhi).—Ed.

[2] At first it seems curious that the third root is passed over. But the Commentators explain by saying that 'pi' (also) implies the inclusion of 'moha' (dulness) as a root common to all the ten vices It is not expressly stated, for the reason that this root of roots does not serve to distinguish the three classes of karma under consideration, one from another.

[3] Cittuppādavasena.

[4] Part I., § 2.

[5] Pattidāna. See Childers's Dict., *s.v.* Patti..—Ed.

[6] On these ten, *cf.* Childers's Dict., *s.v.* Puñño. The seventh (pattānumodana) is there given as abbhānumodanā puñño, and rendered as 'acceptance or use of transferred merit.'—Ed.

[7] *I.e.*, twelve bad and eight good. On the eight, see Part I., § 6.

action. It, too, consists in mental culture, and involves the attaining of ecstasy. It is fourfold, corresponding to the kinds of [Arūpaloka] object.

Finally, bad karma, omitting distraction,[1] produces rebirth on the plane of misfortune.

And further, during a lifetime, all the twelve kinds [of bad karma] take effect as seven kinds of bad results anywhere in Kāmaloka and in Rūpaloka, according to circumstances.

Again, good Kāmaloka karma produces rebirth under fortunate conditions in Kāmaloka. And similarly during a lifetime, it produces the great resultants[2] [in Kāmaloka]. But[3] it produces the eight [good] resultants, unaccompanied by their hetu's, anywhere in Kāmaloka and in Rupaloka, according to circumstances. And further, good [karma] of the highest class[4] accompanied by its three good 'hetu's,' both gives rise to rebirth similarly accompanied, and takes effect during [that] lifetime in sixteen kinds of resultants. Again, good [karma] of a lower class,[5] accompanied by the three hetu's of good, as well as good karma of the highest class, accompanied by two[6] of these three hetu's, both give rise to a rebirth attended by those two hetu's, and also take effect, during that lifetime, in twelve kinds of resultants, omitting those accompanied by these three hetu's.[7] Lastly, good [karma] of a lower class, which is accompanied by two of these hetu's, both gives rise only to such rebirth as is not accompanied by any hetu, and also takes effect, during that lifetime, in resultants also unaccompanied.

[1] Commentators explain that distrait action is too feeble to effect rebirth.

[2] *I.e.*, the eight named in Part I., § 4.

[3] According to the Burmese MSS. the text has 'pana,' which, in the J.P.T.S. text is omitted.—Ed.

[4] Ukkaṭṭhaŋ; the only occurrence of this term.—Ed.

[5] Omakaŋ. See previous note.

[6] Alobha and adosa.

[7] Tihetuka-rahitāni. The four ñāṇa-sampayutta's are now excluded from the foregoing sixteen.

§ 9. *Mnemonic Note.*

Some teachers[1] hold that automatic thought
  Cannot result in willed or prompted [deed],
Nor that self-willed or prompted thinking aught
  That's merely automatic act can breed.
To meet their views:—by twelve and ten, or eight,[2]
  Replace the sixteen and the twelve above—
Results, be it remembered we did state.
  [Let each compare and, as he will, approve.]

---

§ 10. *D.* 3 *and* 4.

One who has practised in a minor degree good Rūpaloka karma, which consists of the first jhāna, is reborn in the heaven of Brahmā's retinue; one who has practised it in a moderately high degree, in the heaven of Brahmā's ministers; one who has practised it in a surpassing degree, in the heaven of the great Brahmā's.

Similarly, practice in a minor degree of second and third jhāna [results in rebirth] among the gods of minor lustre; practice in a moderately high degree, among gods of infinite lustre; practice in a surpassing degree, among the radiant gods.

Similarly, practice in a minor degree of fourth jhāna [results in rebirth] among the gods of minor aura; in a moderately high degree, in rebirth among the gods of unlimited aura; in a surpassing degree, among the gods full of steady aura.

Lastly, practice of fifth jhāna [results in rebirth] among the gods of the Great Reward. The same practised

[1] The Ceylon Cy. (*Abhidhammattha-Vibhāvanī*) mentions the teachers of the school of **Mahādhammarakkhita Thera** of Moravāpī Monastery in Ceylon. Ledi Sadaw names Mahādatta Thera as the head of this school of thought.

[2] Replace 16 and 12 by 12 and 10 respectively and we get 12, 10, and 8, according to the school of thought in question.

with a view to extirpate lust for consciousness[1] [results in rebirth] in the heaven of the unconscious; but Never-returners [practising fifth jhāna] are reborn[2] in the Pure Abodes.

Further, one who has practised good Arūpaloka karma is reborn, in corresponding order, in one of the four Arūpaloka spheres.

§ 11. *Mnemonic.*

E'en thus our merit, waxing great and for this plane, or that one bound,
Brings forth results like to itself, in rebirth and the vital round.

So far for the fourfold [classifying of] karma.

---

§ 12. IV. *Of the Advent of Death.*

Four are [the grounds for] the advent of death.[3] It comes through the expiration of the span of life, through the extinction of karma, through the expiration of both, and through destructive karma.

Now to those thus about to die there is present in consciousness, at the hour of death, by the power of karma, at one or other of the six 'doors,' according to circumstance,[4] either—

(*a*) A presentation[5] of such karma from past existence as is bringing about rebirth; or

[1] Saññā-virāgaŋ—an adverbial phrase meaning, literally, 'till the lust for consciousness is extirpated.'

[2] Uppajjanti—spring into being. Ledi Sadaw would have us to translate this last clause into 'but in the pure abodes, the Anāgāmi's *alone* are reborn,' in order to indicate that, while the pure abodes are exclusively reserved for those of the Anāgāmi's who practise the fifth jhāna, those who practise the lower jhānas may be reborn in the lower planes.

[3] *Cf. Milinda*, 301.—Ed.

[4] See Part III., § 10.

[5] Abhimukhibhūtaŋ, 'what has become face to face.'—Ed.

(*b*) A (sign, or) token of that k a r m a, such as a visible, or other object, which was got at the time when the k a r m a was performed and became an instrument therein;[1] or

(*c*) A sign of the destiny which, as their lot in the existence immediately impending, is by them to be undergone.

After that, attending to just this object which has fixed itself [in consciousness], there usually goes on an uninterrupted continuum[2] of consciousness, which is either [morally] pure, or corrupt, according to the k a r m a that is being matured, and which, in conformity with the existence that is about to be undergone, tends thither.

Only such k a r m a as is capable of producing rebirth is able to arrive at 'the door' [of presentation] as a *re-presentation*[3] of itself.

To one who is at the point of death, at the end of his mental processes, or expiry of his life-continuum, the death-thought,[4] or last phase of his present being arises, and with his decease, ceases. At the end of this cessation, and just after it, mental action,[5] which is called rebirth, because it consists in a joining together[6] the past existence [with the new], arises and is set up in the next existence,[7]

[1] The Commentators instance the shrine where the dying one worshipped, the tank he had made, the flowers offered in worship, the knife with which he murdered, etc.

[2] C i t t a s a n t ā n a ŋ. On s a n t ā n a, which occurs also on p. 161 in this work, see De la V. Poussin: 'Dogmatique Bouddhiṣte,' *Journal Asiatique*, Sept., Oct., 1902, discussed in J.R.A.S., 1903, pp. 584 *ff*.; 1904, p. 370.—Ed.

[3] A b h i n a v a k a r a ṇ a v a s e n a: lit., 'by way of renewing itself.' *I.e.*, not of imagining, but of repeated original experience.

[4] C u t i c i t t a ŋ.

[5] M ā n a s a ŋ. In *Dhs.*, § 6, described as equivalent to m a n o and v i ñ ñ ā ṇ a.—Ed.

[6] P a ṭ i s a n d h i, 'rebirth,' but=lit., uniting (*i.e.*, of lives).

[7] 'Past' and 'next existence' are both 'b h a v a n t a r a ŋ' Apparently the Commentators make no allusion to any tradition of an intermediate state, such as we meet with in more animistic thanatology.—Ed.

according to circumstances and capacities. This mental action is engaged upon the object presented as described; it has either a [physical] base, or no base; it is brought forth by a mental activity[1] which is rooted in such craving as is dormant,[2] and is wrapt in such ignorance as is latent;[2] it is surrounded by its mental associates, and it becomes the foregoer, by being a fixed [*locus*],[3] of all that is co-existent with it.

§ 13. *Of Rebirth.*

In the process of dying consciousness[4] apperception proceeds feebly, and only five moments may be looked for. Therefore, in the case of death coming when objects are *actually present*[5] in the avenues of consciousness, the rebirth-consciousness and also [a few succeeding moments of][6] the life-continuum are then in a state to obtain actual presentation. And so it comes that, on occasion of rebirth in Kāmaloka, there is obtained, by way of the six 'doors,' either a token of karma, or a sign of destiny,[7] as an

[1] Sankhārena janiyamānaŋ. See Appendix: Sankhārā.

[2] Anusaya: lit., 'that which sleeps continuously.' See Par. VII.

[3] Adhiṭṭhānabhāvena.

[4] Maraṇāsannavīthiyaŋ: lit., 'in the process (of thought) at the time of *near* death.' *Cf.* Part IV., § 11.—Ed.

[5] The translator's text reads dharantesu, lit., 'while the object which has entered the avenue of consciousness stands, *i.e.*, lasts.' I was inclined to read marantesu, but this cannot be a correct reading, for marantānaŋ is required by grammar.—Ed.

[6] See Introd. Essay on Maraṇāsanna-kamma, p. 73.

[7] The sign of destiny, according to the Ceylon Cy., consists only of the visible object (rūpārammaṇaŋ ekameva) laid hold of by the mind-door (manodvāragahitaŋ), and is actually present (ekantapaccuppannaŋ). Its presentation is compared to a vision in a dream (vaṇṇāyatanaŋ supinam passantassa viya). But as the dream-phenomenon is not confined to sight and sight alone, the sign of destiny, in all probability, consists of any of the six classes of object. So Ledi Sadaw of Burma contends, on the authority of the *Mahāṭīkā*, the great Commentary on the *Visuddhi-magga.* But our humble opinion is that this dream-like vision is seen by the mind's eye, and is not laid hold of by the six 'doors,' as the latter also contends.

object either present or past. But the karma itself is obtained only as an object of past experience, and it is laid hold of by the 'door' of mind.

But all the foregoing is concerned with objects of a minor character (*i.e.*, of sense-experience).

In rebirth only a token of karma, in the shape of a concept,[1] becomes an object.

Soo, too, in rebirth in Arūpaloka, the only form of object presented is a sign of karma, which is either a sublime cognition itself, or a concept according to the classes of rebirth-consciousness.

In the case of rebirth among unconscious beings, only the vital 'nonad'[2] is reincarnated, hence they are called the materially reborn. Beings reborn into the Arūpa spheres are called materially-and-mentally reborn.

§ 14. *Mnemonic Note on Death and Birth.*

If from th' Arūpa plane you pass away,
You may be reborn in the selfsame way,
If not in higher formless spheres ; but not
In lower plane will be your lot ;
Or else you may find birth in this our sphere
With threefold 'root.'[3] From Rūpaloka gone,
Of luckless rebirth you inherit none.
From Kāma - world, if bound to hetu's three,
All rebirths open are to you. But here,
To Kāma, others all reborn must be.

So far for the order of re-decease and rebirth.

§ 15. *Of the Stream of Becoming.*

So to those who have thus got rebirth, the same kind of consciousness [as attended rebirth], occupied with the same

[1] Attha-paññatti is here intended. See above, Part III, § 10; below, Part VIII., §§ 14, 15.

[2] See next Part. *Cf.* also p. 136, *n.* 2.

[3] *I.e.*, the three good 'hetu's.

[field of] objects, starting straight away after [the moment of] rebirth, goes on, in the absence of any *process* of cognition, in unbroken flux like the stream of a river till the uprising of death-consciousness. [And this flux of] mind, because it is a condition of being, is called continuance of the condition of being.[1] At the end, by reason of dying, it becomes consciousness of re-decease[2] and then ceases. After that, rebirth-consciousness and the rest, revolving according to circumstances, like the wheel of a chariot, go on and on.

§ 16. *Mnemonic.*

Birth, life-flux, processes of thought, decease,
Both here and in existence yet to be,
Birth, life again . . . and thus incessantly
Doth this conscious continuum turn round.
But the Enlightened, pondering[3] release
From this that passeth ever by, have found,—
Steadfast down the long years in piety,
All bonds of cleaving severed utterly,—
The Path sublime,[4] where death and rebirth cease ;
And they, so faring, shall attain to Peace.[5]

Thus ends the Fifth Part, in the Compendium of Philosophy, called the Chapter on the Compendium of Cognitions not subject to process.

[1] Bhavanga-santati: lit., 'the continuity of the factor of being.' The Commentators, however, explain 'anga' in bhavanga by kāraṇaŋ, 'a condition,' or 'cause.' See Introd. Essay, pp. 9, 10.

[2] Cuticittaŋ. *Cf.* p. 150, *n*. 4.

[3] Paṭisankhāya. Repeatedly contemplating the transiency of things by paṭisankhā-ñāṇa. On this insight see Part IX.

[4] Adhigantvā padaŋ. The Commentators explain adhigantvā by magga-phala-ñāṇena sacchikatvā—realizing by means of the understanding of the path-consciousness and fruition-consciousness—and explain padaŋ to mean the sa-upādisesa-nibbāna. See Pt. V., § 14.

[5] Samaŋ. The Commentators say that by this word the anupādisesa-nibbāna is meant.

PART VI

THE COMPENDIUM OF MATTER[1]

§ 1. *Introductory.*

ANALYSIS of thought and thought's adjuncts
Thus far has set forth class and process all.
Now form[1] material must be described,
Enumeration, aspects, origins and groups,
And natural procedure:—these do form
The five divisions of this summary.

---

§ 2. *Of the Kinds of Material Quality.*[1]

Material quality is twofold, to wit, the four great essentials,[2] and material qualities derived therefrom, the two making up eleven species.

How [eleven]?

(1) *Essential material qualities*—viz., the element[3] of

[1] 'Rūpa,' in its generic sense, means 'matter,' and in its specific sense, 'quality.' But, in popular language, it means 'form.'

[2] Mahābhūtāni (bhū=esse). This is nearer the Pāli than our 'elements'—a term reserved for dhātu, below. *Cf. B. Psy.* xlviii., and on Rūpa and its forms, xli.-lxiii., and Book II.—Ed.

[3] Dhātu is defined by the Commentators as that which carries its own characteristic marks or attributes (attano sabhāvaŋ dhāretīti dhātu). See Appendix: Dhātu.

extension,[1] the element of cohesion,[2] the element of heat, the element of motion.[3]

(2) *Sensitive material qualities*—viz., the eye, the ear, the nose, the tongue, the body.[4]

(3) *Material qualities of sense-fields*—viz., visible *form*,[5] sound, odour, sapids, and the tangible, the last excluding the element of cohesion, and being held [to lie in the other] three essentials.[6]

(4) *Material qualities of sex*[7] — viz., female sex and male sex.

[1] Pathavī is derived from 'pattharati'—'to spread out or extend.' Extension to us means occupation in space. Tri-dimensional extension gives rise to our idea of a *solid* body. As no two bodies can occupy the same space at the same time, Buddhists derive their idea of *hardness* (kakkhaḷatta-lakkhaṇa) from pathavī, and regard pathavī as a primary quality (pathavī *eva* dhātu).

[2] Āpo. The Commentators explain this term to mean that element which diffuses itself throughout the mass, pervades the whole mass, and increases the bulk of material bodies, keeping their atoms from being scattered about, holding and collecting them together.

[3] Vāyo. The Commentators explain this term to mean the element which causes a body or bodies to change place (desantaruppatti-hetu-bhāvena), or which moves the body, which vibrates, or oscillates (samīreti).

[4] *I.e.*, the dermic skin.

[5] Rūpaŋ. Thus we see that visible *form* in the sense of a certain coloured surface is only *one quality* out of the twenty-four named in this section.

[6] Particles of matter are held together by āpo (cohesion), which cannot be felt by the sense of touch—*e.g.*, when one puts his hand into cold water, the softness of water felt is not āpo but pathavī; the cold felt is not āpo, but tejo; the pressure felt is not āpo but vāyo. Hence Buddhists take only the three essentials or primaries to constitute the tangible. From this one can easily see that Buddhists are not dealing with Thales' water, Anaximenes' air, Herakleitus' fire, or the Peripatetics' matter, of Greek philosophy.

[7] Itthattaŋ, purisattaŋ; in Abhidh. Piṭ., itthindriyaŋ, etc.—Ed. The generic name is simply 'bhāva' (state), abbreviated from itthibhāva+pumbhāva=itthipumbhāva. Ledi Sadaw explains the 'bhāva' as that state by which masculinity and femininity can be distinguished.

(5) *Material qualities of base*—viz., the heart-base.[1]
(6) *Material quality of life*—viz., vital force.
(7) *Material quality of nutrition*—viz., edible food.[2]

All these, amounting to eighteen[3] species of material quality, are also otherwise distinguished :

(*a*) according to their *differential characteristics* ;[4]
(*b*) according to their *salient marks* ;[5]
(*c*) as *determined* by karma and environment ;[6]
(*d*) as *mutable* ;[7]
(*e*) as object fit for *contemplation*.[8]

(8) *Material quality of limitation*—viz., the element of space.

[1] *I.e.*, of mental life. On this common feature in Eastern and Western psycho-physiology, see above, Part III., § 12. In the *Visuddhimagga* (6) precedes (5). The *Dhs.* omits (5).—Ed. According to later commentators its omission is not accidental. See above, p. 128, *n.* 1, and Appendix : Hadayavatthu.

[2] Āhāro is sustenance, physical or mental. Here physical sustenance is intended. *S.*, ii. 11 ; *B. Psy.*, 80, *n.* 1.—Ed.

[3] Eighteen, by counting (8) as only four, the tangible having been enumerated under (1). See *Mnemonic ;* also *n.* 6, p. 155.

[4] Sabhāvarūpaŋ: *attano* sabhāvena siddhaŋ.

[5] Salakkhaṇarūpaŋ: aniccādīhi lakkhaṇehi sahitaŋ.

[6] Nipphannarūpaŋ: kammādihi paccayehi nipphāditaŋ. The conditioning environments are citta, utu, and āhāra.

[7] Rūpa-rūpaŋ: ruppanasabhāvena yuttaŋ. The term 'rūpa' is related to ruppati, 'to change' (under contrary influences of cold, heat, etc.). The first qualifying member of this curious compound retains its etymological sense, whilst the second qualified member is used in its derivative sense of matter. The Commentators therefore explain this compound as indicating the subjection of *matter* to *change of forms* under contrary influences. *Cf.* dukkha-dukkhaŋ. If so, it seems to amount only to a more general form of (*c*) nipphannarūpaŋ.

[8] Sammasanarūpaŋ. The Commentators explain this by the three salient marks, anicca, etc. On the Sammasana-Insight, see Part IX., § 6.

(9) *Material quality of communication*—viz., intimation by the body,[1] and intimation by speech.

(10) *Material quality of plasticity*[2]—viz., lightness, pliancy, adaptability of matter and the two media of communication.

(11) *Material qualities of salient features*[3]—viz., integration, continuance[4] [of integration], decay, and impermanence of matter. But here the [phenomenon of] production[5] of matter alone is described by the two names of 'integration' and 'continued integration.'[4]

Thus the eleven kinds of material quality may be resolved into twenty-eight when considered as so many properties.[6]

§ 3. *Mnemonic.*

How [into twenty-eight]?

The *four* essentials and *nine* wherewithals of sense
Five organs and four objects—*two* of sex-difference,

[1] Kāya=copana-kāya, 'the *moving body*': communication by signs.

[2] Vikārarūpaŋ. Ledi Sadaw explains this term by visesākāro, 'peculiar, distinctive condition.'

[3] Lakkhaṇarūpaŋ: distinguishable logically from (*d*) above, as consisting in the impressively characteristic, the former being that which has these features (salakkhaṇa).

[4] On these two terms, *cf. B. Psy.*, 195, *n.* 2. It must be borne in mind, however, that santati, in this connection, is not the continuance of what has integrated, but of the phenomenon of integration itself. This is explained by the next sentence. Strictly speaking, we have only three lakkhaṇarūpas corresponding to the three phases of organic life, viz., birth, growth-and-decay, and death. Growth begins with birth and decay ends in death. And the entire interval between birth and death is covered by the word jaratā—'the state of growing old.' For this reason, in such works as Saccasankhepa, only twenty-seven species of rūpa are enumerated.

[5] Jāti-rūpaŋ: rupassa+jāti, 'the production of matter;' or jāti eva rūpaŋ, 'the material quality or phenomenon *of* production.' The Commentators adopt the latter.

[6] Sarūpavasena. Classes (8) to (11) are in the translator's original termed Anipphanna-rūpaŋ, the meaning, according to

The heart, the vital force, and food make *eighteen* kinds
Of form material. Besides all these one finds
Matter as bounded, medium of sign or speech,
As plastic, mark essential, *three* and *four* to each,
All properties inherent *a priori*. Now
Ten and eighteen are eight and twenty [you'll allow].

So far for a concise exposition of matter.

---

§ 4. *Of General Aspects of Matter.*

Now all this matter is wholly included under the following categories :—

without [moral and immoral] hetu's;[1]
relative ;[2]
bound up with the āsava's ;[3]
conditioned ;[4]
mundane ;
belonging to the Kāmaloka ;
not subjective ;[5]
not to be got rid of.[6]

But when distinguishing it as internal, or external, and so forth, it may be divided in several ways. How so ?

---

him, being 'not predetermined by karma,' etc. See *n.* 5, on p. 156. Nipphanna is, literally, 'spread out,' 'arranged' (*cf. Jāt.*, iv. 37), implying planned construction. *Cf. Asl.*, 316 : 'Na nipphanna-rūpānaŋ vasena cakkhudasakaŋ.'—Ed.

[1] Ahetukaŋ : 'unmoral.'

[2] Sappaccayaŋ : 'related to causes and conditions.'

[3] Sāsavaŋ : See Part VII., § 2.

[4] Sankhataŋ : paccayehi sangamma karīyatīti : (Ledi Sadaw's *Paramattha-dīpanī*) 'that which is made, conditioned, or caused by a combination of causes.'

[5] Anārammaṇaŋ, lit., 'not *having* an object'—*i.e.*, it only *is* object.—Ed.

[6] Appahātabbaŋ : *i.e.*, 'indestructible.'

Cf. the longer list in *Dhs.*, § 595.—Ed.

The five sensitive kinds of matter (2) are internal material qualities; the others are external.

Six kinds, comprising the sensitives, together with the heart[1] (2), (5), are basic material qualities; the others are not bases.

Seven kinds, comprising the sensitives and the two media of communication (2), (9), are 'door'-forms of matter; the others are not doors.

Eight kinds, comprising the five sensitives, the two sex-states and vital force (2), (4), (6) are controlling[2] forces of matter; the others are not controlling forces.

Twelve kinds, comprising the five sensitives, and the seven[3] objects of sense, are gross,[4] or near, or resisting material qualities; the others are subtle, or remote, or non-resisting material qualities.

Material quality born of karma[5] has been 'grasped at,' all other has not been 'grasped at.'[6]

[1] See p. 123, *n.* 1.

[2] Indriyarūpaŋ: aṭṭhavidham pi indriya-rūpaŋ pañcaviññāṇesu lingādīsu sahajarūpa-paripālane ca ādhipaccayo gato. (*Abhidhammattha Vibhāvanī*): 'The eight kinds are called Indriya-rūpaŋ, because they *regulate* (or *control*) the five senses, as well as the primary and secondary characters of either sex, and keep the co-existent qualities of body from decay.' It must be clearly borne in mind that in cases of sense-control it is not a case of, say, sight controlling the eye, but a case of the eye regulating sight. Cakkhum eva indriyaŋ, the eye is the Indriya.

[3] Seven, and not five, here, because the tangible is now counted as three essentials, or elements. See p. 155, *n.* 6.

[4] See p. 120, *n.* 1. The Ceylon Commentary explains 'oḷārikaŋ,' by vīsaya-visayī-bhāvāpatti vasena thūḷattā —'because of grossness by way of becoming (lit., 'arriving at the state of') sense-organs and sense-objects'; santike, by gahaṇassa sukarattā—'because of easiness to take (the gross matter).' Sappaṭighaŋ, lit., 'with striking' is applied to the 'gross,' or 'near,' species of rūpa, because they mutually strike each other.

[5] For instance, one's own bodily form and features.

[6] Upādiṇṇaŋ, 'grasped at by craving.' See the term discussed in *B. Psy.*, 201, *n.* 4; 323 *n.* The Ceylon Cy. explains this term by 'taṇhādiṭṭhīhi upetena kammunā attano phalabhā-

Coloured object[1] is visible material quality; all else is invisible material quality.

Eye and ear, as not giving immediate access (to their objects[2]), and nose, tongue and body, as giving immediate access, are five kinds of field-holding[3] material quality; the others are material qualities holding no special field.

Colour, odour, taste, nutritive essence,[4] and the four essentials are the eight kinds of inseparable material quality; all the others are separable.

§ 5. *Mnemonic.*

Thus all those eight and twenty kinds do men of vision clear
Group, as 'internal,' and so forth, even as they appear.

So far for aspects of matter.[5]

---

vena ādiṇṇattā: (so termed) 'because it has been grasped at by the karma that is closely attended with craving and erroneous opinion, by way of its own fruit.'

[1] Rūpāyatanaŋ, a synonym of vaṇṇāyatanaŋ; nīlādi vaṇṇa-sankhātaŋ rūpam eva cittacetasikānaŋ uppatti-ṭṭhānattā ākarattā ca āyatanañ cāti rūpāyatanaŋ (*Porāṇa-ṭīkā*). The material quality called the colours of blue, etc., is itself the āyatana, because it is the *place* where mind and its properties operate together.

[2] The *Mahā Aṭṭhakathā* did not distinguish light and sound from other sensibles. The distinction began with Buddhaghosa, probably because he was, to a certain extent, acquainted with the comparatively modern undulatory theory of light and sound. But this distinction has led the author of *Abhidhammattha-vibhāvanī* to commit himself to the view that there is no contact between eye and its object, ear and sound. U. Hlaing, the Yaw-Atunwun, one of the ablest authorities on Buddhism in Burma, rejected the distinction itself on the authority of the *Mahā-Aṭṭhakathā*. Ledi Sadaw, on the other hand, accepts the distinction, and explains that, though there is undoubtedly contact between eye and light, ear and sound, yet the mind, by habit, refers these sensations to the outer objects that do not come in contact.

[3] Gocaraggāhika-rūpaŋ. Some texts read gāhaka.

[4] Ojā. Apart from taste (rasa) every object has its own nutritive essence. What is poison to one is meat to another.

[5] Rūpavibhāgo, lit., 'division of rūpa.'

§ 6. *On the Origins*[1] *of Material Phenomena.*[2]

The four things said to be the origins of material phenomena are:

1. karma;
2. mind;[3]
3. physical change;[4]
4. food.

1. *Material Phenomena born of Karma.*

The twenty-five kinds of good and bad karma, belonging to life in Kāmaloka and in Rūpaloka, cause to come forth, from instant to instant,[5] starting with rebirth, well-produced[6] material phenomena, 'originating in karma,' within our personal continuity.[7]

---

[1] Samuṭṭhānaŋ: By 'origin' is not meant the absolute origin, which is a mystery of mysteries. It is used in the sense in which Darwin used it in the phrase 'origin of species.'

On this subject compare the much older discussion in *Milinda*, 271.—Ed.

[2] The word 'phenomena' (as rūpaŋ, always singular in Pali) is used here instead of 'material quality' to show that rūpa is also connected with rūpayati, 'to show,' or 'to cause to appear.' Rūpayati pakāsetīti rūpaŋ.

[3] Citta, rendered elsewhere by consciousness.—Ed.

[4] Utu, or temperature. As every change in physical nature is attributed to utu, the element or manifestation of tejo (heat), utu, lit., 'season,' has come to be identified with physical nature itself, or with physical causes, including chemical causes, or all physical forces.

[5] Khaṇe khaṇe, lit., 'at every moment.' It is explained in the comments by 'ekekassa cittassa tīsu tīsu khaṇesu nirantaraŋ.' The three instants of each thought-moment are here intended.

[6] Abhisankhataŋ. This term is explained in the *Paramattha-dīpanī* by 'atītakāle yathā kālantare rūpaŋ janeti, tathā visesetvā suṭṭhu kataŋ,' meaning 'as rūpa was produced at a different time in the past, so well-produced.' This comment reveals the conviction that karma-born matter is not produced out of nothing, but from some pre-existing materials.

[7] Ajjhattikasantāne.

2. *Material Phenomena born of Mind.*

Mind, in seventy-five modes—*i.e.*, excluding the resultants of the Arūpaloka, and the twice fivefold cognition—[1] while only in the course of springing up,[2] causes to come forth, from the first moment of our life-continuum,[3] material phenomena 'originating in mind.' Here too[4] apperception during ecstasy serves to strengthen[5] bodily postures. But determining cognition also,[4] Kāmaloka apperception and super-intellection give rise to [the physical media of] communication.[6] And thirteen [kinds of] joyous apperceptions also[4] produce laughter.

---

3. *Material Phenomena born of Physical Change.*

The temperature of heat and cold, named[7] 'the element of heat,' when it reaches its static stage, gives rise to material phenomena, 'originated by physical change,' either internal or external according to circumstances.

[1] *I.e.*, eighty-nine *minus* these fourteen, mind's total number of modes being eighty-nine. See above, Part I.—Ed.

[2] Jāyantam eva. Mind is supposed to be strong at its uppāda-instant, like a gas in its nascent state. See p. 125, § 3.

[3] Paṭhama-bhavangaŋ.

[4] Pi, 'too,' 'also.' The force of pi in these three sentences is to take in, in addition, what has been said in the previous sentence or sentences. On the theory of the Ludicrous, see Introd. Essay, p. 22 *f.*

[5] Sannāmeti. Ledi Sadaw thinks that sandhāreti was the original reading. This sentence is significant in showing that a cataleptic condition can be produced by jhāna.

[6] Gestures and speech.

[7] Samaññātā. The two eminent annotators, Payagyi Sadaw and Mogaung Sadaw, read samaññātā, and they explain the same as follows: Samani-tabbā kathetabbāti samaññā; sā eva samaññātā. Ledi Sadaw reads with a long accent and derives the word from ñātā, known. The Ceylon Cy. is silent on this term.

4. *Material Phenomena born of Food.*

Food, or what is called 'nutritive essence,' gives rise to material phenomena 'originated by food' at the period of assimilation, and only when it reaches its static stage.[1]

Here the material qualities — heart and physical faculties[2]—are produced only by k a r m a. The two media of communication are produced only by mind. Sound is produced by mind and physical change; the triple properties of lightness, pliancy, and adaptability, may be due to physical changes, mind and food.[3] Inseparable material qualities, as well as the space element,[4] are due to all four causes, while material qualities which are essential characteristics[5] are produced by none of the four.[6]

---

§ 7. *Mnemonic.*

Of matter eighteen, fifteen, thirteen, twelve kinds, taken in turn,
Are of k a r m a, or mind, or physical change, or of eaten nutriment born.
But marks, from the very nature of things in process beginning with birth,
Cannot as such, says the doctrine, be themselves anywise brought forth.

So far for the method of the origination of matter.

[1] Ṭhānapatto va=ṭhitipatto va (Ceylon Cy.).

[2] Indriya, lit., 'the controller.' See p. 159, *n.* 2.

[3] Each of these three factors—physical change, mind, and food—has influence on what is called the 'Locomotive faculty'—*e.g.*, hot climate, slow habit of mind, and a heavy meal make a man sluggish.

[4] *I.e.*, the element of space, according to the Commentaries, obtains between the units of mass, called rūpakalāpā, born of all the four causes (*e.g.*, the intra-atomic space in which electrons move about). See Appendix, Ākāsa.

[5] Or salient features or marks (lakkhaṇarūpaŋ).

[6] If these marks are considered as born of the four causes, the marks in turn must be supposed to have similar marks, and so on, *ad infinitum*.

§ 8. *Of the Grouping of the Qualities of Material Body.*

Material qualities may be arranged in twenty-one groups in virtue of there being a common genesis, cessation, dependence, and also co-existence.

1. For instance, vitality and such material qualities as are inseparable [adjuncts], together with the eye itself, are called 'the eye-decad,'[1] Analogously formed are the groups entitled 'ear-decad,' 'nose-decad,' 'tongue-decad,' 'body-decad,' 'female-decad,' 'male-decad,' 'base-decad.'[2] Inseparable material qualities, together with vitality only, are called 'the vital nonad.'[3] These nine groups are said to be 'caused by k a r m a.'

2. The eight inseparable material qualities constitute 'the pure octad.'[4]

They, together with the medium of communication by signs (or gestures), or with the vocal medium of communication and sound, make up the nonad of body-communication and the decad of speech-communication respectively. Again, taken together with lightness, pliancy, and adaptability of material quality, they make up the undecad of plasticity; or, adding to these, bodily communication, the dodecad of plasticity; or, adding vocal communication and sound, the tredecad of plasticity. These six groups are said to be 'caused by mind.'

3. Four groups are said to be 'caused by physical change.' These are the 'pure' octad, the sound-nonad, the

[1] See above, § 4. Buddhaghosa (*Asl.*, 316) enumerates the ten as follows: 'The four essentials,' *colour*, odour, sapids, nutritive essence, the vital force and the visual organ are called 'the eye-decad.' See on this further, *B. Psy.*, p. 173, *n.* 1.—Ed.

[2] *I.e.*, the heart-decad.

[3] The P.T.S. text should obviously read n a v a k a n t i, as does the Translator's original. See p. 160.—Ed.

[4] S u d d h a ṭ ṭ h a k a ŋ. On s u d d h a, *cf.* p. 36, *n.* The eight are those enumerated in *n.* 1 above, excluding the last two. See p. 160. – Ed.

undecad of plasticity, and the dodecad of sound and plasticity.

4. Two groups are said to be 'caused by food.' These are the 'pure' octad and the undecad of plasticity.

Of the foregoing the 'pure' octad and the sound-nonad —the first of these 'caused by physical change'—are got externally as well as internally. All the remainder are got only internally.

---

§ 9. *Mnemonic.*

From karma, mind, 'utu,' and food, produced in order due,
Things fall in one and twenty groups, to wit, nine, six, four, two.
But not within these groups[1] comes space, the 'men who see' do state,
Nor salient marks; [space just sets bounds, the marks just indicate.[2]]

So far for the classification of material groups.[3]

§ 10. *Of the World of Sense.*

Moreover, all these material qualities accrue undiminished, if circumstances permit, [to an individual] during a lifetime in the Kāmaloka. But at the rebirth of moisture-born creatures, and of those of apparitional rebirth,[4] seven groups of ten at most are manifested, to wit, the eye-, ear-, nose-, tongue-, body-, sex-, and base-decads, and *at least* three groups of ten. That is to say, the eye-, ear-, nose-, and sex-decads are sometimes not got. Hence on this wise are such deficiencies in groups to be understood.

[1] Kalāpaṅgaṃ, lit., 'part of group.'

[2] Lakkhaṇattā, lit., 'because they simply mark (matter). The parenthesis is from the Commentaries.

[3] Kalāpa-yojanā, lit., 'union [of qualities] in groups.'

[4] Opapātikā. Such creatures are said to be born with an appearance of fifteen or sixteen years of age.

Such beings were held to appear suddenly, independent of parents.

In womb-born creatures, on the other hand, three decads are manifested, to wit, the body-, sex-, and heart-decads. Sometimes, however, the sex-decad may not be got.[1] Afterwards,[2] during life,[3] the eye-decad and the rest are manifested in due order.

§ 10A. *Material Qualities at Death.*

And thus the groups of material qualities which are produced in four ways: those produced by karma starting from rebirth-conception; those produced by mind starting from the second [moment of] mental life;[4] those produced by physical change starting from the static phase of conception; and those produced by food starting from the diffusion[5] of nutritive essence, go on unbroken in the world of sense, as long as life lasts, like the flame of a lamp, or the stream of a river.

But at the time of death, starting from the static period of the seventeenth thought-moment, reckoned backward from the last dying thought, material qualities produced by karma arise no more. And those karma-wrought material qualities, which came into being before[6] [the static phase of] that thought-moment, persist till the time of the dying thought and then cease. After that the material quality which mind and food have produced is also cut off. After that a series of material qualities

---

The subject is exhaustively dealt with by Professor E. Windisch in *Ueber Buddha's Geburt*, chap. xi., Leipzig, 1908.—Ed.

[1] *I.e.*, as in the case of asexual creatures.

[2] *I.e.*, after conception.

[3] *I.e.*, during the embryonic stage of fœtal life.

[4] Dutiyacittaŋ here is the same thing as paṭhamabhavangaŋ, on which see above, § 6 (2).

[5] *I.e.*, assimilation.

[6] Pūretaraŋ, the nascent stage of the seventeenth thought-moment is here intended. From this it is clear that qualities produced by karma in the earlier thought-moments would have died out before the dying thought is reached.

produced by physical change goes on till [there remains] what is called a corpse.[1]

---

§ 11. *Mnemonic.*

So when we die, begin again, wherever we are bound,
Material qualities, from life's first start, in some such
round.

---

§ 12. *Groups in Rūpaloka.*

But in the Rūpaloka, the decads of nose, tongue, body, and sex, as well as the groups produced by food, do not obtain. Hence, at the time of rebirth in that world, only four groups produced by karma obtain, to wit, the three decads of eye, ear, and base, and the vital nonad. But during life the groups produced by mind and physical change obtain also.[2] Those, on the other hand, who are reborn among the Unconscious Beings, do not even obtain the eye, ear, base, or sound groups. They likewise obtain none of the groups produced by mind. Hence at the time of their rebirth they get only the vital nonad. And during their lives there comes to them in addition, but with the exception of sound, such material qualities as are produced by physical change.

Now, in the three regions, called Kāmaloka, Rūpaloka, and of the Unconscious, thus must the twofold procedure of material phenomena (1) at rebirth; (2) during life, be understood.

---

§ 13. *Mnemonic.*

In world of sense, material forms are eight
And twenty; of these, twenty-three alone
In Rūpa.[3] Of th' Unconscious Ones the fate

[1] This is understood by the Burmese Buddhists of the present day to mean 'till the corpse is reduced to dust.'

[2] Pavattiyaŋ cittotusamuṭṭhānā ca labbhanti. Omitted in J.P.T.S. text.—Ed.

[3] Rūpīsu=rūpesu=rūpalokesu, beings in Rūpaloka.

Is seventeen only; in Arūpa none.
At start of life, sound, modes and signs,[1] decay
And death come not, but during life's brief day
Naught in experience but may come our way.

So far for the order of happening of material phenomena.

---

§ 14. *Of Nibbana.*

Now Nibbana, which is reckoned as beyond these worlds,[2] is to be realized through the knowledge belonging to the Four Paths.[3] It is the object of those Paths,[4] and of their Fruits.[4] It is called Nibbana, in that it is a 'de-parture'[5] from that craving which is called vāna, lusting. This Nibbana is in its nature single, but for purposes of logical treatment,[6] it is twofold, namely, the element of Nibbana, wherewith is yet remaining stuff of life,[7] and the element of Nibbana without that remainder. So, too, when divided into modes, it is threefold—namely, Void, Signless,[8] and Absolute Content.[9]

---

[1] Vikāro covers both 'modes and signs,' comprising the three plastic qualities of lightness, pliancy, and adaptability, and the two media of communication. See above, p. 157 (10).

[2] Lokuttara.

[3] Catumaggañāṇena. The Paññindriya-cetasika, which enters into combination with other concomitants in each Path-consciousness receives the name of Sammādiṭṭhi-right views.

[4] *I.e.*, Path-cognition[s] and Fruition-cognition[s].

[5] Ni(r)kkhantattā, lit., 'because of out-going.'

[6] Kāraṇapariyāyena: kāraṇa means 'cause,' and pariyāya here means 'synonym' (paribyattiŋ) yanti gacchanti anenāti pariyāyo—that by which (a term is made clear). The Ceylon commentaries explain it by paññāpane kāraṇassa lesena—by way of device of the means (of knowing) in the matter of language.

[7] Upādiseso: Lebenstoff.

[8] Animitta. See Part IX., § 10.

[9] Lit., 'not hankered after,' or 'longed for.' *Ibid.*—Ed.

§ 15. *Mnemonic.*

Great Seers, wholly from V ā n a - lust set free,
Declare Nibbana such a path to be :—
Past death, past end [it goes, this blessed way],
Uncausèd,[1] having no beyond, they say.

Thus, as fourfold, T a t h ā g a t a s reveal,
The ultimate kinds of things we know and feel :—
Mind first, and next, concomitants of mind,
Body as third, Nibbana[2] last in kind.

Thus ends the Sixth Part, in the Compendium of Philosophy, being the Chapter entitled the Compendium of Matter.

[1] A s a n k h a t a ŋ. This word is explained in the Ceylon commentaries by p a c c a y e h i a s a n k h a t a t t ā (so-called) because of not being subject to further causation and conditioning. Ledi Sadaw writes s a n k h a r a ṇ a k i c c a r a h i t a t t ā (so-called) because it is devoid of the function of causing, or conditioning well.

[2] The word Nibbana is, in spite of the exegetical derivation above, as doubtful in its etymological history as is our own Heaven, and as vague in meaning. The Translator was willing to let it be rendered by Nirvana, just as we have let Karma replace Kamma. But whereas only an Italian would rightly pronounce Kam'ma, Nibbana goes of itself on any tongue that will make the *a* long and open. Besides this it is a Buddhist term, belonging to Buddhist doctrine, while Nirvana is associated with Pantheistic eschatology, and, moreover, has now become hopelessly vulgarized. Once Europeanized, the accent in Nibbāna will become superfluous, hence I have omitted it.—Ed.

PART VII

THE COMPENDIUM OF CATEGORIES

§ 1. *Introductory.*

'NEATH two and seventy heads have been set forth
Distinctive kinds of states, each with its mark.
These will I now duly categorize.

---

§ 2. *Of Categories of Evil.*

This compendium of categories must be understood as fourfold, to wit:

I. A compendium of evil categories.
II. A compendium of [ethically] mixed categories.
III. A compendium of what pertains to enlightenment.
IV. A compendium of the whole.

How [are they composed]?

(I.) In the compendium of evil, there are, in the first place,

(*a*) the four Āsava's[1]:

1. sense-desires;[2]
2. becoming;[3]

[1] Āsavo is derived from ā √su='to flow,' and the Ceylon commentaries, among others, explain the term as that which flows right up to the topmost plane of existence or right up to the moment of Gotrabhū (Bhavato ābhavaggaṃ dhammato āgotrabhuṃ savantīti āsavā). See Appendix, Āsava. On this and the following 'evil categories,' *cf. B. Psy.*, pp. 291, 304, 308, 310, 323.

[2] Kāmāsavo. Kāma may mean either that which desires (kāmetīti) or that which is desired (kāmiyatīti). But the Commentaries say that here taṇhā (craving) for objects of sense-experience, including the pleasures of the five senses, is meant.

[3] Bhavāsavo. Bhava is either kamma-bhava or upapatti-bhava (Introd. Essay, 42 *f.*). It may be either Kāma-

3. error ;
4. ignorance.

(*b*) the four Floods[1] :—(*same as* 1-4) ;
(*c*) the four Bonds[2] :—(*same as* 1-4) ;
(*d*) the four Ties :—the ties, physical and mental,[3] of

1. covetousness ;
2. ill-will ;
3. practice of mere rite and ritual ;[4]
4. adherence to one's dogmas ;[5]

(*e*) the four Graspings[6] :—the grasping after

1. sense-desires ;
2. error ;

---

bhava, Rūpa-bhava, or Arūpa-bhava. The Commentaries say that by Bhava here is intended the same craving, this time, for any one of the forms of existence. The psychological factor in the two modes of craving is the Cetasika of greed.

[1] Oghā. The Commentaries explain that these four are so termed because they kill the creatures who have fallen into them by drowning them (lit., 'overwhelming and suffocating them'). Anassāsikaŋ katvā ajjhottharanto hanatīti vaṭṭasmiŋ osīdapentā viya hontīti.—Ceylon Cy.

[2] Yoga. The Ceylon Cy. explains this term as that which yokes the creatures to the rounds (of misery), or that which by way of cause and effect (kamma-vipākena), yokes the creatures to other rebirths, etc., in the machine of existence (bhavayantake), or in the round of existence (vaṭṭasmiŋ). Vaṭṭasmiŋ vā bhavayantake vā satte yojentīti.—Ledi Sadaw.

[3] The Commentaries explain that kāya here includes both rūpakāya and nāmakāya.

[4] Sīlabbataparāmāso. The Ceylon Cy. explains this term by 'Gosīlādisīlena vatena tad-ubhayena suddhīti evaŋ parato asabhāvato āmasanaŋ'—the practice (lit., 'the handling') with an incorrect view (lit., 'the opposite or contrary view') that one becomes pure by bovine and canine morality or conduct, or by both. Ledi Sadaw explains 'parato' as 'by way of the view opposed to the truth' (Ettha ca parato 'ti bhūta-sabhāva-paccanīkato' ti attho). *Cf. B. Psy.*, p. 260, *n.* 4.

[5] Idaŋ-saccābhiniveso. The Ceylon Cy. explains this term by 'Idaŋ eva saccam mogham aññanti abhinivesanaŋ daḷhagāho. The firm belief (lit., 'hold') that this (view) is true, and the other futile.

[6] Upādānāni. The Ceylon Cy. explains this term to mean that which tenaciously or firmly grasps the object as a snake does a frog.

3. mere rite and ritualism;
4. a theory of soul;

(*f*) the six Hindrances[1]:—

1. sensual passion;
2. ill-will;
3. sloth-and-torpor;
4. flurry-and-worry;
5. perplexity;
6. ignorance;

(*g*) the seven forms of Latent Bias[2]:—the bias of

1. sensual passion;
2. lust after life;
3. aversion;
4. conceit;
5. error;
6. perplexity;
7. ignorance;

(*h*A) the ten Fetters[3] of the Suttanta[4]:—the fetters of

1. lust after [life in the] Kāmaloka[5];
2. lust after [life in the] Rūpaloka;
3. lust after [life in the] Arūpaloka;
4. aversion;

[1] Nīvaraṇāni (Burm. MSS. niv-). The Ceylon Cy. explains this term as that which prevents the arising of good thoughts by way of jhāna, etc.; or as that which prevents the jhāna itself; or as that which obstructs the eye of wisdom (paññā-cakkhuno vā āvaraṭṭhena). Ledi Sadaw explains the same to be that which hinders all that is good in human nature by preventing the good which has not arisen from arising, or the good which has arisen from being repeated.

[2] Anusaya from anu √seti='to sleep,' lit., 'that which lies dormant or remains latent.'

[3] Both the Ceylon and the Burmese Commentators explain Saṁyojanas, as 'those which bind' (Saṁyojenti, bandhantīti saṁyojanāni), *i.e.*, bind creatures in the rounds of misery (vaṭṭasmiṃ).

[4] Sutta-Piṭaka.

[5] 'Kāma,' when opposed to 'rūpa,' and 'arūpa,' has either 'bhava' or 'loka' understood after it.

5. conceit;
6. error;
7. practice of rite and ritual;
8. perplexity;
9. distraction;
10. ignorance;

(*h*B) the other ten Fetters of the Abhidhamma, viz., of

1. sensual passion[1];
2. lust after life;
3. aversion;
4. conceit;
5. error;
6. practice of rite and ritual;
7. perplexity;
8. envy;
9. selfishness;
10. ignorance.

(*i*) The ten Torments[2] are:—

1. greed;
2. hate;
3. dulness;
4. conceit;
5. error;
6. perplexity;
7. sloth;
8. distraction;
9. impudence;
10. fearlessness of consequence.

[1] Here 'kāma' is opposed to 'bhava,' and is restricted to objects of sensual desire.'

[2] The Ceylon Cy. explains kilesā as those by which the mind is defiled (kilissati), burnt (upatappati), or afflicted (bādhiyati). Ledi Sadaw of Burma adopts the same explanation, but adds that kilesa's are those by which creatures are defiled, or by which they (the creatures) arrive either at the state of being defiled (malīna-bhāvaŋ) or at the state of being debased (nihīna-bhāvaŋ). See *B. Psy.*, 327 *ff*.

Now in the Āsava-category, under the terms 'sense-desires,' and 'becoming,' is implied the Craving which has them as its objects. In the same way, it is just the erroneous opinion that occurs under different conditions, which is described as 'practice of rite and ritual,' 'tendency to dogmatism,' and grasping after a theory of soul.

§ 3. *Mnemonic.*

The Āsavas, the Floods, Bonds, Ties, root in the threefold base;[1]
The Graspings have a twofold source;[1] but eightfold is the case
With Hindrances, with Bias, six, with Fetters, nine, we hold,[2]
With Torments, ten:—thus Evil's List is reckoned as ninefold.

---

§ 4. *Of Mixed Categories.*

II.—In the compendium of mixed categories there are the following:

(*a*) The Six Hetu's (root-conditions)[3]:—

1. greed;
2. hate;
3. dulness;
4. disinterestedness;
5. amity;
6. intelligence.

[1] Vatthuto is explained by the Ceylon Cy. to mean 'dhammato,' and by Ledi Sadaw of Burma, 'sabhāva-dhammato,' The psychological ultimates described in Part II. as mental properties or concomitants are here intended.

[2] Matā.

[3] See above, Part III., § 4.

(*b*) The Seven Constituents of Jhāna :—

1. initial application (vitakka) ;[1]
2. sustained application (vicāra) ;[1]
3. pleasurable interest ;
4. individualization ;[1]
5. joy ;[1]
6. grief ;[2]
7. hedonic indifference ;[3]

(*c*) the Twelve Path-Constituents[4] :—

1. right views ;
2. right aspiration ;[5]
3. right language ;
4. right action ;
5. right livelihood ;
6. right endeavour ;
7. right mindfulness ;
8. right concentration ;
9. wrong views ;
10. wrong aspiration ;
11. wrong endeavour ;
12. wrong concentration.

(*d*) the Twenty-two Controlling[6] Powers :—the controlling power of

1. the eye ;[6]
2. the ear ;

[1] See Parts I. and II.

[2] The mention of grief here shows that jhāna is liable to abuse in the hands of unprincipled persons.

[3] The intellectual tatramajjhattatā, 'balance of mind,' is not meant here. See p. 14.

[4] Magga here includes both the noble and the ignoble path, the last four constituents leading to the planes of miserable existence. *Cf.* *S.* v., 18, 23 ; *Vibhanga*, p. 373.

[5] The psychological ultimate of sammāsankappa is vitakka, which, in the present case, directs the mind towards the right object—viz., the higher ideal.

[6] On Indriya. See *supra*, p. 159, *n.* 2. It must be borne in mind that it is the eye that controls sight and so on for the other four senses. See also below, Part VIII., § 10 (6), *n.* 2.

3. the nose;
4. the tongue;
5. the body (*i.e.*, the skin);
6. female sex;[1]
7. male sex;[1]
8. life;
9. mind;[2]
10. pleasure;
11. pain;
12. joy;
13. grief;
14. hedonic indifference;
15. faith;
16. energy;
17. mindfulness;
18. concentration;
19. reason;
20 the thought:—'I shall come to know the unknown';
21. gnosis;[3]
22. one who knows.

(*e*) the Nine Forces:—the force of

1. faith;
2. energy;
3. mindfulness;[4]
4. concentration;
5. reason;

[1] Lit., 'womanhood and manhood.' Sex controls the primary and the secondary characters of sex described in the Commentaries under linga, nimitta, kutta, and ākappa.

[2] Mind (mano) is called an indriya because it controls or governs its concomitant mental properties.

[3] Aññā may be differentiated from ñāṇa, as the Christian might distinguish 'saving knowledge' from knowledge in general, including knowledge of matters of mere sense-experience. See the eight moral thoughts of the sense-world. Part I., § 6. English is poor beside Pāli in such terminology. *B. Psy.*, xci.—Ed.

[4] Omitted in J.P.T.S.—Ed.

6. modesty;
7. discretion;
8. impudence;
9. fearlessness of consequences.

(*f*) the Four Dominant Influences[1]:—namely of

1. intention;
2. energy;
3. thought;[2]
4. investigation.[3]

(*g*) the Four Foods:—

1. edible food;
2. contact;
3. volitional activity of mind;[4]
4. rebirth-consciousness.[5]

Now, with reference to the 'Controlling Powers' (*d*), the power called the thought, 'I shall come to know the unknown,' is that Path-knowledge possessed by one who has 'arrived at the stream'; the power called that 'of one who knows,' is the knowledge involved in the Fruit of Arahantship; and by the power of gnosis is meant the six

[1] Adhipati. See *Dhs.*, §§ 269, 1034. *B. Psy.*, pp. 77, 269.—Ed. Adhipati differs from Indriya in that the former is supreme, while the latter has its equals. See the text below: Only one dominant influence, etc. (adhipati eko va labbhati).

[2] Citta here denotes javana-cittuppāda, while the other three dominant influences refer to the respective concomitants of this state of apperception.

[3] Vimaṁsa (in Sinh. MSS. vīm-). The psychological ultimate of this is paññindriya-cetasika. The category of dominant influences shows that when a man *acts*, either intention, effort, knowledge, or reason, may predominate. *Cf.* Criminal Law, in which no responsibility is attached to an act without one or other of the foregoing three dominant factors.

[4] Manosañcetanāhāra-sankhātaŋ kusalākusala-kammaŋ (Ceylon Cy.).

[5] Viññāṇāhāra-sankhātaŋ paṭisandhi-viññāṇaŋ (*ibid.*).

intermediate knowledges.[1] Again, the 'vital power' is twofold, consisting of physical and psychical life.[2]

The 'Constituents of jhāna' are not acquired in the five kinds of sense-cognition,[3] nor are the 'forces,'[4] in effortless states, nor the 'constituents of the Path,' in [states] not accompanied by their hetu's. Likewise, in perplexed thought, individualization cannot attain to the state of a Path-constituent,[5] a controlling power, or a force. Only one 'Dominant Influence' obtains at one time, according to circumstances, and that only in such apperceptions as are accompanied by two or three [good] roots.

---

§ 5. *Mnemonic.*

What are the factors of life we know?
These in sevenfold mixed category go.
Of good and bad, six 'Hetu's' at the base;[6]
'Factors of jhāna,' five; but nine[7] we trace
Paving the [good, or evil] 'Path.' Of powers,
'Indriya's,' sixteen, 'Forces,' nine are ours.
'Dominant influences,' are four, 'tis said.
And four the 'Nutriments.' Told is each head.

---

[1] Cha ñāṇāni, the knowledge[s] belonging to the three higher Paths and the three lower Fruition[s]. These, together with the two foregoing, are the same Paññindriya-cetasika cultivated and developed in different degrees, and are collectively known as sammā-diṭṭhi.

[2] Rūpārūpavasena.

[3] That is, at the moment of the operation of any one of the five senses in a process of sense-cognition. See Introd. Essay, p. 54.

[4] Read balāni for phalāni in J.P.T.S. text.—Ed.

[5] Though ekaggatā is synonymous with samādhi (the eighth Path-constituent), that property by which the mind necessarily regards its object as an individual, does not amount to, or is not raised to the dignity of, samādhi, when the mind is perplexed. Hence ekaggatā cannot always be rendered by 'concentration.'

[6] Vatthuto. See p. 174, *n*. 1.

[7] Navaka, not twelve as named in the Category, nor the usual eight. Note the other discrepancies in the Mnemonic.—Ed.

§ 6. *Of that which pertains to Enlightenment.*

III.—In the compendium of the parts[1] of Enlightenment we have the following :—

(*a*) The Four kinds of Earnest Applications[2] in Mindfulness :—

(1) contemplation of the body ;
(2) contemplation of the feelings ;
(3) contemplation of consciousness ;
(4) contemplation of [particular] mental states ;[3]

(*b*) the Four Supreme Efforts[4] :—

(1) the endeavour to put away evils that have arisen ;
(2) the endeavour to prevent the arising of unrisen evils ;

[1] The fear of being fanciful restrains from rendering 'pakkhiyā' by either 'facets' or 'wings.' It means 'sides,' but is used for a 'bird.' On the growth of this designation for the thirty-seven, see my preface to the *Vibhanga*, xv., xvi. *Cf.* also *Jātaka*, i. 275.—Ed.

[2] Sati-paṭṭhānaŋ is the sati which is established on its object, by penetration, so to speak, into it (anupavisitvā ālambaṇe pavattatīti attho.—Ceylon Cy.). Hence close application of the mind. Paṭṭhānaŋ has here a different import from that which it bears in Part VIII.

[3] In 'dhammānupassana,' the word 'dhamma,' according to the Ceylon Cy., refers to the fifty-one mental properties, or factors, exclusive of 'feeling' (vedanā), and the rendering of it by 'law,' or any other term, would be quite wide of the mark; for these contemplation-exercises are with reference to one's own mind and body, and not with reference to any extra-personal object. But Ledi Sadaw of Burma takes exception to the above universally accepted view, and says that 'dhammā' here refers to (1) six Nibbana's; (2) five khandha's; (3) twelve āyatana's; (4) seven bojjhanga's; and (5) four ariya-sacca's. He bases his view on the fact that the Buddha himself spoke of these five categories as dhammā, but never of the saññākkhandha and the sankhārakkhandha alone.

The modifying 'sammā' signifies no ordinary efforts, but the unfaltering concentrated assay of one who vows : 'Let me be reduced to skin and bone ; let my blood dry up, but I'll not stop till I succeed !' Hence the word 'right,' if not inaccurate, is scarcely adequate. (*Cf.* *M.* i. 480 ; *S.* ii. 28 ; *A.* i. 50.)

(3) the endeavour to bring about the arising of unrisen good ;

(4) the endeavour to further arisen good.

(*c*) The Four Steps to the Iddhi-Potency[1] :—

(1) desire to act ;

(2) energy ;

(3) thought ;

(4) investigation.

(*d*) The Five Faculties :—

(1) faith ;

(2) energy ;

(3) mindfulness ;

(4) concentration ;

(5) reason.

(*e*) The Five Forces :—

As in (*d*).[2]

(*f*) The Seven Factors of Enlightenment :—

(1) mindfulness ;

(2) searching the truth ;[3]

(3) energy ;

(4) pleasurable interest ;[4]

[1] See this term discussed in Rhys Davids's *Dialogues of the Buddha*, I., 272. *Cf.* also definition of Iddhi in *Vibhanga*, p. 217. Ledi Sadaw writes (p. 314): 'Iddhi is accomplishment. The meaning is "accomplishment of such and such effort." And pādo is "the means by which one arrives at," "attains to" (iddhi). On the ten . . . [as above]. The "potency" is of will (cetanā), not of insight (vipassanā).'

[2] Commentators distinguish, in the Bala's, a more positive and militant aspect of these five instruments of restraint or control (Indriya's).

[3] 'Searching the truth' is paraphrased by vipassanā-paññā (Ceylon Cy.).

[4] If there is any truth in the Hamiltonian law of the inverse ratio of feeling and intellection, pīti cannot be rendered by 'joy,' since the hedonic element *varies inversely* with 'bodhi.' Besides, the intellectual pīti has always a reference to its object, whilst the edonic joy is more or less subjective. See Appendix, Pīti.

(5) serenity;
(6) concentration;
(7) equanimity.[1]

(*g*) The Eight factors of the Path:—

(1) right views;
(2) right aspiration;
(3) right language;
(4) right action;
(5) right livelihood;
(6) right endeavour;
(7) right mindfulness;
(8) right concentration.

Now in these categories, mindfulness, as four earnest applications, is described as one in 'right mindfulness'; and so are the four supreme efforts in 'right endeavour.'

§ 7. *Mnemonic.*

Desire to do, thought, equanimity
And faith, together with serenity,
And zest, right views and aspiratiön,
Endeavour, also abstinence threefold,
Right mindfulness and concentratiön:
Fourteen according to their nature here are told,
But seven and thirty 'neath seven heads the lists unfold.
Conception and serenity,
Interest, and the balanced mind,
Intent, thought, threefold sanity,
Reveal'd, nine in one way,[2] you find.
Energy works in ninefold guise,
And in eight, mindfulness,

[1] Here, according to the comments, the intellectual '**tatra-majjhattatupekkhā**, and not the hedonic **upekkhā**, is intended.

[2] In J.P.T.S. text read **nav'ekaṭṭhānā**.

Concentration in four, and reason[1] wise
In five, faith, two. Peerless
These seven and thirty members stand,
[In Wisdom's kingdom] noblest band.
All, save sometimes the first and third in [consciousness] transcendent lie.
In mundane thought as well, if fit, in course of sixfold purity.

§ 8. *A Compendium of 'the Whole.'*

IV.—In the compendium of 'the whole' we have the following:—

(*a*) The Five Aggregates:—

(1) material body;
(2) feeling;
(3) perception;
(4) sankhāra's;[2]
(5) consciousness.

(*b*) The Five Aggregates as Objects of Grasping[3]:—

as in (*a*).

[1] Pañca paññā. Paññā shines in (1) vīmaŋsiddhipādo; (2) paññindriyaŋ; (3) paññā-balaŋ; (4) dhammavicaya-sambojjhanga; and (5) sammādiṭṭhi.

[2] Here sankhāra is a *label* given to the fifty mental properties other than vedanā and saññā, but this label derives its title from cetanā, chief of these fifty, and determinant of *action*. Sankhāra and kamma are derived from the same root 'kar,' 'to do.' (Abhisankhataŋ sankharotīti sankhāro—that which makes the made. This is the kattusādhana-definition of sankhāra, and is applied to kamma as in sankhāra-paccayā viññāṇaŋ (Part VIII., § 1). See Appendix, Sankhārā. Sankhariyatīti sankhāro—'that which is made, this kammasādhana-definition refers to the conditioned, 'the world,' as in sabbe sankhārā aniccā.

[3] This category serves to show that the khandha's are generally grasped by erring people as attā, the metaphysical ego-entity.

(*c*) The Twelve Āyatana's[1]:—

The Sense-Organs.

(1) the eye;
(2) the ear;
(3) the nose;
(4) the tongue;
(5) the body (*i.e.*, the skin);
(6) the mind;

The Sense-Objects.

(7) the visible object;
(8) sound;
(9) odour;
(10) taste;
(11) tangible object;
(12) cognizable object.

(*d*) The Eighteen Elements[2]:—

the subjective elements, to wit:
(1) eye;
(2) ear;
(3) nose;
(4) tongue;

[1] Āyat'ană cannot here be rendered by a single English word to cover both sense-organs (the mind being regarded as the sixth sense) and sense-objects.

In commenting on the 'chahi phassāyatanehi phussa,' *D.*, i. 45, § 71, Buddhaghosa defines āyatana to mean 'simply place of production, of resort, opportunity (or ground), range (or genus).' In the Aṭṭhasālinī (p. 140), he gives definitions 1, 2, and 3, and adds place of abode, and species or mode, as fourth and fifth. See also Appendix, Āyatana.—Ed.

[2] This triple distinction rests on the conception of any complete sense-impression being threefold.

'On contact between eye (organ of sight) and the visible object there arises visual cognition,' *M.* i., 111; *S.* ii. 72. On the force of Dhātu, see Part VI., and *B. Psy.*, lxxvi., and *cf.* the striking passage in *Sum. Vil.*, i., 193-196. See also Appendix, Dhātu.—Ed.

(5) body (*i.e.*, skin);
(6) mind;[1]

the objective elements, to wit:

(7) sights;
(8) sounds;
(9) odours;
(10) tastes;
(11) touches;
(12) cognizables;[2]

the intellectual elements, to wit:

(13) visual cognition;
(14) auditory cognition;
(15) olfactory cognition;
(16) gustatory cognition;
(17) tactile cognition;
(18) mind-cognition.[3]

(*e*) The Four Ariyan[4] Truths:—

(1) the Ariyan Truth about Ill;
(2) the Ariyan Truth about the origin of Ill;
(3) the Ariyan Truth about the cessation of Ill;
(4) the Ariyan Truth about the Path leading to the cessation of Ill.

Now, here there are sixty-nine principles,[5] consisting of mental concomitants, subtle material qualities, and

[1] Manodhātu. See Appendix, Dhātu.

[2] Dhammadhātu, synonymous with dhammayātana. See *infra*. These differ from dhammārammaṇa, in excluding citta, and paññatti, and pasādarūpa.

[3] Manoviññāṇadhātu is a collective term given to seventy-six classes of consciousness, omitting the twice-fivefold sense (dvipañcaviññāṇadhātu), and the triple element of mind (manodhātuttika). These seventy-six classes are not confined to processes of representative cognition. See Appendix, Dhātu.

[4] See p. 185, *n*. 2.

[5] Dhammā.

Nibbāna, which are reckoned collectively as the sphere of cognizable object,[1] or the objective element of the cognizable.[2] The sphere of mind[2] alone is broken up into seven[3] elements of cognition.

---

§ 9. *Mnemonic.*

Body, feeling, and perception, and the rest that go with mind,[4]
Fifthly, consciousness:—these Five as AGGREGATES have been defined.
Aggregates of Grasping—viewed 'neath aspect of the Triple Plane.
But Nibbana, lacking parts,[5] to group 'mong Aggregates refrain!
Section into '*door*,' and *object*, gives ĀYATANA'S; again
These *with the result arising*:—ELEMENTS we call them then.
Triple-planed round is Sorrow; Craving's Sorrow's Origin;[6]
Third, Nibbana, called Cessation; fourth of the FOUR TRUTHS herein

[1] Dhammāyatana or dhammadhātu.

[2] Manayātana, rendered above under Āyatana simply by 'mind.'

[3] *I.e.*, the five elements of cognitions on occasion of sense, the (triple) element of mind, the elements of mind-cognition. [(*d*), 6, 13-18]. See p. 184, *n*. 3.

[4] Sesa-cetasikā—*i.e.*, sankhārā, on which see p. 182, *n*. 2.

[5] Abhedā, 'lacking distinctions.' The Commentaries explain that Nibbana is undifferentiated into the eleven aspects—viz., past, present, future, distant, near, gross, subtle, high, low, internal, or external, characterizing phenomena. *M.*, iii. 16, 17; *S.*, iii. 47, 48; *Vibh.* 1.

[6] In J.P.T.S. text, read taṇhā samudayo bhave—*i.e.*, according to the Commentators, hoti.

Meant is Path[1] transcendent, other Path-adjuncts[2] and
Fruits excluded.
Thus the Whole of what we know beneath these Five Heads
is included.

Thus ends the Seventh Part, in the Compendium of Philosophy, entitled the Chapter on the Compendium of Categories.

[1] Maggo here refers to the aṭṭhangika-maggo, the eight-fold Path—*i.e.*, the Eight Path-factors—viz., right views, etc.

[2] Maggayuttā refers to the concomitants, other than the above eight Path factors in Path consciousness (Aṭṭhangikavinimuttā sesā maggasampayuttā phassādayo.—Ceylon Cy.).

PART VIII

A COMPENDIUM OF RELATIONS

§ 1. *Introductory.*

Now let me tell e'en as is fit how such
And such a state of things related stands
To other states[1] conditioned like itself.

---

§ 2. *Of the Law of Happening by Way of Cause.*

In the compendium of relations we have two schemata :

A. The law of happening by way of cause ;[2] and
B. The system of correlation.[3]

Of these, the former [A] is a mode marked by the simple condition of the happening of a phenomenon on the occurrence of its sole invariable antecedent phenomenon.[4]

The latter [B] is so-called with reference to the more striking 'occasion' (*i.e.*, casual circumstance) in any one relation.[5]

[1] Dhammānaŋ.

[2] Paṭiccasamuppāda-nayo. 'Law' is a strong term for nayo, which is usually, in the Commentaries, adequately rendered by 'method,' and by 'system,' § 7. *Cf.* Part IX., § 5. However, the prime categorical importance of [A] in Buddhist doctrine justifies the use of 'law' in the scientific sense.—Ed.

[3] *I.e.*, as treated of in the Paṭṭhāna, the Seventh Book of Abhidhamma.

[4] Tabbhāvabhāvī bhāvo embodies J. S. Mill's first Method of Induction. Mill's second Method would be expressed by tad-abhāvabhāvī bhāvo. All the Commentaries read -bhāva-bhāvī.

[5] Āhacca-paccayaṭṭhitiŋ ārabbha. Here paccaya and ṭhiti are used synonomously and appositionally. Hence, the

Teachers more usually expatiate on these two laws in conjunction.

A. *The Law of Happening by Way of Cause.*

The law of happening by way of cause is as follows :—

Because[1] of ignorance, the actions[2] of the mind.

Because of the actions of the mind, consciousness.[3]

Because of consciousness, mind[4] and body.

'occasion' as a 'cause.' 'Paccaya' is derived from paṭi+ √eti, 'to come.' [Kāranaŋ] paṭicca phalaŋ eti etasmāti paccayo :—that (causal circumstance or relation) from which the 'fruit' derived from [a 'cause'] comes.—Ceylon Cy. 'Paccaya' includes 'hetu,' 'kamma'—*i.e.*, 'condition,' and 'cause'—and all other 'causal circumstances,' under which any phenomenon or event or thing takes place. Hence it means any 'causal relation' between things.

[1] Lit., from the ignorance-*relation*. But the Piṭakas leave no doubt that paccaya is of a causal or conditioning nature. See preceding note.

[2] Sankhārā. This, according to the Commentaries, is used as a synonymous term for kamma, and should not be confounded with sankhārakkhandho. On the kattu-sādhana (definition in terms of *agency*) of this term, see p. 182, *n*. 2.

[3] *I.e.*, rebirth-consciousness, which indicates the connection between the saṇkhārā of the past existence and the initial resultant consciousness of the present.

[4] Nāmaŋ. This psychological nāma should not be confounded with the grammatical nāma (noun), or the popular nāma (name). All the three terms are derived from the same verb, namati, 'to incline or bend.' But the mind is termed nāma, because it inclines, at least according to Oriental ideas, towards its object. The grammatical term 'noun' and the popular term 'name' are also termed nāma, because they incline towards the object named. Generally nāma includes viññāṇa, with the rest of the incorporeal factors of personality.

That they are mutually involved is, in the *Saŋyutta-Nikāya*, illustrated by two sheaves of reeds supporting each other (ii. 114). In the present instance these two sheaves are separately spoken of, at least logically distinguished one from the other.—Ed.

Cf. Introd. Essay, p. 13, the phrase 'sphere of consciousness,' where the common consciousness of a cittuppāda is likened to the outer shell, and the remaining incorporeal factors of that state of

Because of mind and body, the sixfold organ.

Because of the sixfold organ, contact.

Because of contact, feeling.

Because of feeling, craving.

Because of craving, grasping.

Because of grasping, becoming.[1]

Because of becoming, birth.

Because of birth, decay and death, sorrow, lamentation, ill, grief, and despair come to be.

Such is the coming to pass of this entire body of ill.

---

§ 3. *Of Aspects of the Law.*

In this law there are three periods, twelve factors,[2] twenty modes,[3] three connections, four groups, three rounds, two roots [of action] to be taken into account.

How so?

Of the Three Periods :—

'Ignorance,' and 'the actions of the mind' belong to the Past; 'birth,' 'decay and death,' to the Future; the intermediate eight, to the Present.[4]

Each of these twelve terms is a Factor. For the

---

consciousness are distinguished as inner contents. It is by distinctions of this kind that Commentaries justify the segregation of viññāṇa, from nāma.

[1] Bhavo includes kammabhavo (the active side of an existence) and upapattibhavo (the passive side). See *infra*, § 5. And the Commentators say that bhava is a contraction of kammabhava rendered below by 'karma-becoming,' *i.e.*, karmic activity. This indicated the connection between the saṅkhārā of the Present and the resultant rebirth-consciousness of the Future.

[2] Angāni. These factors are sometimes spoken of as the Twelve Nidāna's.

[3] Ākāra, lit., 'condition,' includes causal and resultant states. See *infra*, § 4.

[4] This chronological division of the 'chain,' though not explicit in the Piṭakas, is affirmed by Buddhaghosa in *Sum Vil.*, on the Mahā-Nidāna-suttanta.—Ed.

composite term 'sorrow,' etc., is only meant to show incidental consequences of birth. Again, when 'ignorance' and 'the actions of the mind' have been taken into account, craving, grasping, and [karma-] becoming are implicitly accounted for also. In the same manner, when craving, grasping, and [karma-] becoming have been taken into account, ignorance and the actions of mind are [implicitly] accounted for also; and when birth, decay, and death, are taken into account, even the fivefold fruit, to wit [rebirth-], consciousness and the rest are accounted for. And thus:

§ 4. *Of Cause and Fruit.*

Five causes in the Past and Now a fivefold 'fruit';
Five causes Now, and yet to come a fivefold 'fruit,'

make up the Twenty Modes, the Three Connections,[1] and the Four Groups.[2]

§ 5.[3] *Of the Three Rounds.*

The Three Rounds are:

1. the Round of Torment—viz., ignorance, craving, and grasping.

2. the Round of Karma—viz., one part of 'becoming' reckoned as 'karma[4]-becoming,' together with the 'actions of the mind.'

3. the Round of the Result [of karma]—viz., one

[1] The Three Connections are: (1) Between sankhārā and viññāṇa; (2) between vedanā and taṇhā; (3) between bhava and jāti. (1) and (3) are between separate existences, past, present, and future; (2) is between two factors in the same span of life.

[2] The Four Groups include one causal group in the Past, one resultant group in the Present, one causal group in the Present, and one resultant group in the Future, each group consisting of five modes.

[3] This § number and the preceding one might well have been omitted in the P.T.S. Edition.—Ed.

[4] Kamma-bhava. If there is any doubt as to the close connection between 'kamma' and 'sankhārā,' it should be settled by this passage.

part of becoming reckoned as renewed existence,[1] together with the remaining factors.

The two Roots are ignorance and craving.[2]

---

§ 6. *Mnemonic.*

Never, till those Twin Roots shall cease to be,[3]
Can cease the incessant round of misery
For sons of men, for aye oppressed beneath
The long gleaned harvest of decay and death;
For ignorance, as the Āsava's arise,
Holds on its way. And so the Seer wise
Pronounced this Round, this universal chain,
Where ne'er beginning was, round triple plane,
To be the Law, that whatso doth befall
Must happen through a Cause [or not at all][4].

---

§ 7. *Of the System of Correlation.*[5]

The system of correlation comprises the following relations:

The relation of—

1. condition;[6]
2. object;[7]
3. dominance;[8]

[1] Upapatti-bhava. See p. 189, *n*. 1.

[2] =dulness (avijjā=moha) and greed (taṇhā=lobha).

[3] In J.P.T.S. text read mūlā na.

[4] These two lines merely amplify the one term 'Paṭicca-samuppādo,' 'happening because-of.'—Ed.

[5] The following section is a summary of the twenty four relations constituting the subject-matter in the exercises of the Paṭṭhāna-the last or 'Great Book' of the Abhidhamma.—Ed.

[6] Hetu, rendered above by 'root,' or left untranslated. The hetu's primarily *condition* kamma (cetanā), and, secondarily, the kamma's effect. See Appendix, Hetu.

[7] *I.e.*, as presented to a subject, or, for Buddhists, to a personal (ajjhattikaŋ) locus of access or 'door.' See Introd. Essay, p. 2.

[8] Adhipati. *Cf. supra*, Part VII., § 4 (*f*).

4. contiguity ;
5. immediate contiguity ;
6. co-existence ;
7. reciprocity ;
8. dependence ;
9. sufficing condition ;[1]
10. antecedence ;[2]
11. consequence ;[2]
12. succession ;[3]
13. karma ;
14. effect ;
15. support ;
16. control ;[4]
17. jhāna ;
18. means ;[5]
19. association ;
20. dissociation ;
21. presence ;
22. absence ;
23. abeyance ;
24. continuance.

§ 8. *Of Mind and Body as Correlates.*

[For example :—]

Mind may to *mind* SIXFOLD relation bear,
FIVEFOLD to *mind-and-body*,[6] ONE alone
To *body*. Body is to *mind* ONE way
Related. Two relations bear to *mind*

[1] Or *sine quâ non* of sufficing efficiency. See Childers's Dict., 'Upanissaya.'—Ed. The Ceylon Cy. defines 9 as a stronger species of 8.

[2] Or priority and posteriority. Consequence implying merely *post hoc*, not *propter hoc*.—Ed.

[3] More lit., 'repetition of an action.' It is used for 'recurrence.

[4] Indriya. See p. 159, *n*. 2.

[5] Magga, lit., 'path.'

[6] For greater lucidity 'nāma' and 'rūpa' are rendered by the Western concepts 'mind' and 'body.'—Ed.

Mind-body-name-and-notion,[1] while to *itself*
Mind-body may in NINE relations stand.
Sets of relations, SIX.

How may this be?

---

§ 9. *Of how Mind and Body may be Related.*

First, mind is related to mind in six ways:

States[2] of consciousness and their mental concomitants which have just ceased are related to present[3] states of consciousness and their mental concomitants by way of (1) contiguity; (2) immediate contiguity; (3) absence; and (4) abeyance. Again, antecedent apperceptions are related to consequent apperceptions by way of (5) succession (or recurrence), and co-existent states of consciousness and their mental concomitants are mutually related by way of (6) association.

Next, mind is related to mind-and-body in five ways:

The hetu's, jhāna-factors, and Path-factors, are related to co-existing states of mind and body by way of (1) condition; (2) jhāna; and (3) means (respectively). Co-existent volition[4] is related to co-existent states of mind and body by way of (4) karma. So also asynchronous volition is related to states of mind and body brought into existence through karma by way of karma.

Again [mental] aggregates of effects[5] are mutually related, and are related *also* to co-existent states of body by way of (5) effect.[5]

[1] Or 'term-and-concept.' Here both nāmapaññatti and atthapaññatti are intended.

[2] Citta-cetasikā dhammā. See Introd. Essay, p. 25 *f.*, on the succession of states of consciousness in the processes of thought.

[3] Paccuppannānaŋ is paraphrased by Ledi Sadaw as follows: punuppannānaŋ paṭipātiyā uppannānaŋ vā. Literally then, it means 'occurring again.' Burmese translations render by 'succeeding.'

[4] On the twofold functions (psychological and ethical) of Cetanā, see Introd. Essay, pp. 16, 42 *f.*

[5] Vipāka, 'result of karma.' This is not a relation of effect to its cause, but a relation among the effects themselves.

Thirdly, mind is related to body in one way:

Consequent states of consciousness and their mental concomitants are related to this antecedent body[1] by way of (1) consequence.

Fourthly, body is related to mind in one way:

The six bases during life are related to the seven elements of cognition by way of (1) antecedence, and so also are the five kinds of sense-objects to the five processes of sense-cognition.

Fifthly, name-and-notion-mind-and-body[2] are related to mind in two ways—namely, by way of (1) object, and of (2) sufficing condition. In this connection 'object' is of six kinds, consisting of visible [audible] body, etc. But sufficing condition is of three kinds:—sufficing condition in object, sufficing condition in contiguity, and sufficing condition in nature.[3] Of these three only the object to which weight is attached is the sufficing condition in object. States of consciousness, and their mental concomitants which have just ceased, constitute the sufficing condition in contiguity. Sufficing condition in nature is of many kinds—for instance, states of passion, etc., and of faith, etc., pleasure, pain, a person[4], food, physical change, residence—conditions, internal or external, as the case may be—are related to (internal or external) moral and other states. K a r m a, too, is related to its results as sufficing condition in nature.

§ 10.[5] Sixthly, states of mind and body are related to states of mind and body in nine ways, to wit, by way of:

(1) dominance;
(2) co-existence;
(3) reciprocity;

[1] K ā y o, lit., 'an aggregate.' *Cf.* the *Dukapaṭṭhāna* where this phrase recurs so often.—Ed.

[2] P a ñ ñ a t t i - n ā m a - r ū p ā n i, as above, p. 193, *l.* 1. On p a ñ ñ a t t i, see Appendix *s.v.*

[3] P a k a t ū p a n i s s a y o.

[4] Instances of this and the following cases are a friend, wholesome food, agreeable climate, comfortable bed and housing, etc.

[5] Here, again, the P.T.S. edition's division of paragraphs is at fault.

(4) dependence ;
(5) support ;
(6) control ;
(7) dissociation ;
(8) presence ;
(9) continuance,

according to circumstances.

(1) In this connection, the first of these relations occurs in one of two ways :

(i.) The object to which weight is attached is related to states of mind, by way of objective dominance.

(ii.) Co-existent dominant influences, which are of four kinds,[1] are related to co-existent states of mind and body by way of co-existent [dominance].

(2) Next, the relation of 'co-existence' is threefold, thus : states of consciousness and their mental concomitants are related both mutually and also to co-existent bodily states as co-existent states. The great essentials[2] are related both mutually and also to the material qualities derived from them, as co-existent. The basis [of mind] and resultant [mental] states are, at the moment of rebirth, mutually related as co-existent.

(3) The relation of 'reciprocity' is also threefold, thus : States of consciousness and their mental concomitants are reciprocally related ; so are the great essentials ; so is the basis of mind with resultant [mental] states, at the moment of rebirth.

(4) The relation of 'dependence' is also threefold, thus : States of consciousness and their mental concomitants are related by way of dependence, both mutually and also to co-existent bodily states.[3] The great essentials are related

[1] Desire to act, energy, thought, and investigation. See above, Part VII., § 4 *f*.

[2] The 'four elements' in popular Western phrase.

[3] This relation expresses the dependence of bodily states on the mind, and not of the mental states on the body. The first member of a pair of correlates is the 'Nissaya,' that which is depended upon and the other member which depends on it is the Nissita.

by way of dependence, both mutually and also to material qualities derived from them. The six bases are related, by way of dependence, to the seven elements of cognition.[1]

(5) The relation of 'support' is of two kinds, thus: Edible food is related to this body, and immaterial supports[2] are related to co-existent states of mind and body, both by way of support.

(6) The relation of 'control' is threefold, thus: The five sentient organs are related to the five kinds of sense-cognition by way of control;[2] so is the controlling power of bodily vitality to material qualities that have been 'grasped at';[3] so are immaterial controlling faculties to co-existent states of mind and body.

(7) The relation of 'dissociation' is also threefold, thus: At the moment of descent into life,[4] the base of mind is related to results [of karma] by way of co-existent dissociation; so also are states of consciousness and their mental concomitants related to co-existent material qualities, viz., by way of co-existent dissociation.[5] Again, consequent states of consciousness and their mental concomitants are related to this antecedent body by way of consequent dissociation. And, thirdly, the six bases during life are related to the seven elements of cognition by way of antecedent dissociation.

(§ 11).[7] (8) and (9) Lastly, the relations of 'presence' and of 'continuance' are each fivefold, thus:

[1] See above, Part III., § 13.

[2] See p. 177 (*g*).

[3] On Indriya. See p. 159, *n.* 2. From this passage it is clear that Buddhists regard the five sentient organs as Indriya's. Though the word 'faculty' includes both mental and physical powers, 'the eye,' 'the ear,' etc., can hardly be called 'physical powers.'

[4] See above, Part VI., § 4.

[5] *I.e.*, of conception.

[6] This is an interesting parallel to modern 'parallelism' of mind and body. In the next sentence, *cf.* § 7, *n.* 2; § 9, *n.* 1.—Ed.

[7] There should again have been no fresh section here in P.T.S.—Ed.

First, co-existence, next priority,
Then, after-sequence, whereso'er it be,
Support nutritive, power of vital state :—
Such is the group of five we now relate.

---

§ 12. *Of the more General Aspect of Relations.*

Further, all these[1] twenty-four relations are reducible to [these four] :—

I. OBJECT.
II. SUFFICING CONDITION.
III. KARMA.
IV. PRESENCE.

But throughout [this exposition of relations], wherever co-existent material qualities are mentioned, two kinds of co-existent material qualities must always be understood : firstly, during life the material qualities related as co-existent are such as are produced by thought ; secondly, at rebirth the material qualities so related are such as are due to deeds done in a former birth.[2]

§ 13. *Mnemonic.*

Thus all we know—phenomena — in threefold stage of time,
Or freed from time,—as personal,[3] or external (keep the rhyme !)
Conditioned, unconditioned,[4] too, beneath the threefold head

[1] Read, for sabbesu, sabbe pi.—Ed.

[2] Kaṭattā-rūpānaŋ. On kaṭattā karma, see p. 144, n. 4. Here, however, the term is extended to all kinds of janaka-karma.

[3] Ajjhattaŋ.

[4] Sankhatāsankhatā. Sankhata is a synonym of sankhāra, meaning, by kammasādhana definition, that which is formed, fashioned, made, conditioned, or caused.

Of term-and-concept, body, mind—'tis in Paṭṭhāna[1] said—
Are as relations twenty-four (by students to be read).

§ 14. *Of the Term 'Paññatti' and its Import.*

Of that 'threefold head,' 'body' is just the aggregate[2] of material qualities; and 'mind' is the five kinds of the immaterial, that is, the four immaterial aggregates reckoned as mind and mental concomitants, and Nibbana.[3]

But the remaining head 'paññatti' is twofold according as it is made known,[4] or as it makes [things] known.[5] How twofold?

There are, in the first place, *ideas*,[6] such as 'land,' 'mountain,' and the like, designated accordingly,[7] and derived from some mode of physical changes in nature. There are, next, *ideas*, as 'house,' 'chariot,' 'cart,' and the like, [named accordingly and] derived from various modes of construction of materials. Then there are such *ideas* as 'man,' 'individual,' and the like [termed accordingly[7] and] derived from the fivefold set of aggregates. Again, there are *ideas* of locality, time, and the like [made known accordingly[8] and], derived from the revolutions of the moon, and so forth. There are *ideas* like 'pit,' 'cave,' etc. [named accordingly[8] and] derived from a mode of non-

[1] See *e.g.*, p. 21 and *passim* of my edition of *Duka-paṭṭhāna*.—Ed.

[2] Khandho. N.B.—'Body' and 'mind,' as before, stand for nāma-rūpa.—Ed.

[3] It is significant that Nibbana is classed under nāma, as showing that Nibbana is a mental state.—Ed.

[4] Paññāpiyattā; atthapaññatti is made known by saddapaññatti or nāmapaññatti. See Introd. Essay, p. 4 *f.*, on the relativity of the two classes of Paññatti.

[5] Paññāpanato. This has reference to the nāma-paññatti, which makes the atthapaññatti known.—See Introd. Essay.

[6] *I.e.*, ideas or notions (paññatti) corresponding to *things* named or designated.

[7] Tathā tathā paññattā, lit., 'named according to such and such [circumstances].'

[8] See *n.* 7.

contact.[1] There are ideas[2] corresponding to the images of the Kasiṇa-circles, etc. [termed accordingly[1] and] derived from the special exercise of mental culture on this or that Kasiṇa-object.[3]

All such distinctions, though they do not exist in the highest sense, have, nevertheless, as modes of shadowing forth the meaning[4] [of things], become objects of thought-genesis[5] [as our ideas]. And the *idea* is referred to, derived from, or determined by, this or that [*thing*], and is called 'idea of thing,'[6] because it is conceived and reckoned, named, currently expressed, or *made known*.[7] This idea of thing is designated 'atthapaññatti,' because it is *made known*[7] [by term, word, or sign].

In the next place, term,[8] as designating (symbol), is illustrated by the various classes of names, to wit, name, name devised, etc. Any of these classes of names is sixfold according as it is—

[1] Asamphuṭṭhākāraŋ.

[2] Kasiṇa-nimitta. The paṭibhāga-nimitta is intended. This, of course, corresponds to the uggahanimitta, which is the image of the parikamma-nimitta (*cf.* p. 54).

[3] Taŋ taŋ bhūtanimittaŋ. This refers to the parikamma-nimitta of the kasiṇa, 'circle of earth,' etc. On the special exercises of mental-culture on these objects see Part IX. and Introd. Essay, p. 54 *f*.

[4] Atthachāyākārena, 'images or ideas as shadows (*i.e.*, copies) of things.'

[5] Cittuppādānaŋ ārammaṇabhūtā. This and parikappiyamānā (conceived) below show that we are here dealing with the *ideas* of things named.

[6] Paññattīti pavuccati and paññatti nāma refer to atthapaññatti, notion or concept.

[7] Paññāpīyatīti, and paññāpiyattā.

[8] Paññatti. There are six classes of names known to native logico-grammarians. These are (1) nāma, name (of a thing); (2) nāmakamma, name made (or given to a thing); (3) nāmadheyya name long established (on a thing); (4) nāmanirutti, name, expressed in language by means of a term; (5) nāmabyañjana, name showing (the meaning of the thing named); (6) nāmābhilāpa, name suggesting (the meaning of the thing named).

1. a naming of something that exists;
2. a naming of something that does not exist;
3. a naming of something that does not exist by something that does exist;
4. a naming of something that exists by something that does not exist;
5. a naming of something that exists by something that also exists;
6. a naming of something that does not exist by something that also does not exist.

That is to say, when, by a given term, people name something which in the highest sense exists, such as [the aggregates of personality—*e.g.*], body, feeling, etc., then this term is called a name of something existing. When by such a term as 'land,' 'hill,' or the like, people designate something which in the highest sense does not exist, then this term is called a name of something non-existent.[1] And by combination with [these alternatives], the remaining kinds may be understood, as for instance in such terms as 'a *possessor* of sixfold super-intellection,'[2] '*woman's* voice,' 'visual cognition,' 'a *king's son*,' taken in order.

Cf. with this list the older and different classes in the Aṭṭhasālinī. *B. Psy.*, pp. 340, 341, *nn.*—Ed.

[1] Buddhists do not recognize the existence of the Platonic *Idea*, corresponding to any name they may give to a thing. They countenance Nominalism by denying to names existence as a fact in Nature; they countenance Conceptualism by holding that copies of things exist in mind as ideas; they countenance Realism by holding that the four Essentials and their derivatives do exist as a reality. In denying the existence of 'land' or 'hill' therefore, Buddhists must not be understood as denying the existence of the four Essentials and of derivatives known as earthy matter. See this note developed in Appendix, Attha.

[2] Read chaḷābhiñño; lit.: 'a six-super-intellect-*or*.' *Cf.* Part IX., § 4.—Ed. In this compound name Buddhists say that the sixfold Abhiññā is a fact, but that 'possessor' is a *name* given to the five aggregates. So also in the compound term 'woman's voice,' the voice does exist as a sound, but 'woman' is a name also given to the five aggregates. Thus, though they admit the existence of the five aggregates as things in the highest sense, they deny this sort of existence in the possessor or the woman.

§ 15. *Mnemonic.*

By following the *sound* of speech thro' hearing's path
brought to our ken,
By following next the *sign*, when mind forthwith its door
flings open,[1] then
The *sense* of things cognized becomes. But of the signs
themselves, 'tis said
They [in the far-off ages] were by world-convention
fashionèd.

Thus ends the Eighth Part in the Compendium of Philosophy, being the Chapter entitled the Compendium of Relations.

[1] On the sequence of the processes of thought involved in understanding the meaning of the word heard, see Introd. Essay, p. 85.

PART IX

THE COMPENDIUM OF THE STATIONS OF RELIGIOUS EXERCISES.[1]

§ 1. *Introductory.*

HENCEFORTH the twofold stations will I tell
Of exercises whereby we may reach
The Calm and Insight [of the holy life].

§ 2. *Of Calm.*[2]

The Compendium of exercises in calm comprises—

I. The seven stations of exercise in calm :

1. the ten hypnotic circles ;[3]
2. the ten impurities ;
3. the ten recollections ;
4. the four illimitables ;
5. the one notion ;[1]

[1] Kammaṭṭhānaŋ. This term, not occurring in this specialized sense, in the Piṭakas, means, lit., 'place and occasion of work (or action).' (*Cf. M.* ii. 197, where it refers to agriculture and trade.) The use of the circles for inducing the quasi-hypnotic states, and of intense visualizations prescribed for this or that exercise, suggested to me the Catholic system of 'stations' for meditation, station and [s]ṭhāna being moreover alike in meaning and etymology.—Ed.

[2] Samatho. Kilese samathetīti samatho. Called calm because it *lulls* the passions. Samatha is a course of auto-hypnosis in which the Five Hindrances are, so to speak, *put to sleep*.

[3] Kasiṇa-maṇḍalaŋ.

6. the one discrimination ;
7. the four stages of Arūpa-jhāna.[2]

II. The six characters :[3]

1. the passionate ;
2. the malevolent ;
3. the muddle-headed ;
4. the trusting ;
5. the understanding ;[4]
6. the imaginative.[5]

III. The three stages of mental culture :

1. the preliminary ;
2. the accessory ;
3. the ecstatic.

IV. The three symbols :

1. the preliminary ;
2. the image ;
3. the transformed after-image.[6]

How [are the classes detailed] ?

I.—1. The ten Circles are of earth, water, fire, or air, blue, yellow, red or white, of space or of light.

2. The ten Impurities are a bloated, discoloured, or festering corpse, one with crackled skin, gnawn and

[1] Saññā. Notion corresponds better than 'perception' to the psychologically vague meaning here of the Pāli word.—See Introd. Essay, p. 40, on this term.—Ed.

[2] Called Āruppa (adjectival form) for short.—Ed.

[3] Caritā. The nearest Western equivalent I know is the German 'Wandel,' but in this case disposition (of character) or temperament—*i.e.*, Wandel of mind, rather than of concrete life, is meant.—Ed.

[4] Buddhicaritā. Is 'buddhi' a Sānkhya survival? It is very late Pāli.—Ed.

[5] *I.e.*, constructively imaginative. On Vitakka, see II., § 2 and Introd. Essay.—Ed.

[6] Paṭibhāganimittaŋ, 'the image conceptualized,' or 'the concept, similar to the image,' but free from the faults of the original symbol.

mangled, bitten in pieces, or mutilated and in fragments, a bloody corpse, or one worm-infested, or a skeleton.[1]

3. The ten Recollections[2] are those of the Buddha, the Doctrine, the Order, virtue, liberality, the gods, peace,[3] death, mindfulness regarding the body, mindfulness regarding respiration.

4. The four Illimitables are love, pity, appreciation,[4] and equanimity.[5] They are also called the Sublime Abodes.

5. The one Notion is that of the offensiveness of material food.

6. The one Discrimination is that of discriminating (in a compound) the four Essentials.[6]

7. The Four Stages of Arūpa-jhāna are the conception of the infinity of space, etc.[7]

Thus there are, in all, forty stations of exercise in the exposition of 'Calm.'

---

§ 2A. *Of the Suitability of Different Exercises.*

Among these forty the exercises reckoned suitable (1) for a passionate habit of mind are the ten impurities and mindfulness regarding the body; (2) for a malevolent habit of mind, the four illimitables, and the four coloured circles; (3) for a muddle-headed, and for an imaginative habit of mind, respiration exercise;[8] (4) for a trusting habit of mind, the six recollections of the Buddha, etc.;

[1] These sights were easy to meet with in a cemetery or charnel place, to which flesh-eating beasts and birds had access, such a spot being among those prescribed for meditation.—Ed.

[2] Or Meditations.

[3] Upasama, implying past struggle to win it. Nibbana is here intended (Ceylon Cy.).

[4] Sympathy with joy and success. See Part II., § 2.

[5] The intellectual tatramajjhattalupekkhā, and not the hedonic upekkhā, is here intended.

[6] *I.e.*, elements. See Part VI., § 2.—Ed.

[7] See Part I., § 10.

[8] This is described in *D.* ii. 291 . . ., *M.* i. 56; iii. 89 . . ., *Paṭis.* i. 162 *f.* . . .—Ed.

(5) for an understanding habit of mind, the recollections of death and peace,[1] the one notion, and the one discrimination.

The remaining stations of exercise are all suitable for every one. Moreover, in choosing the hypnotic circle, a wide one is suitable for a muddle-headed habit of mind, a little one for an imaginative habit of mind.[2]

So far for the section on suitability.

---

§ 3. *Of Mental Culture.*[3]

In all these [forty exercises] the preliminary stage of culture is attainable. In the first eight Recollections and in the two single exercises, only the accessory stage of culture is attained; there is no ecstasy. In the remaining thirty stations of exercise the culture of ecstasy is also attained.

Again, the ten circles and the exercise in respiration pertain to all five jhānas. The ten Impurities and mindfulness regarding the body pertain to the first jhāna, the three first Illimitables pertain to the fourth jhāna; equanimity to the fifth jhāna. Thus twenty-six stations of exercise can induce Rūpaloka jhānas, while the four Arūpa exercises can induce their respective stages of Arūpaloka jhāna.

So far for the section on mental culture.

[1] Here vūpasama. See prev. p. n. 3.

[2] Ledi Sadaw, probably following earlier authorities, prescribes the size of a threshing-floor (khala-maṇḍalādi-pamāṇaṃ) for the muddle-headed, and a diameter of a span and four inches (vidatthi-caturaṅgula-pamāṇaṃ) for the imaginative.

[3] Bhāvanā.

---

§ 4. *Of the Hypnotic Symbols.*[1]

Of these three, loosely speaking,[2] the preliminary symbol and the image are attainable, according to the nature of the object, when practising any of these stations; but the transformed after-image is only got in the [twenty-two][3] exercises with the [ten] circles, the [ten] impurities, the [one] mindfulness regarding the body,[4] and the [one] mindfulness regarding respiration. For it is by attending to the transformed after-image that accessory and ecstatic concentration develops. How is that?

For a beginner who, in [gazing at his] earth or other circle, grasps the sense-symbol, that object is called his preliminary symbol, and that exercise his preliminary culture. But when the symbol is thoroughly grasped by the mind, and when it appears to the mind-door as if one saw it with the eye,[5] then it is this object which is termed the symbol of the image, and that culture becomes well established. Again, in the case of one who is thus well established, and who, after that advanced stage, gives himself to sustained contemplation concerning the image-symbol, with the [degree of] concentration gained from the preliminary stage, then, when that object similar to the image-symbol,[6] freed from its physical base,[7] reckoned as a

[1] Lit., gocara is 'cattle-range,' but is used to mean 'range,' 'field,' *Gebiet* of any specific kind.—Ed.

[2] Pariyāyena. Or, by way of concession—*i.e.*, not necessarily, not strictly speaking.

[3] See § 2, (1).

[4] Koṭṭhāsa, lit., 'part,' 'section,' applied to any organ of body. Buddhists regard the body as made up of the thirty-two koṭṭhāsa's. Here it stands for the kāyagatāsati. Under kāyānupassanā both the kāyagatāsati and the ànāpānāssati are included.

[5] The eye being then closed, or the object absent (Ceylon Cy.).

[6] Tappaṭibhāgaŋ, lit., 'similar to *that*,' hence a copy.

[7] Vatthu-dhamma-vimuccitaŋ. Freed, too, from the imperfections of that base, a purified, ideal copy (Ceylon Cy.).

concept,[1] and accomplished by culture-practice,[2] is well established in, and well driven into, the mind, the transformed after-image-symbol is said to have been well-developed.

Of Jhāna concerned with the Rūpaloka.

Thenceforth contemplation by way of the accessory stage, stripped of obstacles and called concentration of Kāmaloka experience, is said to be accomplished. After that, to one who has maintained that transformed after-image by accessory concentration, the first jhāna of the Rūpaloka plane supervenes.[3] After that, to one who has cultivated that first jhāna by means of the five habits, to wit, turning[4] the attention to the first jhāna, inducing and maintaining it,[5] pre-determining the period of its maintenance,[6] emerging from it, and reflecting on it,[7] for the purpose of putting away the grosser features beginning with the initial imagination, etc.,[8] and of striving to bring about the subtler features, beginning with sustained imagination, etc.,[8] the second, and higher jhānas supervene, in due order.

[1] Paññatti sankhātaŋ. Here attha-paññatti is intended. The after-image, though similar to the image, being freed from its physical base, cannot be depicted to sense or imagination. Hence it is best rendered by concept.

[2] Bhāvanāmayaŋ, 'brought into existence by practice,' or, as Ledi Sadaw writes, 'accomplished by the force of the cultured thoughts' (kevalaŋ bhāvanā-citta-balena pasiddhaŋ).

[3] Appeti, explained in the comments by appanāvasena pavattatīti, 'occurs by way of ecstasy.'

[4] Āvajjana-vasitā. On Āvajjana, see p. 85, *n.* 3.

[5] Samāpajjana-vasitā, lit., 'the habit of entering into jhāna.' *Cf.* p. 59 on Samāpatti.

[6] Adhiṭṭhānavasitā. Without this habit of predetermining the period of jhāna, the last habit would tend to maintain it for an indefinite period.

[7] Paccavekkhanā vasito, lit., the reviewing habit, which is post-jhānic. On these habits see Introd. Essay, p. 58.

[8] Vitakka is here rendered by 'imagination' to show that the object of jhāna is the transformed after-image. By 'etc.,' the other jhāna-factors in order are to be understood, See Part I., § 8.

Thus, in the circles of earth, etc.—twenty-two stations of religious exercise in all—the transformed after-image may be acquired. Of the remaining [eighteen stations], the Illimitables are carried on in dependence on the concept 'beings.'[1]

Of Jhāna concerned with the Arūpaloka.

Now to one who, by way of infinity,[2] practises his preliminary exercise on space obtained by abstraction[3] from any of the circles except the space-circle,[4] the first stage of Arūpa-jhāna supervenes. To one who, by way of infinity,[2] practises this preliminary exercise on the cognition of the first Arūpa stage, the second stage of Arūpa-jhāna supervenes. To him who practises the preliminary exercise on the non-existence of the [aforesaid] cognition of the first Arūpa stage, mentally repeating 'there is naught whatever!' the third stage of Arūpa-jhāna supervenes. To him who practises the preliminary exercise on [the cognition of] the third Arūpa stage, mentally repeating: 'This is calm! this is excellent! the fourth stage of Arūpa-jhāna supervenes.

And in the ten[5] remaining stations of exercise, when one has practised the preliminary exercise of meditating on the attributes of the Buddha, etc., and when that symbol-

[1] Sattapaññattiyaŋ pavattanti. Here atthapaññatti is intended.

Cf. any description of the procedure in these exercises—*e.g.*, *Paṭisambhidā II.*, 130 *ff.*; '*Mettakathā*'; *D.* ii. 186; *Dialogues of the Buddha*, ii. 219-20.—Ed.

[2] The formula for repetition in this exercise is 'space is infinite!' 'space is infinite!' and that in the following exercise is 'consciousness is infinite!' 'consciousness is infinite!'

[3] Ugghāhetvā laddhamākāsaŋ—*i.e.*, amanasikāravasena uddharitvā, prescinding by way of inattention (to the kasiṇa).—Ceylon Cy.

[4] Because we cannot abstract space from space.—(Ceylon Cy.)

[5] *I.e.*, the first eight Recollections and the two single exercises.

notion is well grasped, then the preparation in that symbol-notion is firmly set up, and the accessory stage is also attained.

§ 5. *Of Supernormal Intellection.*[1]

Now, if one has emerged from the fifth stage of jhāna [*used as*] the foundation for supernormal intellection, and performs the preliminary exercise of meditating on the phenomenon determined on, etc.,[2] then the fifth stage of jhāna proceeding by way of that intellection supervenes, with a visible, or other object as its object according to circumstances. By supernormal intellection we mean :

> The powers named Iddhi,[3] the Celestial Ear,
> Discerning others' thoughts. Reminiscence
> Of former births, and fifth, the Heavenly Eye.

So far for the section on the scope of the exercises. Here end also the methods for exercise in calm.

[1] Abhiññā. The reader who is conversant with Pali should not fail to consult *Paṭisambhidā-magga*, i., pp. 112 *ff.* (Mahāvagge Ñāṇakathā), where occurs the oldest account we have of the process of inducing abhiññā. Each of the five modes named in the verses above are dealt with in the same order, nor is the sixth, the certificate of Arahantship, omitted: 'that insight which is knowledge in extinction of the āsava's.' In each case the brother has to begin by so exercising himself in the Four Steps to Iddhi (*supra*, p. 180), that mind and body become 'perfected in training, wholly in subjection, pliant and adaptable' to the will. It is interesting, too, that 'reminscence of former births' is ushered in by meditation on the Paṭicca-samuppāda. See also Appendix: Abhiññā.—Ed.

[2] Adhiṭṭheyyādikaŋ, 'any phenomenon *willed*,' and others. See Introd. Essay, p. 62.

[3] On the ten kinds of Iddhi in general, and on Iddhi-vidhā in particular, see Introd. Essay, p. 60 *f.* On the kinds of Abhiññā, see *S.* ii. 216; i. 191; ii. 217; v. 282, and detailed account in *D.* i., 78-84. The sixth Abhiññā, it will be noted, is purely ethical perfection (see *n.* 1). Abhiññā is called vijjā *D.* i., 100; and paññā in *D.* i., 124; *Dialogues of the Buddha*, i, 157, *n.*—Ed.

This proves once more that Paññindriya-cetasika is the underlying principle or psychological ultimate of every form of knowledge.

§ 6. *Of Insight.*

In the stations for exercises in insight there is

I. The sevenfold category of 'Purity,'[1] to wit:

1. Purity of morals.
2. Purity of mind.
3. Purity of views.
4. Purity of escaping from doubt.
5. Purity of vision in discerning what is Path and what is not.
6. Purity of intellectual vision which is knowledge of progress.[2]
7. Purity of vision which is knowledge [possessed by those in the Four Paths].

II. There are also the Three Marks:[3]

1. The Mark of Impermanence.
2. The Mark of Ill.
3. The Mark of No-Soul.

III. There are also the Three Contemplations:

Of (1-3) Impermanence, Ill, No-Soul.

IV. There are also the Ten Knowledges[4] of Insight:

1. Knowledge of things [in general], as composite.[5]
2. Knowledge of [composite] things as waxing and waning.

[1] Purging the whole being, and so attaining Insight, is the theme of Buddhaghosa's great work *Visuddhi Magga.* In it this category is discussed in great detail, parts i. and ii. being occupied with (1) and (2), part iii. with (3)-(7).—Ed.

[2] Paṭipadā is that by which one arrives at higher distinctions, being the way leading to the Path. It is the whole course of the Vipassanā-practice. See IV., below.

[3] Or salient features. See Part VI., § 4.

[4] Ñāṇāni. 'Knowledges—in common use with Bacon and . . . till after . . . Locke—ought not to be discarded.' Hamilton on Reid. Note A, sec. 5.—Ed.

[5] Sammasana-ñāṇaŋ, lit., 'handling-knowledge,' resulting from the 'handling' of things as composite. It supersedes the older

3. Knowledge of [waning] things, as dissolving.[1]
4. Knowledge of [dissolving] things as fearful.
5. Knowledge of [fearful] things as dangerous.
6. Knowledge of [dangerous] things as something wherewith to be disgusted.
7. Knowledge of [disgusting] things as something wherefrom to wish to escape.
8. Knowledge of things as something to be reconsidered[2] [in order to escape therefrom].
9. Knowledge of things[3] [reconsidered] as something concerning which to feel indifference.
10. Knowledge which is qualification[4] [for the Path].

V. There are also the Three Emancipations :[5]

1. Emancipation [by the concept of] 'Empty.'
2. Emancipation [by the concept of] 'No-Sign.'
3. Emancipation [by the concept of] 'Not hankered after.'

---

term sankhata (conditioned). The knowledge of things as composite, and the knowledge of things as conditioned, have reference to the Three Marks, which both the conditioned and the compound unmistakably bear.

[1] Read for bhavanga (J.P.T.S.) bhanga, as in *Vis. Magga* meaning, lit., 'rupture.'—Ed.

[2] Paṭisankhā—*i.e.*, reconsidered with reference to the very same Three Marks.

[3] Sankhārā, *i.e.* sankhariyatīti, 'that which is made'), and not, here, the sankhataŋ sankharotīti sankhāro, 'that which makes what is made,' of the kattu-sādhana, or agency-definition). See p. 182, *n.* 2, and Appendix Sankhārā, on the different significations of this term. Although sankhārā is not expressly mentioned in the foregoing, the student should bear in mind that the whole course of Vipassanā up to this deals with 'things' under the aspect of one or other of the Three Marks, not necessarily under all the three aspects together. The upekkhā here is the intellectual tatramajjhattatā, and not the hedonic upekkhā—that is, equanimity or mental equipoise among environing 'things.'

[4] Anuloma, lit., 'fitting,' is that which fits, equips, or qualifies one for the higher. See Introd. Essay, p. 55, and p. 129, *n.* 2.

[5] On these three, see *B. Psy.*, 91, 92, *n.* and references—Ed.

The second, animitta, is explained by the Commentators as

VI. There are also the Three Channels[1] of Emancipations.

1-3. Contemplation of these Three Emancipations.

How [are these heads detailed]?

§ 7. *Of the Divisions of the Exercises in Purity.*

I.—1. Purity of morals is the four kinds of utterly pure conduct entitled:

(*a*) discipline as prescribed by the Pāṭimokkha.[2]
(*b*) discipline of [mental and bodily] faculties.[3]
(*c*) utter purity of conduct connected with livelihood.
(*d*) conduct in connection with the necessaries of life.[4]

2. Purity of mind is the twofold concentration of the accessory and the ecstatic stage.[5]

3. Purity of views is the comprehension of mind-and-body with reference to their [respective] features,[6] essen-

---

the absence of the signs of (1) permanence (niccanimitta-abhāvato); (2) passions, etc. (rāgādīnimittarahitattā); (3) all conditionings (sabbasankhāranimitta-abhāvato); (4) hallucinations (vipallāsanimitta-abhāvato). Thus there are four kinds of nimitta's to be reckoned with. The first of these thoughts is, perhaps, intended to get rid of the sassataditṭhi, according to which people often regard impermament things as permanent. Anicce niccanti pavattaŋ vipallāsanimittaŋ. Ceylon Cy. Thus (1) and (4) are taken in conjunction. On the three kinds of vipallāsa, see p. 216, *n.* 4. The third concept might be positively rendered by 'absolute content,' as in Part VI., § 14.

[1] Lit., 'mouths,' mukhāni, also 'faces.'

[2] See Childers's Dict., *s.v.* Pāṭimokkha; Rhys Davids's *Buddhism*, p. 162.

[3] Lit., 'discipline of control'—*i.e.*, sense-control.

[4] Clothing, food, lodging, medicine.

[5] See Part IV., § 7.

[6] Lakkhaṇa here is explained in the comments by sāmañña-sabhāvo, the ordinary feature of *each* thing.

tial properties,[1] resulting phenomena,[2] and proximate causes.[3]

4. Purity of escaping[4] from doubt is the comprehension of the causal relations of mind and body comprehended as aforesaid.[5]

5. After escaping from doubt, the meditator, bearing in mind the method of aggregates, etc.,[6] groups, by way of those syntheses, the triple planed [universe of] things, which are differentiated into past [present], etc,[7] and the causal relations of which have been comprehended as aforesaid.[8] Understanding 'Impermanence' by reason of dissolution,[9] 'Ill,' by reason of fearfulness, and 'No-Soul,' by reason of the absence of a [substantial] entity,[10] he contemplates[11] the Triple Mark by the 'knowledge of things as composite' (§ 6, IV., 1) by way of duration, continuity, or moment.[12] Next he contemplates again and again[13] the waxing and waning [of things] by the know-

[1] Raso, lit., 'taste.' Rasa is either kiccarasa, 'function,' or sampattirasa, 'property.'

[2] Paccupaṭṭhānaŋ, lit., 'that which re-appears.' Its two aspects are: upaṭṭhānākārā-paccupaṭṭhānaŋ, 'resulting modes,' 'state or condition which appears'; phala-paccupāṭṭhānaŋ, 'resulting effect which appears.

[3] Padaṭṭhānaŋ, omitted in J.P.T.S. The four terms here named are used in post-Piṭakan exegesis as constituting a scheme of definition at least as definite as the post-Aristotelian scheme of genus, species, property, and accident.—Ed.

[4] Vitaraṇa, lit., 'transcending,' from 'tarati', 'to swim across.'

[5] Tesaŋ eva nāmarūpānaŋ.

[6] Khandhādi-nayam ārabbha.

[7] Atītādibhedabhinnesu. See p. 185, *n.* 5, for the eleven (Piṭakan) aspects of differentiation into past, present, future internal, external, gross, subtle, high, low, distant, and near, which Nibbana lacks.

[8] Tathā pariggahitesu sapaccayesu.

[9] Aniccaŋ khayaṭṭhena, lit., 'impermanence,' because of the meaning of dissolution.

[10] Lit., 'because they have no pith' (sāra).

[11] Lit., 'handles,' sammasati.

[12] *I.e.*, by way of space or point of time.

[13] Samanupassati.

ledge so designated (§ 6, IV., 2), by way of their causal relations and of moments. To such an one come

Aura,[1] zest,[2] serenity, firm faith,[3] and effort[4] too,
Ease, knowledge, mindfulness,[5] indifference,[6] and heart's desire.[7]

Now purity of vision in discerning what is Path and what is not, is the discrimination of what bears the characteristic marks of Path-consciousness and what does not. This is done by the understanding of these [ten] inimical influences which corrupt Insight.

6. Purity of vision in knowledge of progress comprises the Nine Knowledges[8] of one who, thus set free from inimical influences, contemplates[9] the Triple Mark by a regular progression in Insight,[10] from the knowledge of the

[1] Obhāso: 'rays emitted from the body on account of insight.'—Ceylon Cy. (§§ 7, 8 are misplaced in J.P.T.S. text, and omitted.—Ed.)

[2] Pīti (pleasurable interest).

[3] Adhimokkha, the controlling faculty of strong or resolute faith (balavasaddhindriya).

[4] Paggaho, sammappadhāna-kicca-sādhako, viriyasambojjhangasankhāto.—Ceylon Cy.

[5] Upaṭṭhānā, anussarana-samatthā upaṭṭhānasankhātā sati.—Ceylon Cy. A word oftener in *Paṭisambhidā Magga* than in the earlier Piṭaka books.—Ed.

[6] The Ceylon Commentator says that this represents *both* the tatramajjhattatā and the āvajjanupekkhā. But as 'balance of mind' is a useful adjunct of vipassanā, I am inclined to take only the latter—viz., absence of pleasure or pain in reflection.

[7] Nikanti. These ten phases which 'defile' and are inimical to vipassanā, and therefore termed vipassanupakkilesaparibandhā, are dealt with in the *Visuddhi Magga*, part iii., chap. xxi. One who has practised the first two kinds of insight, in the order and manner indicated, is liable to these defilements while practicing the next stage—*e.g.*, he may feel pleasure at having an aura and think that this constitutes Path-experience, and so stay his progress by self-deceit.

[8] In IV., the last nine.

[9] Paṭipajjati, lit., 'practises.'

[10] Vipassanāparamparāya, lit., 'by a succession of Insights.'

waxing and waning of things up to the knowledge with which he fits himself [for the Path].[1]

When he, thus progressing, has come to full maturity of Insight [he can discern]: 'Now will the ecstasy of the Path arise.'[2] Thereupon, as the reflection by way of the mind-door suspends the life-continuum, two or three [flashes of] consciousness [revealing] insight concerning any one of the Three Marks occur, by name 'preparation,' 'approximation,' and 'qualification.'[3] That 'knowledge of things as something concerning which to feel indifference' which, when its climax is reached, is coupled with the 'knowledge by which one qualifies oneself [for the Path]' is also described as 'Insight that leads to Emergence.'[4]

After this, the consciousness of the Initiate[5] leaning upon Nibbana occurs, over-mastering kinship with the worldly, and evolving kinship with the Ariya's.

Immediately after that consciousness, THE PATH, namely, [consciousness] discerning the fact of Ill, expelling the fact of its Cause, realizing the fact of its Cessation, cultivating the fact of the Way [to Cessation], descends into the avenue of ecstatic thought.[6] After that Path-consciousness, when two or three [flashes of] the consciousness of fruition have taken their course, there comes subsidence into the life-continuum; and then, again, the life-

[1] Udayabbayañāṇato paṭṭhāya yāvānulomā.

[2] Idāni appanā uppajjissatīti. Here appanā stands for the Lokuttarā Appanā. On the significance of Appanā, see p. 129, and Introd. Essay, p. 56 *f.*; 68.

[3] Anuloma. See Part IV., § 7, and Introd. Essay, p. 55.

[4] Vuṭṭhāna, lit., 'standing up out of,' is usually applied as a religious term, to revival from jhāna-abstraction, implying a rest or fruition after toil. (*Cf.* its use in 'rising after childbirth,' Childers's Dict.) Here it stands for the Path, as a 'coming out of more' worldly views.—Ed.

[5] Gotrabhu, meaning 'who has become kin.' 'Ariya's,' as already said, refers to the Buddhas and their eight classes of elect followers, the kinship being the new higher ethical nature evolved.—Tr. and Ed.

[6] This is described as the process of thought-transition to the Path (Magga-vīthi). See Introd. Essay, p. 68.

continuum is interrupted and the knowledges concerned with 'review' occur.

§ 8. *Mnemonic.*

On Path and Fruit and on Nibbana blest
The wise doth meditate. As to the rest—
The 'torments' put away and other ills—
Now and again[1] reflection ('s cup he fills).
The fourfold Path, that thus by right degree
With sixfold Purity must practised be,
Is Purity of knowledge making us SEE.

So far for the section on Purity.

§ 9. *Of Emancipation.*

Here, the contemplation of No-Soul,[2] as letting go the firm belief in a soul,[3] is a channel of emancipation, called the 'contemplation of Emptiness.' Again, the contemplation of Impermanence, as letting go the sign of hallucination[4] [is a channel of emancipation], called the 'contemplation of the Signless,' and the contemplation of Ill, as letting go that 'hankering-after' which is craving, [is a

[1] Read, vā na vā.—Ed. Hīne is the contraction of pahīne: 'those that have been got rid of.'—Ceylon Cy. The Ariya now reviews (1) the Path he has just attained; (2) the Fruit of that Path he has just enjoyed; (3) the Nibbana he has intuited, though not quite realized, as an object of the consciousness called of the Path and of Fruit. The upakkilesa's he may, or may not review.

[2] The word 'attā' means 'self,' but whereas the Buddhists accepted and used the term 'self' as a convenient abstraction for the personal unity of a moment or a lifetime, they only rejected a permanent personal unity such as is implied, less ambiguously, in 'soul.' —Ed.

[3] Attābhinivesaŋ-abhiniveso=daḷhagāho, lit., 'strong hold.'—Ceylon Cy.

[4] Vipallāsa. There are three kinds of vipallāsa—namely, saññā-vipallāsa (erroneous perception), citta-vipallāsa (erroneous ideas), and diṭṭhi-vipallāsa (erroneous views), by which people regard impermanent things as permanent (anicce niccan ti). And these three vipallāsas are called nimitta, 'sign.' Hallucination is itself the 'sign.'

channel of emancipation] called the 'contemplation of the "Not-Hankered-after.'"

Hence the Path receives three names according to the course taken by 'Insight leading to Emergence':—namely, when that Insight discerns [things] as without soul, the Path is called 'Empty-release';[1] when it discerns [things] as impermanent, the Path is called 'Signless-release'; when it discerns things as evil, the Path is called 'Not-hankered-after-release.' The Fruit likewise receives these three names according to those three ways of coming into the Path along the avenues of the Path.

However, in the process of attaining full fruition, it is only the means — namely, insight by which respective 'fruits' arise to those exercising insight after the manner above described—that gives the names, 'Empty-release,' etc. Nevertheless, the fact of the [common] object,[2] and of common essential properties, causes this triad of names to be applied equally to all everywhere.[3]

So far for the section on emancipation.

§ 10. *Of the Individual.*

Now here, he who has cultivated the Path of Stream-Attainment, and by putting away erroneous views and doubt, goes with all rebirth-to-misery banished, is called Stream-winner to the limit of seven times.[4] And he who has cultivated the Path of Once-Returning, from the attenuation [to which he has brought] lust, hate, and

[1] *I.e.*, release [through discernment of] emptiness [as to soul]. It is difficult to get renderings less uncouth but equally faithful, of these terms, so full of home-truth to a Buddhist. We need a John Bunyan here, or at least the aid of glosses, *e.g.* 'Void-of-soul Release,' 'No-lasting-sign Release, 'End-of-Baneful-Longing Release.'—Ed.

[2] Nibbana.

[3] Sabbattha sabbesaŋ—*i.e.*, to all the eight classes of Ariya's attaining the Path or enjoying the Fruit thereof, in every process of Path-thought, or Fruit-consciousness.

[4] Paramo, 'at most'—*i.e.*, limited to seven more rebirths, at the very outside, in the happier forms of Kāmaloka existence.

nescience[1] is called Once-Returner, once more only to come back to this world.[2] And he who has cultivated the path of Never-Returning, by putting away utterly the lust of sense and ill-will, is called Never-Returner, coming no more back to things as we know them[3] (in Kāmaloka). And he who has cultivated the path of Supreme Worth, by putting away utterly the 'Torments,'[4] is called Arahant, he who with āsavas extinct is in all the world WORTHY of its offerings.

So far for the section on the Individual.

§ 11. *Of the Great Attainments.*

Of these, the process of the full attainment of fruition is common to all [in the Paths] according to the fruit which each man wins. But the full attainment of Cessation[5] is only won by Never-Returners and Arahants. In this [process] such an one successively induces the sublime[6] attainment of the first jhāna, etc.,[7] and on waking from each jhāna he contemplates [by way of the Triple Mark] the conditioned phenomena implicated therein.[8] And [by this alternative procedure] he goes as far as [the jhāna of] the Sphere of Pure Nothingness. And after

[1] Dulness is not sufficiently strong to express the degree of Moha attenuated by the Once-Returner. *Cf. Dh. S.*, §§ 362-64.

[2] Imaŋ lokaŋ is, according to commentators, applicable to all the seven happier realms of Kāmaloka.

[3] Itthattaŋ is exactly the 'this thusness' of Artemus Ward, and it is regrettable that so good a word should as yet be outside the pale of serious English.—Ed.

[4] Part VII., § 2, I. (i.).

[5] Nirodha—*i.e.*, of consciousness in trance.

[6] Mahaggata. See p. 101, *n.* 4.

[7] Yathakkamaŋ paṭhama-jhānādi mahaggatasamāpattiŋ samāpajjitvā. By 'ādi,' 'etc.,' it is intended to include the first eight jhāna-samāpatti's.

[8] Tattha-gate sankhāradhamme tattha tatth'eva vipassanto. The conditioned phenomena implicated in each jhāna, from which the meditator has just awakened, are now contemplated under the aspects of the Triple Mark. The word vipassati is invariably associated with the Triple Mark.

the preliminary function of resolving what should be resolved, etc.,[1] he attains to the jhāna of the Sphere of Neither Consciousness nor Unconsciousness. In him after two apperceptive flashes of ecstasy [of this jhāna] the continuum of thought is suspended. Hence he is called 'Winner of Cessation.'

At the time of reviving, if he be a Never-Returner, consciousness of the Never-Returning 'fruit' occurs to him but once. Or if he be an Arahant, consciousness of the Supreme Worth occurs to him but for a single moment. Then follows lapse into life-continuum. Thereafter comes the review [of the respective 'fruit'].

So far for the section on the great attainments.

Here end also the stations of exercise in insight.

On this wise must he cultivate who would attain
The supreme Dual Discipline, if he be fain
To enjoy the Doctrine's essence, and its mastery gain.

Thus ends the Ninth Part in the Compendium of Philosophy, entitled the Compendium of the Stations of Religious Exercises.

[1] Adhiṭṭheyyādikaŋ. The four preliminary functions according to the Commentary are: (1) Resolving that such of his necessaries of life as are not connected with his own body, be not injured or destroyed by fire, etc.; (2) reflecting on the probable requirements of his service by the Sangha and resolving that he should wake up in time; (3) reflecting on the probable summons by the Buddha and resolving that he should wake up in time; and (4) looking forward to the time when he would die, with a view to ascertain whether he would live or die within the next seven days, the usual period of the 'Cessation of Consciousness' with human beings. It will be borne in mind that this preliminary is performed during the interval between the two highest jhānas, when the person is in his normal senses and not rapt in reverie.

NOTE ON JHĀNA IN PATHS AND FRUITS.[1]

I HAVE said that jhāna was not absolutely necessary for the four Paths and the four Fruits. But when they happen to be conjoined with jhāna, the stages of that jhāna are said to be determined by the Apperception of insight leading to emergence (vuṭṭhāna-gāminī-vipassanā-javana). And that determination is, according to one school of thought, regulated by the *basic* jhāna (*cf.* p. 62) entered into immediately before the transitional process. According to another school of thought, it is regulated by sammasita-jhāna—*i.e.*, by such basic, or other jhāna, wherein contemplation may be carried on by the above-named apperception. According to a third school, it is regulated by the kinds of jhāna specially desired by the contemplator (puggalajjhāsaya-jhāna). The last variety may or may not be similar to the first.

---

1 *Cf.* p. 215 with pp. 55, 67 *f.*

APPENDIX

CONTENTS

ATTHA.

Buddhists maintain that all physical bodies, as primarily composed of the four 'great essentials' (m a h ā - b h ū t ā), and, secondarily, of the four derivatives [*cf.* pp. 154 *f.* (1) and (3)] do exist as p a r a m a t t h a - r ū p a, or matter in an ultimate sense (*cf.* p. 1, *n.* 1). But so soon as the same matter is called by different names, the composite things corresponding to these names are held to exist only in the mind. It is not supposed that there is a (Platonic) idea corresponding to any such name that may be given to forms of matter. Take the word 'table.' We call by that name a certain combination of wood. Buddhists say that the Essentials and the Derivatives 'exist,' but the table, *quâ* table, does not. Whether it be a work-table, dining-table, writing-table, these exist only in the mind. Take, again, a piece of silver. We may call it, as it assumes several shapes in succession, bullion, coin, cup, etc., but only the metal itself exists otherwise than in the mind.

In saying that such concrete things are mere names, Buddhists countenance Nominalism. In saying that they exist only in the mind, they countenance Conceptualism. But in holding that the four essentials and the four derivatives exist in these aggregates, they countenance Realism. Buddhism, therefore, is able to reconcile all these scholastic doctrines.

And by the foregoing, the statements in § 14 of Part VIII., that seem irrational, are seen to admit of simple rational explanation. 'Woman's voice,' for instance : Woman is but a name applied to an aggregate varying in age, size, and appearance. But 'voice' is a sound which strikes on the ear, the existence of which, therefore, cannot be denied. Hence the compound word is a name of something that *does not 'exist'* (as an essential or derivative), applied to something that *does exist.*

ABHIÑÑĀ.

[The translator originally rendered this term by 'ultra-thought.' In my translation I used the phrase 'intuitive knowledge,' having Spinoza's *scientia intuitiva* more or less in mind, as being our nearest designation of *insight conceived as transcending normal perception and not consciously ratiocinative.* Spinoza uses the term to mean knowledge, which '*proceeds from* an "adequate" idea (*i.e.,* "an idea having all the properties or intrinsic marks of a true idea") of the absolute essence of certain attributes of God *to* the adequate knowledge of the essence of things.'[1] And he illustrates his meaning by one who solves a mathematical problem through previous knowledge of a general truth respecting the properties of relations involved in the problem. The particular instance is deduced from, or referred to, the bigger truth. In simpler cases, Spinoza goes on to say, 'we *see* the relation *with one glance.*' 'What he really means,' comments that ardent Spinozist, the late J. A. Picton, 'is, that if we see things as God sees them, we see them truly.' And *this* means 'seeing things as in themselves they really are.' But this is precisely the Buddhist ideal knowledge or 'vision': *yathābhūtaŋ sammappaññāya disvā,* repeated over and over in the Sutta-Piṭaka.

In spite, however, of this amount of similarity between abhiññā and 'intuitive knowledge,' the latter term may deflect the European reader from the traditional import of the former. Intuition may get lumbered up with our traditional view that knowledge is 'higher' (abhi-) in proportion as

[1] *Ethica,* II. xl., *n* . *Cf.* Locke's *Essay,* iv, 2.

it is more 'general.' Again, 'intuition' was much brought down to earth and sense through Hamilton's and Mansel's use of it. And my colleague evidently learned to know British psychology largely through Mansel. The Indian notion of 'higher' knowledge, as compared with that of our philosophies, is more akin to vision through the telescope as compared with the revelations attained by the astronomer through mathematics on paper. It is an extension of *per*ception rather than of *con*ception, the percipient seer using, as it were, another sense—the paññā-, or dibba-cakkhu—not the 'eye of flesh.'[1] Anyway I readily abandon 'intuition,' 'intuitive knowledge.' Similarities are interesting, but differences are far more enlightening.—Ed.]

Abhiññā = abhi (*i.e.*, visesato) jānātīti (Ceylon Cy., p. 230):—'one knows beyond (*i.e.*, pre-eminently, distinctively).' I am not clear in what sense you use 'intuitive' to express visesato, which connotes superiority over other kinds of knowledge. Surely not in the Mansellian sense? Or are you restricting 'intuitions' to perceptions *à priori?* I do not see much *à priori* knowledge in the abhiññā processes described in my Introductory Essay. Nor do I think you have used the phrase 'intuitive knowledge' in a Lockean sense, since there is no immediate comparison of two ideas; much less, therefore, is Spinoza's usage compatible. Martineau, in his *Types of Ethical Theory*, wrote that 'the name (intuition) prepares us to meet some mode of apprehension at a glance, in which all process is dispensed with, and the end is struck by a flash' (i., p. 312). Now we have not dispensed with all process, but, on the contrary, have to resort to a very peculiar and complicated process to win a momentary flash of abhiññā, by which the phenomenon desired is effected.

Abhiññā, for us, is undoubtedly associated with *power* (see Introd. Essay, pp. 60 *ff.*), and Warren was nearer the mark when he used 'high power' (*Buddhism in Transla-*

[1] *Cf. Dialogues of the Buddha*, ii., p. 357, *Iti-vutt*, § 61, and my 'Intellect and the Khandha Doctrine,' *Buddhist Review*, April, 1910.

tions, § 65), though this is, of course, not a literal rendering. I would not force on you my non-committing 'superintellection,' but would ask you to reconsider the matter in connection with my Essay.

ĀKĀSA.

Ledi (p. 248) derives this word from ā + √kās, 'to shine,' or 'appear.' Te te dabba-sambhārā vā rūpakalāpā vā visuŋ visuŋ bhuso kāsanti pakāsanti etenāti ākāso. 'Space is that by which objects or material groups are perceived as mutually distinct.' Ākāsa is a niccapaññatti—*i.e.*, a permanent *mental* element, through which we perceive objects. How is it that this paññatti is now spoken of as if it were a paramatthadhamma or 'real' thing? According to Buddhist philosophy, it has no objective reality. But it is usually projected from mind to object perceived, and spoken of as that by which an object is limited and bounded (pạricchedā-rūpaŋ). The curious dictum that space is born of all the four causes (*supra*, p. 163, § 4) is explained by Ledi (pp. 270, 271) as follows: Rūpakalāpā nāma ekasmiŋ paramāṇusmim pi bahuvidhā hutvā pavattanti. Tasmā catuja-rūpakalāpesu ghanabhānena pavattamānesu kalāpantarabhūtā ākāsadhātu pi dissamānā eva hotīti katvā catujesu tassā gahaṇaŋ kataŋ. 'That which we call rūpakalāpa's are units which occur in several ways. Therefore, whenever rūpakalāpa's born of four causes obtain by way of a mass, then the element of space-interstices between them also appear. Hence it (space) is regarded as born of four causes (also).'

Our rūpakalāpa is therefore more of an electron or etherwhirl, of the modern electrical theory of matter, than an atom of the atomic theory. Of course, the former theory did not enter the heads of our commentators; I merely point to a certain amount of resemblance to that theory. If an atom of hydrogen contains 700 electrons, each electron would be a rūpakalāpa, and the atom itself, the smallest known ghana.

Again, on p. 274, Ledi writes: 'ākāsadhātu does not form part of any rūpakalāpa; it merely limits the kalāpa (-units).'

ĀVAJJANA.

The equivalent of 'meditation,' given as the meaning of āvajjana in Childers's *Dictionary*, must not mislead when this word is employed as a technical term in psychological nomenclature. It does *not* connote representative cognition, but is the reaction of mind or consciousness to an impression, the 'ad-verting' to a new objective something that has come within its ken. In the Ceylon Cy. āvajjeti is paraphrased by: tattha (*i.e.*, cakkhādi pañcadvāre ghaṭṭitam-ārammaṇe) ābhogaŋ karoti: 'attends to [or apprehends] the object that impinges on the fivefold door of eye, etc.' A little further on āvajjeti is explained by pariṇāmeti, 'to bend' or 'incline' (see Childers). That is, there is a bending or inclining of the mind in order to give rise to the thought, or process-consciousness (vīthicitta), without giving an opportunity for the continuance of mere life-continuum, or bhavanga.

ASAVA.

We agreed to let this term, infamously famous, remain untranslated. Nothing to fit has yet been discovered. Warren's 'depravities' and Neumann's 'Wähnen' make no pretence to be literal. 'Floods' and 'Taints' (Rhys Davids) convey the idea of spreading movement, of disaster, of defilement, my 'Intoxicants' and 'Drugs' that of poison. The former idea seems alone active in the minds of the Commentators (*supra*, p. 170, *n.* 1); and yet, if *A.* i., 124, § 7, be compared with *Jātaka* IV., 222 (3):

'There is in the world an Ā s a v a[1] called strong drink,'

the latter idea may claim some canonical support (*cf. Dialogues of the Buddha*, i. 92; ii. 28). To the general Buddhist, Ā s a v a probably conveyed no more 'visualizable' meaning than *sin* does to the Christian, although, in either case, the *moral* vibration in consciousness is heavy enough.—Ed.

INDRIYA.

I n d r i y a literally means 'a controlling principle or force.' In the Ceylon Cy., p. 175, occurs this definition: Aṭṭhavidham pi indriyarūpaŋ pañcaviññāṇesu lingādīsu sahajarūpa-paripālane ca ādhipaccayogato:—'And the eighteen [are called] r ū p a -that-controls, because they exercise sovereignty [or control] over the five senses, over sex-characters, and because they preserve coexistent bodily qualities [from decay].'

The Commentary then explains how this controlling power is exercised. Eye controls sight, ear hearing, and so on, because each sense *depends upon* its respective organ. If the organ be weak, the sense is weak. Elsewhere, p. 169, the control of sense-characteristics is explained. And that vital force (j ī v i t i n d r i y a) preserves the body from decay is evident.

Here, again, is Ledi Sadaw's comment (p. 305): Ādhipaccaṭṭhena indriyāni; kiñca ādhipaccaŋ? Attādhīnavuttike dhamme attano gatiyaŋ sabbaso vattetuŋ samatthabhāvo. Iti tesu tesu kiccesu attano ādhipaccasankhātaŋ indaṭṭhaŋ karonti sādhentīti indriyāni. . . . Tattha pañca-

[1] Jātaka Comy.: *I.e.*, 'a poison' (v i s a ŋ), from flower-ā s a v a and the like.

cakkhādīni dassanādikiccesu cakkhuviññāṇādīnaŋ issarā honti, balava-dubbala-manda-tikkhādīsu attākārānuvattāpanato:—Indriya's are so called because of sovereignty [or control]. What is sovereignty? It is the ability to make all that is connected with it follow itself always in its own career. Thus indriya's are the exercisers, the performers of lordship called sovereignty over this and that function. . . .' Here the five (sense-organs), eye, etc., are lords of sight, etc., in the functions of seeing, etc.

I have quoted at such length to point out just this: Cakkhundriyaŋ is *not* cakkhussa+indriyaŋ, 'the power *of* the eye,' but cakkhum eva indriyaŋ, 'the eye *which is* a power.' The term has been rendered 'faculty of sight.' But we are not here speaking of the sense of sight, but of the eye itself, *as exercising a certain control over that sense of sight.*[1]

UPEKKHĀ.

This term is too important to be passed over, grazed only by the brief comments in the footnotes and Essay (pp. 14, 66), especially as there seems to be some vagueness of thought about it in the minds of scholars like yourself and others.

There are three principal kinds of upekkhā. First, the anubhavana-upekkhā (*u.* of sensation or physical sensibility): the neutral feeling or zero-point between bodily pain and pleasure (kāyika-dukkha, -sukha). Anuruddha Thera indicates this class, in (*supra*)

[1] That indriya, as here shown, imports regulative or controlling power, and not bare δύναμις, shows it to be no perfect equivalent of the Greek term (*cf.* my *Bud. Psy.*, lvii.). Buddhaghosa's definition in the Atthasālinī shows this too (p. 119):—'Indriya means sovereignty, or, again, indriya, in its characteristic mark of deciding (adhimokkha) in that which exercises lordship.' Any sense is regulated by, or subject to, the structure, range and condition of its organ.—Ed.

Part III., § 2, when he uses the expression adukkha-m-asukha. This kind of upekkhā is applicable to all sensory stimuli, except those of Touch (Part I., § 4).[1]

The second kind is the indriyappabheda-upekkhā, or upekkhā dividing the (ethically) regulative forces of somanassa, or joy, and domanassa, or grief (or of *mental* pleasure and pain). This class of upekkhā is found in the forty-seven classes of consciousness (*i.e.*, fifty-five classes called 'accompanied by indifference,' *minus* those where four senses are involved, pleasurably or painfully, = eight), referred to in Part III., § 2.

Of these two kinds of upekkhā, the former is sensational, the latter is emotional, and both are hedonic.

Lastly, there is a third class of upekkhā, and that is a cetasika, of the nineteen sobhaṇa-cetasikā;[2] in other words, a mental property or element, of the nineteen 'morally beautiful' properties. I refer to tatra-majjhattatā, 'balance of mind,' 'mental equipoise.' It is intellectual and not hedonic, and appears as a nuance in conscious experience, when the object is of a 'higher' kind than those which evoke the hedonic upekkhā. It is, *e.g.*, a bojjhanga, or factor of Wisdom, in the consciousness of Ariya's, and a factor of higher knowledge than the average, in the consciousness of average minds (*Three Ṭīkā's*, p. 195). It is this tatra-majjhattatā which we meet with in the phrases brahma-cariyupekkhā, or religious equanimity, and sankhārupekkhā, or indifference to the world.

Hedonic upekkhā enters into the composition of fifty-five classes of consciousness; intellectual (not ethical) upekkhā enters into the composition of fifty-nine such classes. These two groups of classes sometimes overlap each other, as in the case of the 'moral resultant,' or 'inoperative classes of kāma-consciousness,' which are 'accompanied by indifference,' and again in fifth jhāna. In

[1] See note at end of this article.

[2] As hedonic, upekkhā comes under the cetasika of feeling (vedanā).

these overlapping classes of consciousness hedonic indifference was taken as the chief basis of division, though intellectual indifference was present as well. This applies to the upekkh'ekaggatā—'hedonic indifference and individualization'—characterizing fifth jhāna (Part I., § 8, class 5).

I have said that 'balance of mind' is intellectual, not ethical. Nevertheless, it associates itself with moral (kusala) thoughts and higher classes of consciousness which are ethically *neutral*, though not with immoral (akusala) consciousness. Your rendering 'equanimity,' 'equableness,' or 'impartiality,' applies well enough when upekkhā is associated with ethical sentiments, but the morality of the sentiment is not due to the upekkhā. There is little of ethical value—as I understand the term—when an object deserving of pity is viewed with upekkhā. But though I may be mistaken as to the exact import of the term, I do not quite appreciate 'disinterestedness' for tatramajjhattatā. This word is paraphrased by tesu tesu dhammesu majjhattatā:—'the *mean* with respect to these or those things.' Dhammā may mean 'any things.' Hence, if you substitute this, or that set of things, with respect to which, or among which, the mind is balanced, you get different shades of meaning—*e.g.*, in the brahmacariyupekkhā, one's mind is indifferently affected with regard to persons *as* objects of love, pity, or moral appreciation; in sankhārupekkhā, one's mind is indifferently affected with respect to conditioned things, *as* objects of desire or aversion. You may be equally interested, or disinterested, concerning any two sets of things, and yet in both cases there is upekkhā. If you do not like 'indifference,' 'neutrality' would perhaps cover both hedonic and intellectual upekkhā.

Note.—With reference to hedonic upekkhā being incompatible in consciousness with tactile sensations, please permit me to criticize your version of the classic simile of cotton-wool between hammer and anvil (*B. Psy.*, lvii., and 127, *n.* 1). You say that 'they,' referring to other senses, and not, as was correct, to the secondary qualities of body, 'are as balls of cotton-wool on four anvils, deadening the impact of the hammer.' In the case of those other senses, there is *no hammer at all*, the impact of which is to be deadened by the intervening cotton-wool. Another ball of cotton-wool takes the place of the hammer in each of these four senses, and the impact between two balls of cotton-wool does not reach the anvil below; whereas, in the case of Touch, the impact of the hammer on the cotton does not stop with the latter, but is imparted to the anvil below. The secondary qualities of Body within and without in the case of the other four senses are likened to the two balls of cotton-wool, and the anvil below is likened to the primary qualities within. In the case of Touch, the object (which is composed of three primary qualities, pathavī and so forth) is compared to the hammer.[1]

[1] I am much indebted to Mr. Aung for this kindly criticism. The hammer, as he rightly says, is reserved by Buddhaghosa, for the relatively direct and therefore weighty impressiveness of the sense of touch. In the case of the other four senses, in which the 'derived' material qualities (upādā-rūpa) in both sense organ and sense-object impinge on each other, it is as if a ball of cotton-wool struck another similar ball on an anvil. There is bare contact, but no forcible impact. 'Feeling occupies the medium position (of upekkhā). But in touch the external "great essential" strikes as object on the tactile sense, and this recoils on to the great essentials related to it. As if one struck the cotton-wool on the anvil with a hammer, and this, breaking through the wool, grips the anvil, and the impact is forcible. Such, too, is the impact in touch, pleasant touch arising concerning a desirable object, painful touch concerning an undesirable object.'—*Asl.* 263.

Of all this Europeans will say it is more consistent with the logic of a theory than with fact. Next to sight, touch is precisely the sense that gives us the greatest scope for sensations which are hedonically neutral. Our finger-tips are not, perhaps, equal to antennæ, but they, too, are instruments of *knowledge* to a very large extent, informing us mainly through neutral stimuli.

In reply to this, my colleague refers me to both the Ceylon Cy. (*Three Ṭīkā's*', p. 102 *f.*) and Ledi's Cy. (p. 106 *f.*), in which the

KRIYĀ-CITTĀNI (p. 2).

As every action has its reaction (*i.e.*, consequences), the rendering 'action-thoughts,' in the translation of *Dhamma-saṅgaṇi*,[1] does not appear to me a happy expression. The term kriyā (in older Pali, kiriyā), was made technical by Buddhaghosa, if not by some earlier authority, to express the idea of mere doing—karaṇamattaŋ. The apparently contradictory phrase which I have seen used by an English writer—'inaction in action'—is very expressive of this idea. Kriyā-citta is characteristic of the Buddha and his Arahants, whose character is not ethically modified one way or another by it. The reason is that cetanā (volition) in kriyā citta, being affected by a different set of conditions—a-lobha, a-dosa, a-moha—is no longer operative—

---

absence of upekkhā in touch is discussed. Here, however, a footnote must leave the matter. He adds the following :—'As cold is but the absence of heat, so in the Buddhist view of the universe, sukha is but the absence of dukkha—a theory known to our own ethical controversies. Even the Nibbana-sukha is but freedom from suffering.'

We speak of a lukewarm state between heat and cold in ordinary parlance, but not in scientific speech. In strict logic, as in point of fact, there is *no room for* upekkhā in touch. Upekkhā is purely a *mental* feeling, according to our classification of vedanā, and is therefore subjective. Objective pleasure or pain may be *mentally* regarded as indifferent according to the degree of *physical* affection. In my Essay, p. 14, I should have been more accurate had I said not vedanā, but dukkha or sukha is either bodily or mental. (Vedanā *covers only the hedonic aspect of feeling and emotion.*) I tabulate the different aspects of vedanā thus :

Anubhavana.	*Vedanā.*	*Indriyabheda.*
1. Dukkha	kāyika.	1. Dukkha.
	cetasika.	2. Domanassa.
2. Adukkham-asukha	cetasika.	3. Upekkhā.
		4. Sukha.
3. Sukha	kāyika.	5. Somanassa.
	cetasika.	

[1] *Buddhist Psychology*, p. 156 *f.*, xcii. *f.*

i.e., no longer transformed into karma. Is this connotation intended in the expression: 'No karma can be set free?'[1] since the expression seems to convey also that kriyā-citta has karma locked up in it.

Kriyā-citta is a species of abyākata, which is often rendered, with etymological literalness, 'undetermined,' but of which a better rendering for an ethico-philosophical system, as Buddhism is, would be 'un-moral.' Abyākata is that which is neither kusala (good or moral), nor a-kusala (the opposite). But moral and immoral thoughts alone constitute karma[2]—*i.e.*, attach any moral responsibility to a thinker or actor. Kriyā-citta, therefore, which is by its nature unmoral, is conceived as entailing no such responsibility, and thus no karma at all.

CITTA, VIÑÑĀṆA.

These two terms are for us synonymous.[3] The manner in which Buddhist writers connect them in meaning may be seen from my Essay. By them they are used interchangeably, in psychological discussion. And they hold that Part I. of the Manual, enumerating cittāni of all kinds, is dealing with the viññāṇakkhandha. Whether Anuruddha Thera is using citta or viññāṇa, it does not affect the common idea of *consciousness* or *awareness* in its more general expression. I incline to think that you may attribute too much emphasis to the prefix *vi*, being guided by such terms as visena, visiṭṭha, or even vividhena. Whatever may be the *dictionary* meanings of these words, vi, in viññāṇa, does not connote superiority of ñāṇa. A cittuppāda,

[1] Yes. 'Set free' not from, but through the kriyā-citta, from or in the life of which the citta is a factor, a passing phase.—Ed.

[2] *B. Psy.*, lxxxiii. *f.*—Ed.

[3] See *Saŋyutta-Nikāya*, ii. 24: cittaŋ iti pi mano iti pi viññāṇaŋ. —Ed.

or state of consciousness, is made up of so many cetasika's, each of which is 'citta-with-a-difference,' or consciousness-and-something-more. And the term viññāṇa simply represents the totality of consciousness, which differs from the phassa-consciousness, vedanā-consciousness, etc., which make it up. It is this difference which is all that the 'vi' can serve to connote.

If 'consciousnesses' be bad English for cittāni, we must keep to 'classes of consciousness,' remaining grammatical if unwieldy. We want no word implying 'products,' such as 'cognitions' might perhaps imply. And 'thought,' except in the popular form which was inevitable, *metri causā*, for your mnemonic rhymes, must be reserved for processes of reflection and representative cognition.

CETANĀ.

Cetanā is derived from 'ceteti,' to cause to think, the causative of cintenti, from the root cita. Ceto and cetasika are derived from the same root, the former meaning 'mind,' the latter 'mental property.' Cetanā means 'the causal principle of thought.' And 'will,' in Buddhism, is the chief element of causation in karma.

Now, ceteti is explained by the verb abhisandahati,' 'to connect.' *Cf.* cetāpeti, 'to collect or get together.' So the *Ṭīkā's*[1]: ceteti attanā sampayuttadhamme ārammaṇe abhisandahatīti cetanā :—'cetanā is that which connects the concomitants with itself on the object of consciousness.' Again, the active import of cetanā is brought out in the same passage thus: sankhatābhisankhāraṇe vā byāpāraŋ āpajjatī ti cetanā :—cetanā is that which arrives at action (or exertion) in the matter of conditioning (what ought to be) conditioned (or causing what ought to be caused). And the Commen-

[1] P. 87, Saya Pye's ed. of *Three Ṭīkā's.*

tary goes on to explain: 'Because this very cetanā is conspicuous, or prominent in such conditioning the conditioned, the Buddha, in the Suttanta method of classifying the khandha's, explained sankhārā, in the compound sankhārakkhandha, as sankhataŋ abhisankharontīti sankhāro.[1]

This passage throws light on why sankhārakkhandha came to be so called. It was merely a convenient name given to a certain group *because of* the chief feature in it, to wit, cetanā, and *not* because forty nine mental properties besides cetanā show more 'activity,' or more 'tendency,' or 'predisposition' than vedanā or saññā. Phassa, *e.g.*, is not necessarily more active than either of these. But cetanā has been compared to a head carpenter, doing his own work as well as well as those of his workmen.[2]

Ledi (p. 78), after slightly elaborating the foregoing by pointing out that cetanā determines the respective functions (tasmiŋ tasmiŋ kicce va) of its concomitants on this or that object (tasmiŋ tasmiŋ ārammaṇe va), goes on to explain that cetanā acts on its concomitants, acts in getting the object, and acts in accomplishing the task—*i.e.*, determines action. It focusses its concomitants on to an object. It has āyūhana-rasa, or the function of exertion, and saŋvidhāna-paccupaṭṭhāna, or appears as the phenomenon of determination of what is determined. When cetanā acts, all the remaining concomitants act also.

Thus all points to cetanā as volition or conation. On the development of cetanā from bare element to such higher phases of will as adhiṭṭhāna, see the Introductory Essay, (pp. 43, 45, 62).[3]

[1] *Saŋyutta-Nikāya*, iii. 87.

[2] Atthasālinī, l. 8, quoted in *B. Psy.* 8, *n.* 1. See *infra* art.: Sankhārā.

[3] Mr. Aung adds: 'I was surprised that you found no term for 'will' in your article 'The Will in Buddhism,' and that cetanā was conspicuous by its absence.' The Buddhist Society (Buddha-sāsana-samāgama) of Rangoon did me the honour of reprinting this inquiry (J.R.A.S., 1898) some years ago. I therein remarked

CETASIKA.

The Fifty-Two C e t a s i k a's (Mental Properties or Elements).

Here we are dealing with the basic principles, the bare elements, the psychological ultimates of consciousness. This cannot be too carefully borne in mind, nor the renderings too scrupulously selected. That, for instance, we *may* render e k a g g a t ā by 'concentration,' when enumerating the mental factors in j h ā n a, does not permit us to use the same rendering when we speak of the consciousness of an amœba. And yet this little creature is not entirely destitute of e k a g g a t ā, or capacity to individualize among sense-impressions. This remark applies to all the c e t a s i k a's. We must select the simplest meaning applicable to every possible case. And if we cannot fit terms to every one of these protean shapes, it is better to retain the Pali, and content ourselves with explanatory glosses.

The protean character of each c e t a s i k a, considered logically as the basic principle, the bare element, into which a thought complex may ultimately be resolved, may be gathered from the study of any one c e t a s i k a, say v i t a k k a.

---

that (as in Matthew Arnold's well-known instance of Soli and solecisms), whereas Buddhism was essential a *culture* of will and desire, there seemed to be in Pali no term tantamount to our will or volition—none at least nearer than c h a n d a. Groping by the uncertain guidance of etymology, I found c e t a n ā too intellectual in *form* to represent will. And with regard to the Commentarial definition, I paid too much attention to its p a c c u p a ṭ ṭ h ā n a (reappearance) of s a ŋ v i d a h a n a, and its a t t h a (meaning) of a b h i s a n d a h a t i, and too little to its r a s a (function) ā y ū h a n a, effort (*Vis. Mag.*). The light thrown for me by my critic and colleague on the matter has been gladly hailed, and I can now go with other European translators who had not hesitated as I did. It is to me a matter of regret that correction from Burma did not reach me when the reprint was circulated. The very intimate connection, to revert to etymology, between the 'words' for consciousness or cognition, c i t t a, c e t o, and will, c e t a n ā, may prove suggestively interesting to investigation in comparative psychology.—Ed.

I use the word 'protean,' not in the sense of 'variable in the meaning *assigned by different authors,*' but in the sense of 'variable in meaning *according to the nature of the object, or according to circumstances.*'

In Part II. (§ 4) of this Manual we learn that vitakka is present in fifty-five classes of consciousness, and that these classes take part in different processes (described in the Introductory Essay). In the process of presentative visual consciousness, vitakka is present in each phase, short of cakkhuviññāṇa, or full visual cognition. Then, in several other classes of consciousness, the element of vitakka is present as a *directing of concomitant elements* to a sensible object. In imagination vitakka directs to an image; in conception, to an idea; in symbolical conception, to a concept; in judgments (vinicchaya-vīthi), to a proposition; in reasoning (takka-vīthi), alluded to, but not discussed in my Essay (it belongs to the province of logic); to a syllogism or an inference. In doubt, vitakka is a directing now to one object, now to another, back again, etc. In distraction, vitakka is a directing of mind to several objects one after another. In first jhāna, vitakka is a directing of mind to the 'after-image,' etc., and in transcendental consciousness, vitakka is a directing of mind to Nibbana, the Ideal. So engaged it is called sammā-sankappa, perfect aspiration. And in this connection your rendering of 'conception,' is not amiss. I only maintain that 'intention' is *not* the correct word for this term, but should serve (as an alternative with 'desire-to-do') for chanda.[1] Again, as a jhāna-factor, vitakka might be not incorrectly rendered by 'imagination,' when its

[1] It is, notwithstanding, interesting to find the Commentator Dhammapāla paraphrasing sankappa by chanda. This is in the Commentary on the Therīgāthā, p. 234, on verse 329:—tava pabbajāya sankappo, pabbajāya chando, ijjhatu. According to this passage, intention might serve for either. But I prefer, for sammā-sankappa, perfect aspiration, the lifting of the mind on to (abhiniropanā) higher objects. My colleague replies that Abhidhamma usage of a term is not always on all fours with that found in the Suttas.—Ed.

object is the uggaha-nimitta (the image), and by 'conception,' when its object is the paṭibhāga-nimitta (transformed after image). But the object of vitakka is *not always* an image or an idea, as may be seen from the fact that presentative cognitions, having sensibles as their objects, include the factor of vitakka. Hence neither imagination nor conception is sufficiently wide to cover the implications of vitakka.

Thus we see that 'the directing of mind towards an object' is the basic meaning common to all. Hence it is clear that we must assign a simple *elemental* meaning to these psychological ultimates called 'mentals' (cetasikā), so as to make them applicable to every possible case where the 'mental' in question is discernible. If, as an example of how *not* to do it, we render paññindriya by wisdom in a philosophical manual, it would not be applicable to the classes of consciousness said to be simply 'associated with knowledge' (ñāṇasampayuttā). And yet we know that the Manual uses paññā and ñāṇa as interchangeable terms. If we render paññindriya by that elusive English word 'reason,' or by 'understanding,' it would meet somewhat better the protean character of the Pali term.[1]

[1] In the Sutta-Piṭaka, the word cetasika hardly ever occurs. In *Anguttara Nikāya*, i. 81, 157, it is used simply to distinguish 'mental' from 'bodily' dukkha or sukha. *Cf.* *Jātaka*, iii. 143. In *Dīgha Nikāya*, i., 213 (Kevaḍḍha-Suttanta). it is used as a parallel to citta, vitakkita, vicārita, the four together representing mano, or mind. 'Suppose,' the Buddha is saying, 'a brother makes manifest the citta, and the cetasika and the vitakkita and the vicārita of others, saying: "So-and-so is your mano, your citta"' . . . I believe this is a unique instance of cetasikaŋ (note the singular!) used in this way in the oldest Pali. Cetasikaŋ is distinguishable from cittaŋ, but there is as yet no definite group of cetasikā. In the *Paṭisambhidā-magga*, however, we find the Abhidhamma phrase: citta-cetasikā dhammā (p. 84, = *Vibhanga*, 421). This is explained in *Dhamma-sangaṇi* (§§ 1187-90; *cf.* § 1022) to mean the four khandha's, citta for viññāṇa, and cetasikā for the other three mental, or arūpinā khandhā. Finally, in the Kathā-Vatthu, latest increment to the Canon, we find the plural cetasikā, with and without dhammā, implying a number of

To revert to ekaggatā,[1] I do not think 'self-collectedness' is the best rendering. No idea of self is

certain mental properties or states, which, it was a matter of orthodox theory to hold, both happened in mental procedure, and happened as coexistent accompaniments or adjuncts of citta (p. 338). It is of some interest, as a question in psychological evolution, to compare the cetasikā's in this passage, so far as they specified, with the fifty-two given in the medieval teaching of our Manual ('pe' = 'and so on'):

Kathā-Vatthu.		*Compendium.*
	phassa	
	vedanā	
	saññā	
	cetanā	
'pe'		ekaggatā
		jīvitindriya
		manasikāra
		vitakka
		vicāra
		adhimokkha
		viriya
		pīti
		chanda
		moha
		ahirika
		anottappa
		uddhacca
		lobha
		diṭṭhi
		māna
		dosa
		issā
		macchariya
		kukkucca
		thīna
		middha
		vicikicchā
	saddhā	
viriya		
	sati	
		hiri
		ottappa
		alobha
samādhi		adosa
		tatramajjhattatā
paññā		kāyapassaddhi
rāga		pe
dosa		cittujukatā
moha		viratiyo (3)
pe		appamaññāyo (2)
anottappaṃ		paññindriya

[1] In *Dhamma-saṅgaṇi*, invariably preceded by cittassa: 'of mind': cittass'ekaggatā. *Cf. supra*, p. 36 of text: citte ekaggatā.—Ed.

here involved. You point out that it is an abstract noun, and literally so it is, because it means singleness of object, or individuality in object. Bu' in reality it is that state of mind which is conscious of one and only one object, because it is not distracted by a plurality of possible objects. As Ledi Sadaw's literal rendering has it, it is the fact in [a given state of] consciousness, of having a single point [e k - a g g a] as object. In other words, it is the *germ* of all attentive, selective, focussed, or concentrated consciousness. 'The individual,' as we say with your Mansell, 'is the ultimate object of all consciousness.' And e k a g g a t ā, *quâ* c e t a s i k a, is the subjective counterpart of 'this one as distinct from the rest.'

ADHIMOKKHA.

A d h i m o k k h a,[1] decision, is another term that needs to be carefully discriminated when denoting an 'elemental' of consciousness. As such it does not amount to a process or product of judgment (v i n i c c h a y a - v ī t h i), in

A whole essay might be indited on all that these two lists suggest, especially in the light of Mr. Aung's valuable exposition of the Commentarial tradition. And the inquiry might well be pushed further into the apparent supersession of the factors of the s a n k h ā r a k k h a n d h a, or, indeed, of all five k h a n d h a s, by the c e t a s i k a - category, for purposes of psychological training. The doctrine of the five k h a n d h a s, as we know, was a logical instrument wherewith to oppose Ātmanism (*cf.* J.R.A.S., 1902, p. 48). The c i t t a - c e t a s i k a theory is, *psychologically* speaking, a considerable advance.—Ed.

[1] This is one of the terms for mental elements that came from the background in *Dhamma-sangaṇi* to a relatively front rank in the evolution of Buddhist psychology during the centuries between the compilation of that work and the Compendium. In the older book it is one of the supplementary 'or-whatever (other)' (y e - v ā - p a n a k ā) elements of consciousness in a c i t t a, and is omitted from the s a ṅ k h ā r a k k h a n d h a. It is listed in that k h a n d h a in the *Vis. Mag.*, and among the c e t a s i k a 's in this work (*Bud. Psy.*, 5, *n.* 1).—Ed.

presence of two or more concepts. Just as the cetasika of vicikicchā, doubt or perplexity, denotes awareness of an unsettling, distracting nature, so is adhimokkha a name for the nuance in consciousness of the opposite awareness—the settled state of a mind 'freed from'[1] that unrest, or from a plurality of possible objects—freed from the questioning 'is it thus or not (evaŋ nu kho no nu kho?)?'[2] It is deciding to attend to this, not that, irrespective of more complicated procedure as to what 'this' or 'that' appears to be, etc.

VIRIYA.

Viriya, 'effort,' or 'energy,' is less easily misunderstood in its bare elementary sense as cetasika—*i.e.*, as distinguished from its sublimated rank as a bojjhanga or other bodhipakkhiya factor). With the definition quoted by you (*Bud. Psy.*, 15, *n.* 1) we may compare the vīrānaŋ bhāvo: 'state of those who are strong in effort,' of the Ceylon Cy., p. 88, and Ledi's 'valiant in work' (p. 82). Both hold that reference to action (kamma) is intended. The Ceylon Cy. explains its function as ussāha, or 'support of concomitant element.'[3] Ledi also repeats Buddhaghosa's lakkhaṇa's. I have used 'effort,' or I suggest 'exertion,' without wishing to find your 'energy' unsuitable.

[1] The term = lit., 'release-on-to.'—Ed.

[2] Thus it appears almost as the volitional counterpart of the more cognitional ekaggatā. Buddhaghosa's definition is given in *Bud. Psy., loc. cit.*—Ed.

[3] It would have been more in keeping with the subtle introspection of Buddhist analysis had the Commentaries defined it as the subjectively-felt nuance, in a given conscious complex, of activity put forth.—Ed.

PĪTI.

On pīti I have enlarged to a slight extent in my Essay (p. 56). Pīti is not hedonic but intellectual, having reference to an object in consciousness. And this is why I earnestly dissent from the now almost classical rendering in England of this word by 'joy.' Pīti has as its invariable concomitant somanassa, with which joy fits well enough, since the Pali term means pleasure (sukha) *plus* excitement. But pīti abstracted means *interest* of varying degrees of intensity, in an object felt as desirable, or as calculated to bring happiness. By kattu-sādhana definition,[1] pīti is a creating of interest—*i.e.*, it is the *zest* felt by an agent in his occupation, or *pleasure*, if we follow Fleming and Calderwood's *Vocabulary of Philosophy*. Webster's Dictionary, again, describes 'interest' as 'excitement of feeling, whether pleasant (or painful) accompanying especial *attention to some object*.' This is exactly our pīti, if we omit the 'painful' alternative, since pīti is felt always with reference to an object of *desire*. By bhāvasādhana definition, pīti is the interest created in such an object: Ārammaṇaŋ kallato gahaṇa-lakkhaṇāti vuttaŋ (*Three Ṭīkā's*, p. 75)—'It is said that [pīti] has, as its characteristic mark, grasping the object *quâ* desirable.' So also in similar terms, Ledi, p. 50.

Pleasure (sukha) is, as a rule, preceded by, is derived from, a certain amount of interest. Without this precursor one would not pay especial attention to the object. If, therefore, we may eliminate 'painful excitement'—as the Vocabulary quoted from does—in our definition of interest, I hope you will retain 'pleasurable interest' for pīti. If neither this, nor even 'prospective pleasure' be accepted in the West, it were better to retain the Pali word rather than to confound the intellectual zest in an object, or objective with a purely emotional state of the subject.

[1] Definition in Buddhist logic is in terms either of agency or of state. This is the former. See Introd. Essay, p. 2.—Ed.

At the same time pīti must not be misunderstood to mean a complex phenomenon. Even when present in the sublimated form of a bojjhanga, or wisdom-factor, it is still a factor or element, a simple element in a complex.[1]

CHANDA.

Chanda = the bare element of 'wish-to-do' (kattukamyatā, as our Commentators say), the germ, so to speak, of 'intention.' We have translated it by intention, when it is raised to the dignity of an 'adhipati,' or dominant influence, in Part VII., p. 177. I do not mind if chanda be rendered by 'desire-to-do,' instead of 'intention,' if only 'intention' be *not* reserved for sankappa (see above, on VITAKKA). But I fear that 'desire' unqualified may overload the meaning of chanda *as a* cetasika. So many Europeans translate taṇhā by desire, and taṇhā is the ethical concept for that which, psychologically considered, appears as the mental element or cetasika of lobha (greed). And our Commentators are careful to distinguish between chanda, when it stands in ethical discourse for the passion of taṇhā, and the element, subjectively discernible in a mental complex, of 'wish-to-accomplish.'[2]

[1] 'The forward view' of the mind, as we might say with George Meredith, the nuance of anticipation, that may be hypothetically postulated as an original element, and not as a resultant of simpler elements. This correction of 'joy' is of very great 'interest,' and accords well with the supremely intellectual note in Buddhist religious psychology.—Ed.

[2] Of all the highly instructive distinctions in Buddhist philosophy pointed out by the translator, none perhaps is more valuable than this for English readers or those of the Latin races. The ambiguity lurking in the Anglo-Latin word 'desire' is not perhaps so great a stumbling-block for those of other European nations. On the other hand, there may not be for these, as there is for us Anglo-Latins, any equivalent so splendid in content (*Inhalt*). See the breadth and force of it in George Sand's *Lélia*, where Prometheus is apostrophized: 'Prométhée, Prométhée, est-ce toi, toi qui voulais affranchir l'homme

JAVANA.

This is one of the most important terms you have invited me to discuss, and I think I had better strike at the root of the matter.

The term is derived from the root j u, 'to be swift,' or 'to go.' So Ingan Sadaw, in the *Dhātvattha-sangaha:*

---

des liens de la fatalité ? . . . Les hommes t'ont donné mille noms symboliques : audace, désespoir, délire, rébellion, malédiction. Ceux-ci t'ont appelé Satan, ceux-là, crime ; moi je t'appelle DÉSIR ! Vérité ! vérité ! tu ne t'es pas révélée ; depuis dix mille ans que je te cherche. . . . Depuis dix mille ans l'infini me répond : désir, désir !'

Now we cannot afford to impoverish our ethical (and æsthetical) concepts by squandering this term outright on t a ṇ h ā, and thereby, so to speak, making the devil a present of all desire—even of that d h a m m a c c h a n d a that drove Prometheus to fight Zeus, that drove the Buddha from home to the Bo-tree, that drove the Christ to bring down heaven to earth. Much harm hereby has been wrought by translators, whose cheapening of the word 'desire' has justified the superficial criticism which perennially speaks of Buddhist ethics as the 'negation,' or 'extinction of all desire.' Craving (or unregenerate desire, *Begierde*) serves admirably for t a ṇ h ā. Desire belongs to our psychology of feeling + will as a term of *un*moral import, *as such*. Hence it seems to me most important to retain it for c h a n d a, which (as I have repeatedly pointed out elsewhere) is, as a c e t a s i k a, *un*moral, as d h a m m a c h a n d a is moral, and is only *im*moral as k ā m a c c h a n d a, or when substituted for t a ṇ h ā (*e.g.*, *S.* v., 272 *f.* —*i.e.*, Brāhmaṇa-sutta, Iddhipāda-Saṇyutta).—Ed.

To Europeans the inclusion of the three 'abstinences' will seem a psychological incongruity. (1) How are perfect speech, action, and livelihood to be classed as phases in, or properties of, consciousness? And (2) why not the corresponding immoral opposites (since for Buddhism immoral phenomena are as ultimate as the moral)? My colleague replies (*a*) that his traditional culture defines perfect speech, action, and livelihood as *that by which* we speak, act, and live well. I judge this to mean that, in their *ultimate* terms, the abstinences are three mental dispositions following, or according to, which the three specified forms of activity follow. I may be wrong, and our letters discussing these matters have a weary length of way to go. (*b*) Classification is made by the classifier *according to his requirements.* Bad c e t a s i k a's sufficiently cover all bad speech, thoughts, and acts. But Buddhists require the three V i r a t i's to differentiate l o k u t t a r a (saintly) from l o k i y a (mundane) consciousness.—Ed.

(jū jave ca gati ca). But Warren's literal rendering, 'swiftness' and 'swiftnesses' (*Buddhism in Translations*, pp. 177, 245, etc.), have for us Buddhists *no meaning whatever*. What philosophical significance, then, can the other alternative—'to go'—have? In Pali roots or words implying a *going* often mean also a *knowing*. Knowing is considered a sort of mental going. And so, in the Commentaries, we find such passages as 'ye gatyatthā te buddhyatthā.' '"I" gatiyaŋ tad-atthā ye pavattipāpunesu pi te buddhiyam pi.' Javana therefore means 'knowing,' or 'cognition.' Primarily, it denotes a function (kicca), and only secondarily a functional state of consciousness (kiccavanta). Hitherto I had used *cognition* to express the former, *cognitive* to denote the latter. That the javana-function lasts seven mental moments, while others may be briefer, shows that the idea of swiftness is not essential. Somehow, notwithstanding, this foreign idea of swiftness has crept into the discussions about the term; possibly there is an allusion to the rapid succession of several vīthi-citta's, in which javana goes on. Let me make this clearer.

Vīthi, in our philosophy, means a *road*, along which the mind travels by marked and unalterable stages. The fixity of these stages gives rise to the term citta-niyama, corresponding to that which Mansell termed 'the form of consciousness,' and which he distinguished from the matter of—*i.e.*, the variable element in—consciousness. As there are several distinct forms of consciousness, each form is termed 'a process of thought,' and the term vīthi-citta is applied to the whole process, and not to any particular mental state functioning in that process. For instance, in the one mental act of sense-perception indicated by the words 'I see a rose,' we distinguish four vīthi's:

vision, or cakkhudvāravīthi;
reproductive sequel, or tad-anuvattaka-mano-dvāra-vīthi:

conceiving the name, or nāma-paññatti-vīthi; discerning the meaning of the name, or attha-paññatti-vīthi.

All four constitute the vīthi-citta of perception of a rose.

Now, in each of these processes several classes of consciousness function. And sometimes there is javana, and sometimes not. In the first process, if the object be very vivid, or vivid, javana functions. Javana functions also in all other processes of representative or reflective consciousness (manodvāravīthi) except dream-consciousness. And the four processes described above in the sight of a rose occur in such *quick* succession that we fancy the object is perceived instantaneously. Hence, in popular speech, we say a man has good javanañāṇa, if he has quickness of perception. But I do not think we are justified in transferring the epithet of quick or swift from the processes to any particular functioning arising in those processes.

It must be remembered that javana, as a kiccavanta, or functional state of consciousness, is composed of several mental properties, among which cetanā (volition) is common to all. Buddhist writers often, in using the word javana, are referring to the active or conative factor (cetanā) in the act of cognition rather than to the intellective side of the process. The context shows clearly enough what they mean. Your 'conative impulse' of javana in *Buddhist Psychology*, 132, *n.*, savours of this usage, though the usage is not philosophically exact. Again, if, on p. 156, *n.*, you had said 'javana is the effective act (*not* outcome of an act) of cognition, the stage when the mind of the percipient,' *or by which* his 'character (kamma) is modified ethically in one way or another,' the description would be correct so far as it goes. But it would still leave the nature of kriyā-javana and phala-javana untouched. It must be remembered that, in *these* javana's, there is no more any determining of the passive side of one's future existence, because of the presence of certain conditions or h e t u's—to wit, a l o b h a, a d o s a, a m o h a. I have already pointed out, under KRIYĀ, that the character of an Arahant is not modified ethically by his k r i y ā-thought (thought inoperative in making k a r m a).

J a v a n a pertains to the active side of *present* existence, and determines the passive side of *future* existence. The other stages in the cognitive process pertain to the passive side of *present* existence, and have already been unalterably determined by the active side of *past* existence. To Europeans, the latter functions, as well as j a v a n a, would all count equally as acts of mind. But we Buddhists distinguish j a v a n a as a determining, free, causal act, from s a m p a ṭ i c c h a n a and the rest, which are predetermined, fixed resultant (v i p ā k a) acts.

In the absence of any English word capable of expressing what j a v a n a imports for Buddhist psychology, I had fallen back on a term so elastic and untechnical as 'cognition.' Our essential need is, after all, only a word to express the meaning of ordinary knowledge, *provided that* this word is applicable to j a v a n a's in *every* kind of v ī t h i. For instance, on referring to the simile of the man and the mango-tree in the Introductory Essay (p. 30), illustrating the normal process of cognizing an impression, j a v a n a is likened to tasting the mango. J a v a n a thus implies experience, appreciation, satisfaction. But you object that, for the European psychological reader, it is impossible to dissever from a 'process' of cognition the phases immediately preceding the phase of j a v a n a: the 'adverting' of the mind (ā v a j j a n a), the 'receiving,' 'examining,' and 'determining.' Cognition covers them all, and I have myself spoken of the whole v ī t h i - c i t t a as the act or process of cognition. Hence I consent to adopt your suggestion that 'apperception' is less of a misfit than most other words. But it should be understood that by 'apperception' I understand a voluntary or free determining act or phase of mind.[1]

[1] Apperception is most familiar to us in the works of Leibniz, Kant, Herbart, and Wundt. It will suffice to recall the *psychological*

Reversal of Javana.

The excitement of pleasure by a disagreeable object or of displeasure by an agreeable one is a case of the reversal of the apperceptional act. We have remarked that the apperceptional act is *free*, and that resultant acts of mind are *fixed*. The former is compared to an alligator which can swim with or against the current, just as it pleases, and the latter are likened to lifeless objects which merely float up and down with the tide. That is to say, the quality

(rather than metaphysical) force of the term as used by the first and last of these thinkers. In the *Principes de la Nature et de la Grace* we read, 'la perception qui est l'état intérieur de la monade représentant les choses externes, et l'aperception, qui est la conscience ou la connaissance réflexive de cet état intérieur, laquelle n'est point donnée à toutes les âmes, ni toujours à la même âme.' In other words, perception for Leibniz was '*I know*,' 'aperception' was '*I know* that I know.' Now Wundt: 'When we are conscious of a mental content (*Inhalt*), we say that it is perceived by us; when, on the contrary, besides perceiving it, we concentrate ourselves upon it, so that it stands out as distinctly as possible, we say that it is apperceived. When the impression which we perceive most distinctly is perceived with an effort of will called attention, it is said to be "apperceived"' (condensed from Wundt's works by G. Villa, *Contemporary Psychology*, pp. 214, 235 *ff.*).

In both these definitions there is to this extent agreement with the Buddhist javana-moments: apperception is a fuller or more complete cognition than perception (*cf.* Introd. Essay, p. 29). The relation with both its terms is realized, and the phase is understood as deliberate or voluntary. The misfit arises in the way this last feature is envisaged by East and by West. Wundt sees will in the effort of full attention. The Buddhist sees cetanā in the action of javana on karma. As elsewhere, it is the *afferent* stage that interests the European, the *efferent* mystery that interests the East.

I have spent many hours over javana, and am content to throw apperception overboard for a better term, or for javana, untranslated and as easy to pronounce as our own 'javelin.' It suffices to remember that it is the mental aspect or parallel of that moment in nerve-process, when central function is about to become efferent activity or 'innervation.' Teachers in Ceylon associate it with the he word 'dynamic.' And its dominant interest for European psychologists is the fusion of intellect and will in Buddhist psychology, to which I adverted under 'cetanā.'—Ed.

of the latter is determined by that of the object. If the object be agreeable, resultants of good deeds done in a former birth take part in the process; otherwise, resultants of bad deeds.

A process *ending* in an act of apperception occurs to the five classes of beings whose consciousness-at-rebirth was accompanied by hedonic indifference on the happier planes of the Kāmaloka, *whenever a very agreeable, vivid object excites anger.*

The reason why retention does not follow here is that an agreeable object requires retention of the joyful class, which, however, is incompatible with the class of apperception—namely, that of anger (dosajavana)—that obtains.

DASAKA (*Decad*).

You take exception to my use of the modern term 'cell.' Of course, the cellular theory is a modern development. Nevertheless, the physiology of the kalāpa's (groups, p. 164) is very similar to, if not identical with, that of cells. Jīvita-navaka-kalāpa is a unitary mass of living matter. Add to it sentience by way of sight, etc., and we get cakkhu-dasaka-kalāpa, and so on. Add to jīvita-navaka sex, and you get bhāva-dasaka. Add thought-basis, and you get hadaya-vatthu-dasaka (decad of the heart basis). Buddhists speak in terms of these dasaka's as so many units in the case of sentient beings. The units are supposed to live for seventeen thought-moments—*i.e.*, for fifty-one thought-instants, of which the first (or genesis of rūpa) is termed jāti; the last, aniccatā (or cessation [bhanga] of rūpa). The forty-nine intermediate instants or phases constitute the jaratā (or static [ṭhiti] stage of rūpa).[1] Thus the static stage of rūpa is of longer duration than that of citta.

[1] *Cf. Dh. S.*, §§ 642-5. Pronounce the title-word das'ăkă.

At the moment of conception (or 're-birth') or paṭisandhi, three kalāpa-units usually obtain, namely, the kāya-, bhāva-, hadaya-dasakakalāpa's.[1] These, according to certain laws of production set forth in this sixth part of the Compendium, multiply themselves. At each successive moment these three kalāpa's will be in an advanced stage, as newer ones are formed. At the end of the seventeenth moment after conception these initial kalāpa's will have died out. In this way the older kalāpa's die momentary deaths (khaṇika-maraṇa), the younger ones having advanced a stage further in their own brief career. This process of renewal or replacement of kalāpa's goes on in continual succession throughout a lifetime. At and after the seventeenth moment from paṭisandhi, some of tho kalāpa's will be in process of integration; some will be more or less advanced; others will be undergoing disintegration or dissolution. But when life is young, the procedure is favourable to new kalāpa's being formed. Hence growth (vaḍḍhi). A time comes when integration and disintegration balance each other. During the latter part of life there is a *plus* tendency towards disintegration.

Usually a lifetime is logically divided into *two* periods—paṭisandhi (conception) and pavatti (progress [of life]). But we may distinguish three phases: nibbatti (birth), vaḍḍhi (growth), and pavatti. But as these are logical divisions, we may limit nibbatti to paṭisandhi, or extend it to include earlier fœtal life. Again, we may include the whole, or part, of the embryonic stages under vaḍḍhi, and extend vaḍḍhi up to the time when decay sets in. These adjustments do not affect the general principle involved.

Well, the jāti (*i.e.*, nascent or uppāda phase) of the kalāpa's, formed during the nibbatti period of life (however we may have limited that period), would be termed ācaya, and be held comparable to the welling up

[1] Groups of bodily, sexual, and mental 'cells.'

of a reservoir on the river's bank.[1] Hence ā c a y a and n i b b a t t i are practically synonymous. The j ā t i of the k a l ā p a's formed during the v a ḍ ḍ h i-period (however we may have limited it) would be termed u p a c a y a, and held comparable to the brimming over of the reservoir, u p a c a y a and v a ḍ ḍ h i thus being practically synonymous. The j ā t i of the k a l ā p a's formed during the p a v a t t i-period (however we may have limited it) would be termed s a n t a t i, and held comparable to the overflowing of the reservoir, s a n t a t i and p a v a t t i thus being practically synonymous.

Ten'eva pāliyaŋ yo āyatanānaŋ ācayo so rūpassa upacayo; yo rūpassa upacayo sā rūpassa santatīti vuttaŋ (Ledi, p. 254): 'For this reason, therefore, it is declared in the Pali (P i ṭ a k a s) as follows: to ā y a t a n a's (of sight, etc.) there is a certain ā c a y a, and that ā c a y a is the u p a c a y a of r ū p a; to r ū p a there is a certain u p a c a y a, and that u p a c a y a is the s a n t a t i of r ū p a.' Here ā y a t a n a's correspond to the eye-decads, etc., of the Compendium, p. 164.

Now ā c a y a is not the 'cumulative effect,' as you make out in your Dhamma-saṅgaṇi translation.[2] Ledi (p. 254) explains c a y a by p i ṇ ḍ a v a s e n a a b h i n i b b a t t i—'initial appearance by way of congeries or group'—and ā c a y a as a synonym of n i b b a t t i: tattha ekekasantatiyaŋ ādimhi santati-sīsa-rūpānaŋ sabba-paṭhamaŋ uppādo nibbatti nāma; tato vaḍḍhana-rūpānaŋ uppādo vaḍḍhi nāma; vaḍḍhane samatte avaḍḍhitvā pabandha-ṭhitivasena vattana-rūpānaŋ uppādo pavatti nāma: tattha ca nibbatti-vaḍḍhiyo upacayo nāmo, pavatti santati nāma: 'here at the beginning of each and every *series* the foremost genesis of those r ū p a 's which form the head of such a series is termed n i b b a t t i. The genesis of those r ū p a 's which grow after that is termed v a ḍ ḍ h i; when growth has been completed, the genesis of r ū p a's, which

[1] *Bud. Psy.*, p. 195, *n.* 2, where this simile from Buddhaghosa is quoted.—Ed.

[2] *Bud. Psy.*, *loc. cit.*

occur by way of continuity, without further growth, is termed pavatti. Here nibbatti and vaḍḍhi together are called upacaya, and pavatti is called santati.'

So in our Compendium (Part VI., § 2), ācaya is merged into upacaya, to mean the jāti-phase of rūpa's formed in early life. And the Commentators set themselves to explain what 'early life' is. Ledi *e.g.* (p. 254): 'The genesis of the rūpa's, at the moment of conception, in beings of uterine birth, is termed upacaya, because of its foremost appearance; the genesis of the rūpa's during the interval from that time till the genesis of the first set of eye-decad kalāpa's, ear-decad kalāpa's, etc., is also termed upacaya, because of subsequent growth. After that the genesis, throughout the lifetime, of the rūpa's of the four series caused by the four causes—kamma, citta, utu, and āhāra—is termed santati.

For my part I would apply upacaya to the genesis of the *first* kalāpa of each kind in the series, and santati to all *later* kalāpa's in the same series. I will illustrate my meaning by the life of an amœba. When an amœba divides and multiplies itself, the genesis of the parent amœba would be upacaya, that of each of the later amœbas in the series would be santati. Of course, the image of this lowly organism did not enter the heads of our Commentators, nevertheless, their view is of general applicability, applying alike to amœba and any other units of living matter. And I think it is helpful rather than the contrary to interpret old terms by modern thoughts, and explain old thoughts by modern terms — provided, of course, that we do not force new wine into the old wine-skins beyond what these are able to contain.

Take another more pertinent case. A has a son B, who in turn has a son C, a grandson D, and a great-grandson E. The birth of A would be upacaya, the subsequent births santati. The mode of birth being similar in all the five cases, upacaya and santati are but two different aspects of one and the same phenomenon of birth (jāti). They are the same in mode, but differ in time. Hence, if upacaya means 'integration,' santati means 'continuance of integration' (*i.e.*, of the one phenomenon or process). It is certainly *not* 'continuance of what has been integrated.' It is the continued integration, production, generation, or formation of the new rūpa-kalāpa's.

Does not this resemble the multiplication, propagation, or proliferation of cells?

It should now clearly be seen why jāti-rūpa goes by two names. But jāti-rūpa is not 'form organically produced. How can the *process* of integration and re-integration be the product of such a process. It = rūpassa jāti, the birth, production, or generation, of rūpa. But my note has exceeded due limits.

DHĀTU AND ĀYATANA

(*With reference to* MANO *and* DHAMMĀ.)

The Commentaries, ancient and modern, both give the same definition of dhātu: attano sabhāvaŋ dhāretīti dhātu—'dhātu is that which bears its own intrinsic nature.'[1]

You ask me to comment on this comment. Your own suggestion that dhātu was borrowed by Buddhism from current metaphysic, with an implication of noümenon, and that nissattaṭṭhena (in the sense of non-entity), etc., were added by commentators to the definition to correct

[1] Buddhaghosa, in the *Atthasālinī*, defines dhātu somewhat differently, but so as to throw some light on this, to us, not very obvious definition—*e.g.*, p. 263: 'sabhāva-suññata-nissattaṭṭhena mano yeva dhātu manodhātu.' This amounts to stating that mind is an element—that is to say, there is behind it no more primal, noümenal being (satta) or entity of which it is a phenomenal appearance. Ni-aṭṭhena=not in the sense of . . .—Ed.

this implication, commends itself to me as plausible. We might picture the modern chemist, follower of the electrical theory of matter, still calling chemical elements dhātu's, but adding ni-'Daltonian-Atom'-aṭṭhena!

But there is a slight difficulty in the way of accepting your term 'phenomenal ultimate.' If phenomenon be opposed to noümenon in the sense of Kant's 'Ding-an-sich,' I accept. But if 'phenomenal' be opposed to 'real,' I object.

The definition, given in my first sentence, is intended to exclude everything that has no intrinsic nature, that is not paramattha-dhamma (thing in its ultimate sense, not merely a fiction of concept and name, or paññatti-dhamma[1]). Another definition of dhātu, in the *Three Ṭīkā's*, is practically the same as the foregoing: salakkhaṇaŋ dhāretīti dhātu, 'dhātu is that which bears its own characteristic mark' (p. 371). For, earlier in the same work (p. 234), lakkhaṇa is itself defined as the sāmañña-sabhāvo[2] of anything; and again, by Ledi (p. 387), as the paccatta-sabhāvo[3] of anything. Hence dhātu is a term applicable to every paramattha-dhamma. But 'satta,' 'jīva,' in the sense of 'soul,' of current metaphysic, are only *names* or *concepts* (paññatti).

Are we then to look upon paramattha-dhamma as real, or as phenomenal? I think that we may consider citta, cetasika, rūpa, as phenomenal. But we have the term Nibbāna-dhātu. And Buddhists at least must regard that as real.

Now as we are at present constituted, we can only *know* phenomena. But we can look upon phenomena as real, even if our concepts about them change. Chemical elements are no longer looked upon as atoms. But they are no less real to us for that. The sequence of cause and effect is as real as can be. We may therefore indulge in a

[1] *Cf.* art. Attha, and p. 81, *n.* 1; p. 200, *n.* 1.

[2] The essence [in a given] designation.

[3] Intrinsic, own nature.—Ed.

paradoxical phrase that every phenomenon is a reality. I think, then, that 'element' is the best equivalent for dhātu. It is an ultimate (phenomenal or real) which cannot be resolved into a simpler one.

Of Āyatana the Commentaries give no fewer than five definitions, according to the different connections in which this important technical term is used. Of these the following, taken from the Ceylon Cy. (p. 197), best apply to the connection indicated in the title: Āyatanti ettha taŋ taŋ dvārārammaṇā citta-cetasikā tena tena kiccena ghaṭṭenti vāyamanti—'āyatana's are those [places] *where* the mind and mental properties, having such and such doors, and such and such objects, strike (*i.e.*, are active) by such and such functions.' Hence sense-organs and sense-objects are *collectively* termed āyatana's because they serve as places or abodes, of meeting, or mixing, or production, for the several senses.

I should think that āyatana is another term which might well be left untranslated, so impossible is it to find a term sufficiently comprehensive without being too vague and inexpressive. I do not object to your 'sphere,' but I do object to 'field of sight' as a translation of cakkhāyatana. Cakkhāyatana is the seeing eye itself, and not the objective or field of its visual range. To say, for cakkhāyatana, 'the āyatana of eye,' or 'eye, the āyatana,' is alone correct. The same diction holds good for indriya, in cakkhundriya, as I have shown in the Compendium (p. 159, *n.* 2). And manāyatana is similarly formed: mano ca taŋ āyatanañ cāti manāyatanaŋ, 'mind the āyatana.' The same reading holds good for the senses viewed as dhātu's. The eye, ear, etc,, and mano are each of them *the* dhātu. Cakkhādayo ca dhammā . . . dhātuyo nāmāti (Ledi, p. 323). In Part VII., § 8 (*d*), of the triple terms, the first refers to the sense-organ, the second to the sense-object, the third to the 'sense' itself.

Now mano, whether it be called āyatana or dhātu, is not to be restricted to ideation, but covers the entire mind, presentative as well as representative. This is clearly put in the Compendium (p. 185, 'The sphere of mind,' etc.). *Cf.* also Ledi Sadaw's: Tesaŋ sabbesaŋ gocaravisayaggāhakaŋ mano ti (p. 322): 'mind is capable of taking all sense-fields as its object.' Neither can dhammāyatana, dhammadhātu, be limited to images and ideas. Else we find ourselves contradicted by the previous sentence in the Compendium (p. 184, 'Now here,' etc.).

We may tabulate manāyatana thus:

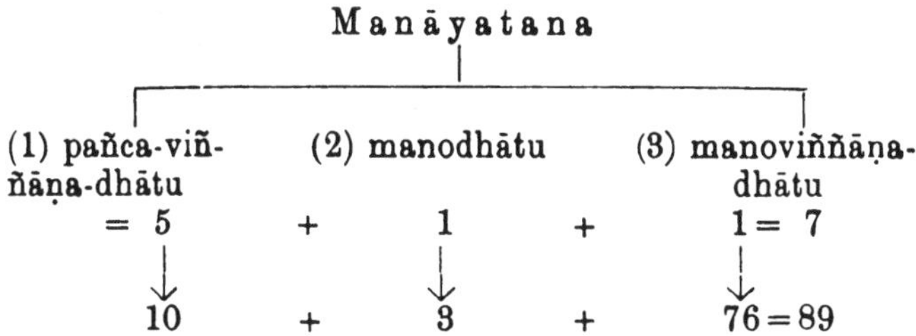

Thus manoviññāṇadhātu is a collective term for seventy-six different classes of consciousness. And these seventy-six take part in presentative classes of cognition. *E.g.*, in Part III. it will be found that forty-six classes may take part in a visual process, where no conscious representation goes on. It is, in fact, difficult to get an English word to cover all these seventy-six classes. I have used element of apprehension and element of comprehension, for want of better terms, to express (2) and (3) respectively. Thus under 'apprehension' we include (*a*) the 'adverting' of mind towards any of the five 'doors' (pañcadvārāvajjana), and (*b*), (*c*) the two classes of sampaṭicchana, or mental 'acceptance' of impressions. These cover all that is called 'bare minding,' manana-matta —*i.e.*, the simpler kind of apprehension,[1] as compared with manoviññāṇadhātu.

Into this term the word viññāṇa is inserted merely to distinguish it from the simpler manodhātu, although

[1] Part iii. of the Compendium shows that the object of manodhātu *is the sensible.*

all the eighty-nine classes in the foregoing scheme are of the viññāṇakkhandha. The group it serves to designate comprises all these eighty-nine classes *minus* the ten covered by the twice fivefold sense-dhātu's and the triple mano-dhātu, leaving seventy-six. But neither may manoviññāṇadhātu be limited to coincide with the representative or re-representative cognition of European psychology. Santīraṇa, the (momentary) stage of investigation following the 'reception' or acceptance of an impression, and preceding the 'determining' moment, is by us considered as belonging to presentative consciousness *only*. Nor have the eight classes called 'great resultant' anything to do with re-representation, when, in the presentative process, they are active in 'retention' (tad-ārammaṇa).[1]

You have asked me to state more precisely the distinction we draw between the function called mind-door-adverting (manodvārāvajjana) and sense-door-adverting (pañcadvārāvajjana). The latter is a 'turning to' the external sense-stimuli which must be *present* in presentative consciousness (pañcādvāra-vīthi). The former is a turning to all *other* objects named in the first part of my Essay, *e.g.*, mano turns to the *image* of a past sense-stimulus in representative consciousness; or it may turn to any idea or concept in representative or reflective consciousness. But I have repeatedly pointed out that the consciousness so implicated is not necessarily representative in order to include cases in which it turns to, say, a state of anger presentatively felt, or, to quote Mansel, 'intuited in a presentative consciousness.' When I know

[1] It is not easy for those trained in physiological psychology to break through the relatively evident, if somewhat materialistic, classification dividing presentations of sense from representative cognition. Some recent teachers, however, have been blurring these hard and fast lines for us. And the regarding, *as presentative*, other conscious experience than that which meets us through channels of sense—the regarding, *e.g.*, images and concepts as other than as *réchauffé*, and re-arranged and mediate—may find not uninteresting this cognate theory in the East.—Ed.

that I have been angry, I merely have an *idea* of my past angry state in representative consciousness. If you look at the list of dhammārammaṇa's in my Essay, you will notice that some of them can be *intuited*—*e.g.*, Nibbana—by an Arahant.[1]

PACCAYA AND PAṬICCA-SAMUPPĀDA.

The Ceylon Commentary derives Paccaya thus: (kāraṇaŋ) paṭicca phalam eti etasmā ti paccayo (202), 'that from which the fruit (effect) derived (from a cause) comes.' I have been tempted to complete the definition by adding kāraṇaŋ (cause). We have, in kamma, hetu, and paccaya, three technical terms meaning kāraṇaŋ. But paccaya includes the first two and adds to them; it includes, namely, all other circumstances under which an event takes place, or a relation among things obtains.

And paccaya-sāmaggiŋ paṭicca samaŋ gantvā phalānaŋ

[1] *C.f.*, *e.g.*, p. 59 with pp. 68 *ff.* My object was to elicit quite clearly the extent to which the functioning of mano-dvāra coincided with the Aristotelian theorizing about *sensus communis* and a *sensorium commune*, or how it came to pass that different sensations combined to give us *one* percept—say, an orange. Buddhaghosa's description of the mano-dhātu seems to limit its range entirely to this fusion of *sensory* impressions. 'The mano-dhātu,' he writes in *Atthasālinī*, 263, 'has the "mark" of cognizing the five kinds of sense-objects immediately after the five kinds of sense-impressions (cakkhu-viññāṇādi); and the "property" of *receiving* the same. Its "recurring appearance" is truth (tathābhāva—lit., "thus-state"); its "proximate cause" is the going-off of the sense-impressions (apagamana). . . . Whatever door-objects come together, the basis of manodhātu—*i.e.*, the heart—is the *locus* having the function of receiving them.' *Cf. supra*, p. 116 (*d*). *Cf.* also the *Kaushītaki Upanishad*: ekabhūyaŋ prāṇā gacchanti, 'the vital forces go into unity, otherwise no man were able to bring into consciousness (prajñāpayituŋ) name by speech, form by the eye, sound by the ear, thought (dhyānaŋ) by the mind (manas). But inasmuch as the vital forces go into unity, all these (things) are one by one (ekaika) brought into consciousness: when speech speaks all the vital forces speak after (Deussen—*i.e.*, with) it,' and so on. According to Max Müller, prāṇā in the plural (vital forces) stands for the

uppādo etasmāti paṭicca-samuppādo: 'p a ṭ i c c a - s a m - u p p ā d a is that from which [there is] the arising of the fruits coming (or derived) from a conjuncture of circumstances' (Ceylon Cy., 201).

All the Burmese texts, including Pye's edition, read t a b b h ā v ă b h ā v ī - b h ā v ā, with short ă (p. 187, *n.* 4, of Manual). The Ceylon Commentary paraphrases the term by 'tassa paccaya-dhammassa bhāvena bhavana-sīlassa bhāvo': 'the occurrence of the habitual happening on (*lit.*, by) the occurrence of a p a c c a y a - d h a m m a, or circumstance under which a relation obtains.'

And Ledi Sadaw writes (p. 332): tasmiŋ tasmiŋ paccaya-dhamme bhāve vijjamāne sati te te bhavanti sīlenā ti tabbhāvăbhāvino sankhatadhammā; tesaŋ bhāvo tabbhāvăbhāvi-bhāvo. imasmiŋ sati idaŋ hoti; imassa uppādā idaŋ uppajjatīti evaŋ pavatto sankhatadhamma-niyāmo: 'On the happening of a causal — *i.e.*, indispensable— antecedent phenomenon (p a c c a y a d h a m m a) certain [effects] which happen inevitably (s ī l e n a = by way of habit) are termed t a b b h ā v a b h ā v ī—*i.e.*, the conditioned things (which follow antecedent causes); the cause (b h ā v o) of these things is t a b b h ā v a b h ā v i b h ā v o. When, namely, *this* [cause] happens, there is *that* [effect]; because this [cause] occurs, that [effect] arises. Thus we get [the N i y ā m a, that is] the constancy, rule, law, or uniformity of conditioned things.' The Commentators had, doubtless, in their minds the canonical e v a ŋ - d h a m m a t ā - n a y a (or method of 'thus is the norm')[1]—the law by which like effects follow like causes.

---

five senses. Now, according to this U p a n i s h a d—and it ranks among the pre-Buddhistic U p a n i s h a d s—p r ā ṇ ā, in the singular —that is, 'breath'—is no other than p r ā j ñ ā, consciousness, or soul, or ā t m a n, whose seat is the heart, m a n a s being merely a function of the soul, like the five senses. The Buddhists retained m a n o as a sixth sense, but assigned it, at the same time, the position of referee, occupied, in the doctrines they opposed, by the a t t ā they rejected, or, at least, rejected under the character assigned to it by Ātmanists.—Ed.

[1] *Cf.* *Dīgha-Nikāya*, ii., 12*f.* (M a h ā p a d ā n a S u t t a n t a).—Ed.

The two bhāva's refer to the antecedent phenomenon as a cause. The bhāvī refers to the consequent phenomenon as effect. Or, according to the Ceylon Commentary, the last bhāva means 'happening.' The meaning should be: 'Of these, the former, A, is a mode marked by the simple condition of the invariable happening of a phenomenon (event, thing, circumstance) on the occurrence of its sole invariable antecedent phenomenon (event, thing, circumstance).

The *positive* aspect of causation is here alone referred to. We are dealing with samuppāda, the 'arising' of effects through presence of a cause. The Ceylon Commentary points out, however, that the negative aspect of causation is implied though not expressed: 'eten'eva tad-abhāvābhāvākāramattopalakkhitatā pi atthato dassitā hoti' (p. 202). The Ceylon Commentator had evidently the truth formulated, for English thought, in J. S. Mill's 'Method of Difference' (*Logic*, III., viii.) in his mind.

The word ṭhiti (p. 187, *n.* 5) is used synonymously with paccaya, and is best rendered by 'occasion.' So the Ceylon Commentary: tiṭṭhati phalaŋ ettha tadāyattavuttitāyāti ṭhiti. Āhacca visesatvā pavattā paccayasankhātā ṭhiti āhacca-paccaya-ṭhiti (p. 202): 'That by dependence upon which the effect (fruit) stands is called the "occasion." In any relation the distinctive, conspicuous, or "striking" causal circumstance is the occasion that is called 'paccaya.' In the title of Part VIII. we have rendered paccaya by 'relation.' So far so good. But when opposed to paccayuppanna, paccaya is 'relating thing' as opposed to 'related thing' (See Introd. Essay, p. 2). Of any pair of correlates, paccaya is the more 'striking' of the two, that which appears as force or power—that which, as it were, renders service: upakārakatā-sankhāto (Ledi Sadaw, p. 332). There are, for instance, many circumstances necessary to the discharge of a gun, both in the gun itself, the charge, the environment, and the agency working the gun. That which we select as the most striking occasion of the explosion we call paccaya. Now the psychological aspect and ultimate of 'ignorance' (avijjā) is moha, one of the three evil hetu's. And in momūha-cittāni, moha acts with the 'conspicuous' force of a paccaya. None the less, by the foregoing, it, as paccaya, is only one among a group of conditions or causal circumstances necessary to the production of an effect (namely, of the sankhārā).

The anomaly in the Paṭicca-samuppāda, of 'becoming' *preceding* 'birth,' is due to the faulty rendering of the word 'bhava,' which is used in different senses. I give the Commentary (pp. 203, 204): kamma-bhavo upapatti-bhavo ti duvidho bhavo. Tattha paṭhamo bhavati etasmā phalan ti bhavo; so kāmāvacarakusalā kusalādi vasena ekūnatiŋsavidho; dutiyo pana bhavatīti bhavo; so kāmabhavādi vasena navavidho. Upādāna-paccayā bhavo ti c'ettha upapatti-bhavo pi adhippeto; bhavapaccayā jātīti kammabhavo vā; so hi jātiyā paccayo hoti, na itaro: bhava is twofold—kammabhava and upapattibhava.[1] The former is that from which the fruit or effect happens; it is twenty-nine-fold (referring to the twenty-nine cetanā's previously termed sankhārā), to wit, good and bad karma of the Kāmaloka, etc. But the latter is ninefold, to wit, Kāma-, Rūpa-, Arūpa-bhava, etc. In the phrase 'upādānapaccayā bhavo' the latter kind of bhava is meant. But in bhavapaccayā jāti the former, or kamma-bhava, is meant. It, indeed, and nothing else, is the only cause of jāti.

Perhaps the appended diagram will serve to illustrate the meaning better than so many words. It must be borne in mind that Paṭicca-samuppāda is a Vaṭṭa-kathā (discourse on evil),[2] not a theory of the

[1] *I.e.*, existence on its active side, shaping the present and future, and existence on its passive or resultant side, as shaped and determined by the past.—Ed.

[2] Lit., on the Round—*i.e.*, of saŋsāra.—Ed.

evolution of the world from primordial matter. Even as a theory of the origin of evil, it does not attempt to show the absolute origin of evil; it only shows how evils originate. And so life is taken as it is.

For the purpose of the discourse it was held sufficient to take any three consecutive existences,[1] considered as past, present, and future, as shown in the innermost circle. Now, although in each existence there are always two sides (kamma-bhava, upapatti-bhava[2]), for the purposes of the discourse it was sufficient to consider the kamma-bhava of the past, the upapattibhava of the future, and existence as a whole in the present. This is shown in the circle next to the innermost.[3] In each of these four sections or 'layers' there are five conditions (numbered 1 to 5), making up the 'twenty conditions.'[4] Of these *twenty*, however, *only twelve* are expressly named as Anga's or Nidāna's (shown in the outermost circle and numbered with Roman figures). And why? Because, with reference to *past* existence, the mere mention of avijjā *implies* taṇhā and upādāna, these three never existing apart; again, because the mention of sankhārā implies kamma, the latter being merely a development out of the former, which has been shown to be practically cetanā, the germ of kamma (or bare element of conation). Hence these two Anga's—avijjā and sankhārā—virtually exhaust the kamma-bhava of the past.

Now, the kamma-bhava of the past determines the upapatti-bhava of the present (as is shown in the diagram by an arrow). The upapatti-bhava of the present must begin with rebirth-consciousness. But the latter can never exist by itself apart from its nāma (mental properties or concomitants), and is accompanied by its karma-born body. All the five factors of the

[1] Called tayo addhā (three periods).
[2] *Cf.* Pt. VIII., § 5 (2, 3).
[3] Called catu sankhepā (four layers).
[4] Called Vīsatākārā.

upapatti-bhava of present existence are fully mentioned. But when we come to the corresponding kamma-bhava, we mention only the three, leaving the others to be understood by implication.

Now, this kamma-bhava must necessarily determine the upapatti-bhava of the future (shown in the diagram by an arrow). Here a single word—jāti—is used to cover all the five factors. Jarā-maraṇa is added to show that it is the usual accompaniment of jāti.

The 'three connections' (ti sandhi) are shown by thick lines. The first and third connections are between separate existences; the second is between two factors in the same existence. The 'four groups' are: one causal group in the past; one resultant group and one causal group in the present; one resultant group in the future.

PAÑÑATTI, VIÑÑATTI.

I have discussed the former term at length in my Introd. Essay, and have tried to show that the word covers both name-and-notion (or term-and-concept) and also a great range of concepts or ideas—anyway, I have used the term 'concept,' in default of a better English word, rather loosely to cover many classes of what with us are called paññatti's.

But paññatti must not be confounded with viññatti. The two are as the poles asunder. Viññatti is a rūpa,[1] and a paramattha-dhamma,[2] to which paññatti-dhamma is opposed. Viññatti is that peculiarity or difference, (vikāra) which constitutes the *purposive* character of a sign, *i.e.*, the movement of body or vocal organs, by which its purposive character is known and its meaning is made known (Ceylon Cy., p. 171).

Paññatti is not concept *plus* expression, but it may

[1] Classed as rūpa in *Dh. S.*, § 596. Translated, in *Bud. Psy.* by 'intimation' (by act or by speech), pp. 178, 192, 193.—Ed.

[2] See Appendix, Attha, and *cf.* p. 6.

be concept *or* term, notion *or* name, according to the context.

V a c ī - v i ñ ñ a t t i is not 'word,' but is the peculiarity (v i k ā r a) of word, when this is used as a sign for the hearer to understand the speaker's meaning. Every spoken word does not possess this peculiarity; but as soon as a man wishes to communicate his wish to another by word, then only does that word have v a c ī - v i ñ ñ a t t i. Similarly with gestures. Every movement does not possess the peculiar character usually manifested in beckoning, nodding, etc. But as soon as a man wishes to communicate with another by showing signs, the movements he employs then possess the character of k ā y a - v i ñ ñ a t t i.

PAṬṬHĀNA.

According to the Ceylon Commentary: nānappakāraṇāni ṭhānāni paccayā etthātyādinā paṭṭhānaŋ; ananta-naya-samanta-paṭṭhāna-mahā-pakaraṇaŋ: 'That *in which* the various circumstances under which relations obtain [are treated of] is termed P a ṭ ṭ h ā n a — *i.e.*, the "Great Treatise," in which infinite modes of universal relations are dealt with' (p. 201). Or more directly expressed by Ledi Sadaw (p. 332): paṭṭhapeti sankhatadhamme nānā-pakārehi paccaya-bhedehi pavatteti deseti etthāti paṭṭhā-naŋ, mahā-pakaraṇaŋ: 'The great treatise "P a ṭ ṭ h ā n a" arranges conditioned things under various kinds of relations, describes, and teaches them.'

BHAVANGA.

In this term (which of course = b h a v a s s a a n g a ŋ) the Commentators explain a n g a to mean, *not* 'part,' but k ā r a ṇ a—the cause, reason, or indispensable condition. In Childers's Dictionary 'cause' is given as one meaning of a n g a. And by b h a v a n g a we mean the cause, reason, indispensable condition, of our being regarded subjectively as continuous; the *sine quâ non* of our existence, that without which one cannot subsist or exist (Ceylon Cy., p. 104).

Primarily bhavanga means function. Ledi Sadaw (p. 111) explains it as the function of being, by reason of which the passive side of existence (upapatti-bhava) continuously exists so long as the janaka-kamma (Manual, Part V., § 8) of the past, which caused that existence, lasts. Thus the Commentators use upapatti-bhava to show that bhavanga does not belong to the category of kamma-bhava to which javana belongs.

Secondarily bhavanga denotes a functional state (or moment) of subconsciousness. As such it is the subconscious state of mind—'below the threshold' of consciousness—by which we conceive continuous subjective existence as possible. Thus it corresponds to F. W. Myers's 'subliminal consciousness.'

There is a grain of truth no doubt in the Cartesian 'cogito *ergo* sum,' as well as in the Hegelian 'identity' of thought and being. But in Buddhist philosophy, being, which is vīthimutta, or process-free—that is, bhavanga—is *contrasted* with thought, which is essentially vīthi (vīthi-citta). And the dividing-line between being (bhavanga) and thought is the 'threshold' of consciousness. Or, to use Buddhist metaphors, the 'stream' of being is contrasted with the 'door' of mind. And mano-dvāra happens when bhavanga is 'cut off' (bhavangupaccheda) or arrested.

There are nineteen different classes of bhavanga-subconsciousness described in Part I. of the Manual. Of these, only ten, it is held, are possible in Kāmaloka, five in Rūpaloka, and four in Arūpaloka. And only one class at a time is possible for each individual being. A flow of momentary states of sub-(liminal) consciousness of such a particular class constitutes the stream of being. And as the beginning and end of a stream are distinguished as source and mouth, though composed of the same watery material as the body of the stream, so the initial and final points of a particular stream of being are termed rebirth and death. In other words, the paṭisandhi-, cuti-, and bhavanga-citta's of an individual life are of one and the same class. They are alike in respect of their cause or conditions precedent (saṅkhārā), their component parts (sampayutta-dhammā) and their object (ārammaṇa). They differ only in function. The stream is liable to be interrupted constantly by thought (vīthi-citta or *processed* consciousness), but it cannot be regarded as a sub-plane *from which* thoughts 'rise to the surface' (see Introd. Essay, pp. 11, 12). Buddhist writers often drop the word stream, 'sota,' when referring to the stream of being, understanding it by the context, as in the expression 'bhavanga-pāto'—'subsidence into . . . being.' It is sota which conveys the idea of flux, not bhavanga. Of what is the flux? Of bhavanga-citta's, or momentary states of subconsciousness performing the function of being subjectively conceived as a stream. For although we may use 'being' as the etymological equivalent of bhu+anga, the term should always be understood subjectively, somewhat after the manner of Hegel, and *never objectively*.

When a being is conceived, Buddhist belief gives him a congenital mind, simultaneously with the inception of physical growth, as the resultant of the past janaka-(generative) kamma. That mind, at the moment of conception, is but a bare state of subconsciousness, identical with the more adult bhavanga-consciousness during dreamless sleep. And this state of subconscious vitality is endowed or informed potentially with hetu's, good or bad.[1]

[1] Bhavanga, as a philosophical term, occurs in the *Abhidhamma-Piṭaka*, viz., in *Tika-Paṭṭhāna* (Paññāvāra):— . . . bhavangaŋ āvajjanāya . . . anantarapaccayena paccayo. The translator has sent me this most interesting reference since my note 2, on p. 9, was printed. I had searched the *Tika-P.* in MS., but had overlooked it.—Ed.

Foreign Element in the Vital Continuum.

(Āgantuka-bhavanga).[1]

In the case of the four classes of beings whose consciousness-at-rebirth was accompanied by joy, a foreign element of vital continuum intervenes as a sort of connective principle between the apperception of anger and the normal vital continuum, as when they are offended with a very agreeable object. As in the previous case retention cannot operate. Neither can the apperception of anger be immediately followed by the normal vital continuum, because the latter is of the joyful class. The passage from a state of anger to one of joy would be too abrupt without the mediation of a *hedonically indifferent* element, which acts as a sort of buffer between two opposing natures. Therefore, any one of the six Kāmaloka continua accompanied by hedonic indifference may intervene, having for its object any Kāma-object which had been habitually experienced in life. The six hedonically indifferent vital continua are 7 and 15 of § 4, and 3, 4, 7, and 8 of § 6, Part I. of the Compendium. (See Part V., § 4, and *cf.* § 9, Part IV.).

MAHĀBHŪTĀ.

(*The Main Principles or Essentials of Matter.*)

I must here differ from you in your choice of earthy, lambent, gaseous, fluid, etc.[2] We are dealing now not with the *states* of matter as met with in nature, but with *properties* of matter common to all the states in which matter is met with. If Buddhist teaching instances earth, water, fire, and air, this is only because, in those four, the properties of paṭhavī, āpo, tejo, and vāyo preponderate. But paṭhavī-adhika,[3] āpo-adhika substances and the like are not themselves paṭhavī, āpo, etc. Greek

[1] *Cf.* p. 131, *n.* 1.

[2] *Bud. Psy.*, pp. xlvii., 197, 241-3.

[3] *I.e.*, preponderating in paṭhavī

philosophy must have influenced you in the choice of the dictionary meanings of these terms. But we must not sacrifice philosophical to historical interest. We must get at the ideas of the Buddhists as distinct from those of the Greeks. Let us hear the Commentators: Āpeti sahajātarūpāni pattharati; appāyati vā brūheti vaḍḍhetīti āpo (Ceylon Cy., p. 167): 'Ā p o is that which diffuses itself throughout its co-existent qualities; or that which increases the bulk of them.' There is no mention here of watery element (ā p o). Again (Ledi Sadaw, p. 240): Āpeti sahajātarūpāni byāpetvā tiṭṭhati; appāyati vātāni suṭṭhu brūheti vaḍḍhetīti āpo; tāni vā avippakiṇṇāni katvā bhuso pāti rakkhati; pivati vā pivanto viya tāni sanganhāti sampiṇḍetīti āpo. 'Ā p o is that which locates itself by pervading its co-existent qualities; or that which greatly increases their bulk; ā p o is that which heaps them well together, without allowing them to be scattered about; or that which imbibes (absorbs) them, or that which holds or collects them together, as it were, by imbibition.'

The last etymology is strained, since water is not that which imbibes but that which is imbibed. At any rate, whether ā p o is derived, according to the alternatives given by the Commentaries from ā p e t i, a p p ā y a t i, p ā t i, or p i v a t i, tradition in both Ceylon and Burma tends to the doctrine that ā p o is 'cohesion'—b a n d h a n a t t a ŋ r ū p a s s a (*Dh. S.*, § 652).[1] If a mass is kept together by the force of cohesion, and if you remove that force by splitting the mass into fragments, what is left in those fragments? Cohesion. So, too, if the fragments are reduced to smaller particles, we find cohesion inhering down to the last indivisible atoms. This justifies the phrases, 'diffuses or locates itself by pervading its co-existent qualities.' That a large body is built up of smaller bodies by cohesion justifies the phrase 'increases the bulk of them.' That a mass of matter is held together by cohesion justifies the remaining phrases.

[1] So Buddhaghosa in commenting on this passage, *Asl.*, p. 335. The punctuation needs some amending in the P.T.S. edition.—Ed.

I am aware that paggharaṇa-sabhāva, or fluidity, is regarded as the characteristic mark (lakkhaṇa) of water,[1] cohesion being looked upon as its *function* (kicca). But if we bear in mind that air possesses still more fluidity than water, paggharaṇa no more distinctively suggests water than it suggests air. Buddhist writers speak of fluid in connection with āpo much as we often speak of magnetism or electricity as a 'fluid.' They do instance water as an āpo-adhika substance (*i.e.*, preponderantly cohesive). I am aware that physicists hold there is more cohesion in solids, and that their firmness is due precisely to this. But Buddhist philosophy considers firmness or hardness (kakkhaḷatta) as the characteristic mark of solids (paṭhavī), for, however apparently cohesive a solid may be, once it is broken up its original cohesiveness is gone and there is no recohesion. But a liquid cannot be divided without tending to recoalesce. It is true that air or gas behaves in the same way to a certain extent, but its capacity of expansion without limit tends to counteract the force of the cohesion holding the particles of air or gas together. And so Buddhist philosophy reserves air as the type of mobility (vāyo = motion).

Tejo is, of course, heat, including cold, or relative absence of heat. Cold is not known to Buddhist thought as a force distinct from heat. 'Lambent' and 'fiery' may only fit occasionally in popular phraseology. Tejo is the element which matures, sharpens, intensifies, or imparts heat to the other three Essentials.

Vāyo is defined as 'that which, as the condition of motion to another place, brings about the impact of one Essential with another.'[2] Again, in Ledi's words, 'that which vibrates or oscillates; that which, as a condition of motion in space, moves the series of elements to a different place, or carries its co-existent qualities from place to place'

[1] *Dh. S.*, *loc. cit.*

[2] Vāyati desantaruppatti-hetubhāvena bhūtasanghātaŋ pāpetiti vāyo (Ceylon Cy., p. 167).

(p. 240). These comments point to 'motion' as the meaning of vāyo.

I suggest, therefore, in English versions of these four terms in our 'natural philosophy,' the renderings:—the element of extension, the element of cohesion, the element of heat, the element of motion. I prefer the first to your 'extended element.' We Buddhists mean the concept extension, not extended things, or things as tending to occupy space. We are here concerned with action, not agent. What I have said on definitions of agency and of state (Introd. Essay, pp. 2, 7) applies to all our philosophical ideas.

RŪPA.

I take objection to rupa being rendered by 'form.' Used for rūpa in the Suttas and in popular language the term may be correct enough. But it is not always safe to render a Pali word by one and the same English word everywhere without reference to the idea to be conveyed. As used in *Abhidhamma*, rūpa, in its generic sense (quite apart from its specific sense of object of sight) means 'that which changes its form under the physical conditions of heat, cold, etc.'[1] When we say that matter changes its form, or passes from one form to another, we mean that it assumes different shapes or figures. Now any one of these would be called saṇṭhāna-paññatti (not rūpa), and is inferentially known in any one of the sequel of thought-processes described in my Essay. 'Matter,' therefore, matches well enough with rūpa, just as mind matches with citta or mano. Nāma-rūpa is hence better rendered by mind and body than by 'name and form.' Here, again, pioneer students have confounded the grammatical nāma (name) with the psychological nāma (mind). Etymo-

[1] See the *Three Ṭīkā's*, p. 59.

logically the word is no doubt identical, meaning to bend, or tend towards.

Another objection to the use of 'form' for rūpa is the ambiguity of form. In European philosophy it has been contrasted with matter, and, when so contrasted, form is considered as a *constant* element as contrasted with the shifting shapes of matter.

If it be objected that matter suggests the hypothesis of substance, there are sufficient indications in the Manual (Part VI.) to show that we understand rūpa in the Berkeleian sense. The twenty-eight 'properties of matter' (§§ 3-5) are really qualities of body. And rūpāyatana (§ 4) = rūpārammaṇa (Part III., § 10) = vaṇṇāyatana[1] is the one dassanarūpa, or visible object. This object of sight is not 'form,' which both for Buddhist and for European psychology is not so much 'seen' as inferentially known, but mere colour (vaṇṇa) —*i.e.*, coloured surface or extension—*i.e.*, vaṇṇa *plus* paṭhavī (see Essentials). 'Form' therefore is not strictly *visible*, but is a dhammārammaṇa (or saṇṭhāna-paññatti: appearance-concept), inferentially known in one of the 'sequels' of the process of sight. A saṇṭhāna-paññatti-vīthi has to intervene, building on the bare messages of coloured extension.

It may interest you to note the following quotation from the Khandha-Yamaka in the *Abhidhamma-piṭaka*: rūpaŋ rūpakkhandho ti [pucchāyaŋ sati[2]]? Piyarūpaŋ sātarūpaŋ rūpaŋ, na rūpakkhandho. Rūpakkhandho rūpañ ceva rūpakkhandho ca. Na rūpakkhandho na rūpan ti [pucchāyaŋ sati[2]]? Piyarūpaŋ sātarūpaŋ na rūpakkhandho rūpaŋ. Rūpañ ca rūpakkhandhañ ca ṭhapetvā avasesā na ceva rūpaŋ na ca rūpakkhandho. 'Does [everything that is called] rūpa [belong to] the "material group?"

[1] 'The eye . . . gives us perception of light and colour, gifts peculiarly its own.' All other elements in vision 'are the work of sight on a basis of touch' . . . 'perceiving by way of inference.' G. C. Robertson, *Elements of Psychology*, pp. 122 *ff*.

[2] 'If it be asked':—a Commentarial gloss.—Ed.

[The eighty-one worldly classes of consciousness and their concomitants called] rūpa that is "attractive" and "pleasant" are called rūpa, but they do not belong to the "material group." The twenty-eight material qualities (Manual, Part VI., §§ 2, 3) that go to make up the material group are designated rūpa, and they belong also to the "material group."'

'[Again] is anything that does *not* belong to the "material group" ever called rūpa? [such is the question.] Things attractive and desirable are called rūpa, though they do not belong to the "material group." Those things and that group apart, the remainder [viz., the eight classes of transcendental, *i.e.*, lokuttara, consciousness, and their concomitants, and Nibbana] are neither called rūpa, nor do they go to make up the material group.'

That rūpa, in the Piṭakas, was used to express states of mind may well shock the literalist, who would use wooden consistency in translating terms. In its generic sense, rūpa, as a philosophic term, means matter, and in its specific sense, quality.

SANKHATA; ABHISANKHATA.

By sankhata we do not intend to convey the notion of 'compound' (as you call it) so much as that of 'conditioned.' Of course, what is compound is always caused. But it is the idea of causation that is *chiefly* implied.

SANKHĀRĀ.

I have pointed, in the Introductory Essay (p. 2), to a roughly approximate identity of cleavage in Western and Buddhist divisions of the mind. I said that the vedanā-ñāṇa-sankhāra division corresponded to European feeling, thought, and volition. But I do not intend to convey that the term sankhārā can be restricted to a technical expression for will. Sankhārā as volitions is one aspect, sankhārā in sankhārakkhandha is another. In the *former* use of the word we mean pubbābhisankhāro—*i.e.*, previous volitional effort or conation (on the part of self or another), or payoga-sankhāro or upāya-sankhāro (motivated or designed operating). *Cf.* the distinction asankhārika and its opposite in § 2, and Ledi Sadaw, p. 26.

In the *latter* term—aggregate of sankhāra's—sankhārā is a collective name given to the fifty mental properties (cetasika's) which go to make up citta or consciousness. They are named sankhāra's, because, as *concomitants, they perform their respective functions in combination*[1] *as one whole*, of act, speech, or thought (Ledi Sadaw, pp. 318 *ff.*). Scholars have thought that under sankhāra's were classed the more *active* expressions of conscious life. But phassa (contact) and vedanā (feeling), the first two of the fifty, are for us anything but pre-eminently active elements. Neither is saññā (perception) active, as compared with cetana (volition). Feeling and perception, however, as broadly distinctive forms of consciousness, have already, in the very ancient khandha-classification, been told off in separate groups. Hence the only other wholly representative property was chosen to be the namesake of the other forty-nine—namely, that volitional activity which we understand by both cetanā and sankhāra. Cetanā, as a cetasika, is a constant. And sankhārakkhandha really means the group of 'volitions and other associated factors.'

But in the Paṭicca-samuppāda (see Appendix, *s.v.*), sankhārā is used as a synonym of the developed cetanā—*i.e.*, of karma.

[1] *Cf.* in this respect European efforts at equivalent renderings: 'confections,' 'syntheses.' Intrinsic variety rather than concomitancy is aimed at in two others—'*Gestaltungen*' 'conformations.' '*Betätigungen*' belongs rather to the former definition. '*Unterscheidungen*' to neither.—Ed.

Thus in all the three foregoing distinctions—pubbābhisankhāra, sankhārakkhandha, and avijjāpaccayā sankhārā—the active or agency-form (kattu-sādhana) of derivation: sankharotīti sankhāro, holds good; 'sankhāra is that, namely, which determines, conditions, operates' (from √kar, 'to do'). But in the (Suttanta) phrases: 'sabbe sankhārā aniccā,' 'sankhārupekkhā,' 'sankhāradhammo,' 'sankhāraloko,' the passive kammasādhana form of derivation is adopted: sankhariyatīti sankhāro, 'sankhāra is that which is determined, conditioned, acted upon.'

I mention all these forms of sankhāra because the over-literal scholars of the West are apt to translate any one of our terms by the same word, regardless of the sense, context, or derivation. And in the last-named passive import of sankhārā we should certainly not restrict the word to mean the fifty psychical elements or cetasika's, but we should understand sankhata, 'things,' or 'the world,' or 'the conditioned.' Our commentators are guided by the context. Let me quote the Ceylon Commentary—*e.g.*, on p. 188 of the Compendium, where we have rendered sankhārā by 'actions' (*i.e*, karma), as referring to the cetanā in the twenty-nine moral and immoral citta's: sankhatam abhisankharontīti sankhārā: kusalākusala-kammāni. Te tividhā: puññābhisankhāro, apuññābhisankhāro āṇañjābhisankhāro ti.[1] Tattha kāmarūpāvacarā terasa kusalacetanā puññābhisankhāro; dvādasa akusalacetanā apuññābhisankhāro; catasso āruppacetanā āṇañjābhisankhāro ti evam etā ekūnatiṃsacetanā sankhārā nāma. 'Sankhāra's condition (determine, act upon) the conditioned; they are good and bad actions (karmas). They are threefold, etc. Thus the twenty-nine cetanā's are called sankhāra's' (p. 203).

To repeat: sankhārakkhandha is, more or less, a *label* given to a collection of varying cetasika's. But the label derives its title from cetanā (otherwise called

[1] *Cf.* *S.* ii. 82, *Paṭisambh.* ii., 178, with *Vibh.*, 135.—Ed.

sankhāra's). If some European label, like your 'syntheses,' be given to the term in translation, when occurring in this connection, I see no objection. But the label must not be suffered to hold good for every application in Buddhist literature of the word sankhāra. Personally I prefer 'karma' to 'syntheses.' Take the comment on sankhāra in consciousness just before death (Pt. V., § 12):

(*a*) Sankhārenāti kusalākusala-kammena kammasahajātaphassādi-dhamma-samudayena, cuti-āsanna-javanasahajātena vā (Ceylon Cy., 161): 'By sankhārena here is meant *by good and bad karma*, or by the collection of mental properties — phassa, etc. — coexistent with karma, or by the [properties] co-existent with death-bed *apperception*.' Now, in each of these significations karma is prominent, for apperception is the stage at which karma is produced.

(*b*) Sankhārenāti paṭisandhi-janaka-kamma-sankhātena cetanā-sankhārena, taŋ-sahajāta-phassādi-dhamma-samūhena pi vā; so pi hi upanissaya-bhāvena paṭisandhiŋ janeti yevāti: 'By sankhārena is meant the cetanā-sankhāra called karma-productive-of-rebirth, or by the collection of mental properties—phassa, etc.—co-existent with that (cetanā-sankhāra). In fact, this [collection] too [can] cause rebirth as an upanissaya condition (principal cause).'

From these quotations it is clear that sankhāra, in such a connection, is synonymous with karma, and is primarily applied to cetanā, but is extended secondarily to the properties concomitant with the cetanā. I take it that your 'syntheses' do not refer to the collection in the above quotations.[1] You have merely used the word as a convenient label for sankhārakkhandha. Now, the Arahant's kriyā-citta (inoperative consciousness) has this khandha, but no longer brings forth the mental action in question—*i.e.*, rebirth.

[1] Yes, they would, *i.e.*, in each *latter* alternative: 'collection, etc.' 'Syntheses' is simply an etymological approximation to sankhārā, like the Commentator's dhamma-samudayo, -samūho above.—Ed.

SUKHA.

I agree with you in using pleasure, pleasurable feeling, for sukha, in psychological analysis, just as dukkha, under the same aspect, means pain, painful feeling. But the ethical sukha is better rendered by 'happiness,' 'bliss,' or your 'ease,' and the ethical dukkha by misery, ill, and so forth. Nibbāna-sukha — *e.g.*, is rather 'bliss' than pleasure. The following is my scheme:

kāyika sukha = pleasurable feeling;
cetasika, or mānasika sukha = pleasure (mental);
the ethical (religious) sukha = happiness, ease, bliss;
kāyika dukkha = painful feeling;
cetasika dukkha = pain (mental);
the ethical dukkha = misery, ill;
sukha, as in sukhapaṭipadā = easy process;
dukkha in opposite = difficult process;
somanassa = joy (pleasure + excitement);
domanassa = grief (pain + excitement).

HADAYA-VATTHU.

(*Heart as Physical Basis of Mind.*)

The omission of 'hadayavatthu' in the *Dhamma-sangaṇi* is very significant to us Buddhists. The doctrines in that work we attribute to the Buddha (I am not now speaking of the *form* of presentation or redaction of those doctrines as we have them in that book), and we hold that the omission is not accidental.[1] In view of the

[1] *Dh. S.* § 6; *Bud. Psy.*, lxxviii., *n.* 3. The omission alluded to is that of 'the heart' from the list making up rūpa, while in Buddhaghosa's corresponding list (*Vis. Mag.*, ch. xiv.; J.R.A.S., 1890-3, p. 123 *f.*), hadayavatthu is *inserted* after jīvitindriya. —Ed.

popular idea—*i.e.*, of the cardiac theory of the seat of mental activity—prevailing in his time, the Buddha preferred to be silent on the point. He did not accept the theory, but if he had expounded his own theory, it would not have been acceptable to his hearers.[1] But he reserved the question of the basis of consciousness for the philosophic teaching handed down in the Paṭṭhāna. Even here he was very careful not to commit himself to the cardiac theory, even by way of concession to the popular view. The Paṭṭhāna doctrine is as follows: cakkhāyatanaŋ cakkhuviññāṇa-dhātuyā taŋ sampayuttakānañ ca dhammānaŋ nissaya-paccayena paccayo: 'the eye is related to sight and its concomitant states by way of base [to that based thereon].' And so on for the other senses and sense-organs. But when he comes to mind (m a n o) the style is altered: '*Yaŋ rūpaŋ* nissāya manodhātu ca manoviññāṇadhātu ca vattanti, *taŋ rūpaŋ* manodhātuyā ca manoviññāṇadhātuyā ca taŋ sampayuttakānañ ca dhammānaŋ nissayapaccayena paccayo—'*That material thing* on the basis of which apprehension and comprehension take place—*that thing* is related to both of them, as well as to their concomitants by way of the relation of Base.' It was quite easy here for the founder of Abhidhamma doctrine to have used the word 'heart' instead of 'that material thing' (r ū p a), had he believed that heart was related to mind as its physical base.

The Commentators had to give a name to this y a ŋ

[1] Christians may be hereby reminded of a similar judgment ascribed to Christ in St. John's Gospel: 'I have yet many things to say unto you, but ye cannot bear them now. Howbeit when he, the Spirit of truth, is come, he will guide you into the whole of truth.' Also of Copernicus, refraining *for thirty-six years* from publishing his heliocentric theory, thinking 'it might be better to follow the examples of the Pythagoreans and others, who delivered their doctrine only by tradition and to friends,' *i.e.*, esoterically. Now the Buddha is declared to have said he had 'no such thing as the closed fist of a teacher who keeps *some* things back.' *Māha Parinibbāna Sta.* This may be interpreted as either that he taught all he knew to all, or that he withheld some things from *everyone* alike. That which no man may see, is not committed to the 'fist' *at all.*—Ed.

rūpaŋ . . . taŋ rūpaŋ, and they wrote 'heart' in accordance with the popular theory. And they doubtless believed they had commented accurately in so doing, since the Buddha himself had used 'hadaya' in his Discourses to express thought or mind. But to use the word thus for edifying exposition is very different from using the same in philosophical language to express 'basis of thought.'

I do not wish to flout history in stating that as far back as twenty-five centuries ago, the Buddha *practically* rejected the universally accepted theory of heart as basis of mind, in advance of Greek theories, and anticipated the modern view of the seat of consciousness. But I look to you, as an exponent of Buddhist philosophy, to do justice to the Buddha and the Abhidhamma.[1]

HETU, HETUKA.

I first thought of the word 'motive' for hetu. But it does not cover all the denotation of hetu as given in Part III. of the Manual. For while greed, hate and love (lobha, dosa, a-dosa) are undoubtedly motives, the West, active in gaining money and land, does not seem to regard a-lobha as a motive. Nor can ignorance or dulness, and the absence thereof (moha, a-moha), ever be regarded as anything so positive in connotation as

[1] After all, we acknowledge an anticipation of an analogous kind in Demokritus's theory of Touch in the evolution of sense. It is true that, on this point, the quoted fragments of the Levantine philosopher are more positive in expression than the (comparatively) intact teaching of his great Indian colleague. Nevertheless, any orthodox Christian ought to admit the possibility and plausibility of a teacher, for whom omniscience is claimed, conforming to popular usage in edifying discourse. For did not Christ declare that 'out of the heart proceed evil thoughts (διαλογισμοί),' and ask: 'Why reason ye these things in your hearts?' He, too, might have said, with the Buddha: 'These are merely names, expressions . . . designations in common use in the world. And of these a Tathāgata makes use indeed, but is not led astray by them' (Poṭṭhapāda Suttanta, *Dialogues of the Buddha*, I., 268).—Ed.

motive. Now when Buddhists give in charity, they are said to be actuated by the motive of a-lobha: alobha-hetu dānaŋ—a gift from the 'motive' of 'absence of greed.' If positive meaning may be conveyed by 'disinterestedness,' and if a-moha be rendered by 'reason,' 'motive' might perhaps serve for hetu. 'Cold' is only absence of heat, yet it is spoken of as a positive cause or condition.

It is indeed nearer to hand to render hetu by 'cause,' according to the common Pali phrase: ko hetu ko paccayo yo . . . What is the cause or reason why. . . . But in ethical doctrine we find this rendering is too loose. The Ceylon Commentary, p. 68, says: 'although anything ahetuka is caused by efficient hetu (nibbattaka-hetu), it is so called because it is devoid of concomitant hetu (sampayutta-hetu). Ledi (p. 39), while adopting the explanation 'sampayutta-hetu *virahato* ahetuka-cittāni,' disapproves of the idea of contrasting concomitant hetu with causal hetu, the latter not being permissible in Abhidhamma—*i.e.*, in philosophy. Grammarians, however, speak of janaka-hetu, ñāpaka-hetu, and sampāpaka-hetu, meaning 'cause,' 'reason,' and 'means' respectively, as distinguishable under nibbattaka-hetu. In other words, this phrase is a term of grammar, and not of philosophy. Be that as it may, it is clear from these comments that sahetuka is a term applied to classes of consciousness which are not devoid of (a-virahita) concomitant hetu.

What, then, is the philosophical import of hetu?

The Ceylon Commentary (p. 208) gives the following definition: hinoti patiṭṭhāti etenāti hetu—'hetu is that by which (the effect) is established.' This is obviously incomplete, but the phala—effect or fruit—is supplied in the commentarial exposition by the simile of a tree. The growth of a tree, namely, is affected by several conditions, viz., the seed, root, soil, water, manure, etc., any one or any *group* of which *may* be considered as constituting a *cause*, and the rest as being *conditions*, of growth. Now, by Buddhists the seed would be invariably considered to be the cause, and the root a principal condition among other conditions of the fruition of the tree. And they usually compare karma to the seed, and hetu to the root. But as the root is dependent upon the seed, so is hetu dependent upon karma (kamma-nidāna-bhūta). Thus hetu is something which affects a cause in the production of the effect of that cause. In other words hetu is a condition, as distinguished from a cause. So in the *Paṭṭhāna*, which expounds our philosophy of Relations, we read: hetu hetusampayuttakānaŋ dhammānaŋ hetu-paccayena paccayo (*Dukap.*, p. 9). This I understand to mean: 'hetu's (greed and the other five) are related to their concomitant mental properties as conditions.' Take a concrete example: Part II. of the Manual tells us that the first class of 'appetitives' (lobhasahagata) is composed of nineteen mental properties among which lobha is conspicuous as the root. But as cetanā, being sabbacittasādhāraṇa, is common to all classes of consciousness, we find in one and the same class both cetanā and lobha. As volition is translated into action (*i.e.*, deed, word or thought), cetanā is transformed into kamma. And if we render kamma by 'cause,' it is clear that we need another term to express hetu as something akin to, and yet distinct from, 'cause.'

Hetu affects cetanā in its transformation into kamma, the cause, and therefore conditions the effect of that cause. And it also imposes a limitation to the application of the remaining concomitant mental properties.

If the word 'condition' be acceded to as the nearest equivalent, the adjectival form 'conditional,' for hetuka, can hardly be objected to.

European ears are no doubt more or less accustomed to 'conditional' as a logical and grammatical term. This may be because Europe has not an ethico-philosophical system like Buddhism. But it is a pity to throw away an expressive term simply for this accident.

TWO SUPPLEMENTARY NOTES

1. *On the Difference between* Vitakka (*Initial Application*) *and* Manasikāra (*Attention*).

I agree to your rendering of vitakka and vicāra by 'initial and sustained application' as on the whole the best, and as leaving 'attention' for manasikāra. The *Three Ṭīkā's* distinguishes the latter term from vitakka as follows[1]: Manasikāra has the 'mark' of carrying the mind well into the object (ārammaṇe samannāhāra-lakkhaṇo). Vitakka merely throws, so to speak, its concomitant properties on to the object (pakkhipanto viya hoti). Its 'mark' is 'lifting its co-existent properties on to the object' (sahajāta-dhammānaŋ ārammaṇe abhiniropana-sabhāvattā). Attention is like a charioteer harnessing two horses (mind and object) into a pair. Initial application is like a favourite courtier introducing a villager (mind) into the presence of the king (object).

What happens then in a-vitakka-citta, or consciousness without vitakka? The mind dispenses with this introduction when it has become *habitually associated* with the object. It was, but is no longer, sa-vitakka with respect to that class of object. The senses get at the object without aid from vitakka by the mere impact of physical base and object (vatthālambaṇa-sanghaṭṭanena). Again, each higher jhāna is a-vitakka in virtue of the lowest jhāna-practice (heṭṭhima-bhāvanā-balena).[2]

[1] *Cf.* my footnote, p. 95, *n.* 1.—Ed.

[2] *Op. cit.*, 87 and 74.

Ledi Sadaw gives a similar explanation (p. 80), but adds that Buddhaghosa, in the *Papañca-Sūdanī*,[1] questioned this explanation, current already in his time, and advanced the following view: 'Mind indeed always gets at its object, its constant companion being attention (manasikāra), without which it would be like a rudderless ship, drifting on to *any* object. With this rudder the senses arrive at their proper destination. It is in the nature of consciousness to cognize object (ārammana-vijānana-sattivasena). When evil thoughts arise, greed, etc., bring mind to their respective objects. In second jhāna, etc., attention, effort, and mindfulness so convey mind. But vitakka is the most powerful of them all. Why, then, are not other (functions of cognition) termed vitakka? Because they have (or rather are) distinguishable functions, while vitakka has the sole function of *directing*. Sa-vitakka-citta directs or applies itself; a-vitakka-citta is directed or applied to its object. But attention, or "action-in-mind" (manasmiŋ kāro) attends to the object in both cases.'

---

2. *On Authority in Buddhist Belief.*[2]

. . . Vīthi's, or processes of thought, are detailed in a Pali-Burmese work called *Vīthi-Letyo*, which was the *vade mecum* of older students in Burma. Ledi Sadaw's views on the same subject, as embodied in his *Paramattha-dīpanī*, are expounded and discussed in detail in the *Vīthi-mañjarī* by his pupil, U. Pandi. Although I owe a great debt to the learning displayed in these and many other works, I should have served no useful purpose in giving references to them in a work such as this. Personally, let me add, I am acting only as the mouthpiece of my country's teachers. I have no theories of my own. At best I am but an interpreter of Burmese views based

[1] Cy. on *M.*

[2] From a letter by the translator.

on the Ceylon Commentary and the works of Buddhaghosa. You may take my essay as medieval Buddhism presented through modern Burmese glasses. And you may consider that the Burmese view, with the sole exception of Ledi Sadaw, is, as a rule, one with Sumangala (*i.e.*, Ceylon Cy.) and Buddhaghosa.

But I fear you would be expecting too much from me if you were to ask me to test our traditional philosophic theories by modern science and criticism, or rather, to adduce evidence to establish what is stated in our books. Our commentators certainly hazarded many a very bold guess, as when they say that one thought-moment is more than a billionth of the time occupied by a wink of the eye, and so on. To be able to measure the duration of thought will be to have placed psychology on the footing of the exact sciences. To recognize that thought is a radiation is, I submit, a great thing in itself. Who can say that this may not one day lead some discoverers to devise an instrument exploiting some substance, yet unknown, which is sensitive to thought, and so to measure our thought-'waves' and their duration?

I do not ask the West to swallow all that is said in Buddhist books. But I think it is just as well that the West should have a candid statement of all that is calmly said by Buddhists on authority. Else a partial study of what we think and say would only give rise to misconceptions as regards Buddhist terminology.

Buddhists accept on faith the teaching that has been handed down from century to century. Now, in matters passing the possibility of verification, the nearest approach to proof is *to show the likelihood* of anything. For instance, our assertions about grades of superhuman beings will be laughed at in the West (*i.e.*, by those who have relinquished their own traditional beliefs of like nature). Such beings cannot be proved to exist. Nevertheless, comparative anatomy has done a little service toward showing the *likelihood* of a regular gradation of beings, which does not necessarily stop at man. Again, we who have been accustomed to associate mind with brain, may scoff at the idea of the Arūpa-world. And yet modern hypnotism, in a small way, shows *likelihood* of the existence of a world with thought, minus brain-activity.[1] How far these Buddhist beliefs are, or are not, borne out by modern science, it is for each scientific generation to declare.

[1] I do not gather that the translator has read Fechner on mind in plants, etc., but his argument is on all fours with Fechner's.—Ed.

INDEX

I

SUBJECTS

[1] The *Dhammasaṅgaṇi* adds *three unmoral* hetu's: § 1,062; *Bud. Psy.*, 283 *f.*

II

PROPER NAMES

III

PALI WORDS (DISCUSSED IN NOTES AND ESSAY)